THE
BOOK OF
ROYAL
LISTS

CRAIG BROWN AND
LESLEY CUNLIFFE

SUMMIT BOOKS

NEW YORK

FOR HUGH MONTGOMERY-MASSINGBERD

Published by SUMMIT BOOKS
A Simon & Schuster Division of Gulf & Western Corporation
Simon & Schuster Building
Rockefeller Center
1230 Avenue of the Americas
New York, New York 10020
Originally published in Great Britain in 1982
by Routledge & Kegan Paul Limited
SUMMIT BOOKS and colophon
are trademarks of Simon & Schuster
Manufactured in the United States of America

10 9 8 7 6 5 4 3 2   1

First American Edition

Library of Congress Cataloging in Publication Data

Brown, Craig.
  The book of royal lists.
  Includes index.
    1. Great Britain—Kings and rulers—Biography—Anecdotes,
facetiae, satire, etc.   2. Great Britain—Queens—Biography—
Anecdotes, facetiae, satire, etc.   3. Great Britain—Princes and
princesses—Biography—Anecdotes, facetiae, satire, etc.
I. Cunliffe, Lesley Hume. II. Title.
DA28.1.B73   1983   941'.009'92 [B]   82-19616
ISBN 0-671-46507-4
ISBN 0-671-47282-8 (pbk.)

THE KINGS AND QUEENS OF ENGLAND

WILLIAM (The Conqueror)	**1066–1087**	*The first Norman King of England*
WILLIAM II (Rufus)	**1087–1100**	*The first bachelor to succeed to the throne until King Edward VIII*
HENRY I	**1100–1135**	*The most prolific king - 24 children*
STEPHEN	**1135–1154**	*The first and last of this name*
HENRY II	**1154–1189**	*The first king to read a book in bed*
RICHARD I (Lionheart)	**1189–1199**	*The last king to visit the East until King George V*
JOHN	**1199–1216**	*Changed the history of government with* **Magna Carta**
HENRY III	**1216–1272**	*The first king to be born in England*
EDWARD I	**1272–1307**	*The first king to commission a national land survey with maps*
EDWARD II	**1307–1327**	*The first king to take a personal interest in the theatre*
EDWARD III	**1327–1377**	*The first post-Conquest king to speak English*
RICHARD II	**1377–1399**	*The first king to use a handkerchief*
HENRY IV	**1399–1413**	*The first king whose parents were both English*
HENRY V	**1413–1422**	*Caused by his own order the deaths of 12,000 non-combatant civilians*
HENRY VI	**1422–1461**	*The first king to use a wooden stamp for his signature*
EDWARD IV	**1461–1483**	*Opened Parliament at the age of three*
EDWARD V	**1483**	*Never crowned; probably murdered in the Tower of London by Richard III*
RICHARD III	**1483–1485**	*The last king to die in battle*
HENRY VII	**1485–1509**	*The first king ceremonially to touch for the 'King's Evil' (scrofula)*
HENRY VIII	**1509–1547**	*The first king to be called 'Your Majesty'*
EDWARD VI	**1547–1553**	*The first king to keep a diary*

Christian IX, King of Denmark (1818–1906)

Princess Louise of Hesse-Cassel (1817–1898)

Grand Duke Constantine Nikolaievitch of Russia (1827–1892)

Princess Alexandra of Saxe-Altenburg (1830–1911)

Prince Alexander of Hesse and by Rhine (1823–1888)

Countess Julie Von Hauke, Princess of Battenberg (1825–1895)

Ludwig IV, Grand Duke of Hesse and by Rhine (1837–1892)

Princess Alice of Great Britain (1843–1878)

Edward VII, King of Great Britain (1841–1910)

Princess Alexandra of Denmark (1844–1925)

Francis, Duke of Teck (1837–1900)

Princess Mary Adelaide of Great Britain (1833–1897)

Claude Bowes-Lyon, 13th Earl of Strathmore and Kinghorne (1824–1904)

Frances Dora Smith (1832–1922)

Rev Charles William Frederick Cavendish-Bentinck (1817–1865)

Caroline Louisa Burnaby (1832–1918)

George I, King of the Hellenes (1845–1913)

Grand Duchess Olga Constantinovna of Russia (1851–1926)

Louis Mountbatten, 1st Marquess of Milford Haven, formerly Prince of Battenberg (1854–1921)

Princess Victoria of Hesse and by Rhine (1863–1950)

George V, King of Great Britain (1865–1936)

Princess Mary of Teck (1867–1953)

Claude George Bowes-Lyon, 14th Earl of Strathmore and Kinghorne (1855–1944)

Nina Cecilia Cavendish-Bentinck (1862–1938)

Prince Andrew of Greece and Denmark (1882–1944)

Princess Alice of Battenberg (1885–1969)

George VI, King of Great Britain (1895–1952)

Lady Elizabeth Bowes-Lyon (1900–)

Philip, Duke of Edinburgh (1921–)

Elizabeth II, Queen of Great Britain (1926–)

Charles, Prince of Wales (1948–)

Prince William of Wales

(1798–1857)	Adelaide Horatia Elizabeth Seymour (1825–1877)	Edward Charles Baring, 1st Baron Revelstoke (1828–1897)	Louisa Emily Charlotte Bulteel (1839–1892)	James Hamilton, 2nd Duke of Abercorn (1838–1913)	Lady Mary Anna Curzon-Howe (1848–1929)	George Bingham, 4th Earl of Lucan (1830–1914)	Lady Cecilia Catherine Gordon-Lennox (1838–1910)	Edmund Burke Roche, 1st Baron Fermoy (1815–1874)	Eliza Caroline Boothby (1821–1897)	Frank Work (1819–1911)	Ellen Wood (1831–1877)	Alexander Ogston Gill (1833–1908)	Barbara Smith Marr (1843–18--)	David Littlejohn (1841–1924)	Jane Crombie (1843–1917)
6th Earl Spencer (1857–1922)	Hon Margaret Baring (1868–1906)			James Albert Edward Hamilton, 3rd Duke of Abercorn (1869–1953)		Lady Rosalind Bingham (1869–1958)		James Boothby Burke Roche, 3rd Baron Fermoy (1851–1920)		Frances Work (1857–1947)		William Smith Gill (1865–1957)		Ruth Littlejohn (1879–1964)	
Albert Edward John Spencer, 7th Earl Spencer (1892–1975)			Lady Cynthia Hamilton (1897–1972)					Edmund Maurice Burke Roche, 4th Baron Fermoy (1885–1955)				Ruth Gill (1908–)			
John Spencer, 8th Earl Spencer (1924–)								Hon Frances Burke Roche (1936–)							
				Lady Diana Spencer (1961–)											
1982–)															

THE KINGS AND QUEENS OF ENGLAND

LADY JANE GREY	**1553**	*The most unwilling queen and the shortest serving*
MARY I	**1553–1558**	*The only Queen Regnant to marry a foreign reigning monarch*
ELIZABETH I	**1558–1603**	*The first monarch to install a loo*
JAMES I	**1603–1625**	*The first king to commission a vernacular Bible*
CHARLES I	**1625–1649**	*The last king to enter the House of Commons*
CHARLES II	**1660–1685**	*The first king to attend a public theatre*
JAMES II	**1685–1688**	*The first king to be succeeded by his daughter in his own lifetime*
WILLIAM III and	**1689–1702**	*The first king to have more than one baptismal name*
MARY II	**1689–1694**	*The only ruling queen to proclaim her husband joint sovereign*
ANNE	**1702–1714**	*The last monarch to refuse the Assent to Parliament*
GEORGE I	**1714–1727**	*The last monarch to be born abroad*
GEORGE II	**1727–1760**	*The last king to lead his troops into battle*
GEORGE III	**1760–1820**	*The last King of America*
GEORGE IV	**1820–1830**	*The first king to wear a kilt*
WILLIAM IV	**1830–1837**	*The last king to dismiss his government*
VICTORIA	**1837–1901**	*The first monarch to be recorded and filmed; to have electric lights and a telephone*
EDWARD VII	**1901–1910**	*The first king to own and drive a car*
GEORGE V	**1910–1936**	*The first monarch to go down a coal mine*
EDWARD VIII	**1936 (abdicated)**	*The first king to install a television; the only king to have written his own autobiography*
GEORGE VI	**1936–1952**	*The last Emperor of India*
ELIZABETH II	**1952**	*The first monarch to have circumnavigated the globe; the first monarch to have acceded to the Throne while up a tree*

Contents

Acknowledgments

We are extremely grateful to David Williamson for all his research, especially in the field of genealogy, to Hugh Montgomery-Massingberd for all his help and encouragement, to Kathy Holme, Sophie Hicks, Barbara Cartland, Adam Plattenberg-Witten zu Meitengen, Peregrine Worsthorne, Stephen Pile, Linda Bell, Jean Rook, David Godwin, Henry Porter, Helen Armitage and Hugo Vickers, to W M Addams Reitwisener and Gary Boyd Roberts for Princess Diana's American genealogy and to all those too modest or well-connected to be mentioned.

Photographs on pages 47, 55, 71, 109, 163, 252 (lower), and 256 are reproduced by kind permission of the Press Association, and all others by kind permission of Keystone Press Agency.

Lines of verse from Eric Clerihew Bentley p. 88 are reproduced from *The Complete Clerihews of E. Clerihew Bentley* (1981) by kind permission of Oxford University Press. Verse by Sir Osbert Sitwell on p. 216 is reproduced by kind permission of Gerald Duckworth & Co. Ltd. Verse by John Masefield on p. 216 is reproduced by kind permission of the Society of Authors as Literary Representatives of the Estate of John Masefield. Verse by C. Day-Lewis on p. 216 is reproduced by kind permission of A. D. Peters & Co. Ltd. Verse by Mary Wilson on p. 216 is reproduced from *New Poems* (Hutchinsons, 1979) by kind permission of the publishers.

Eleven personal requisites the Queen always takes on foreign journeys

1 Her feather pillows
2 Her hot water bottle
3 Her favourite China tea
4 Cases of Malvern water
5 Barley sugar
6 Cameras
7 Her monogrammed electric kettle
8 Her toilet soap
9 A special white kid lavatory seat
10 Jewellery which has a special association with the countries she is going to visit
11 Mourning clothes and black-edged writing paper in case of bereavements

Eight questions you are likely to be asked when meeting Royalty

1 *How long have you been waiting?* The Queen
2 *What exactly are you doing?* Prince Charles
3 *How long have you been working here?* Princess Anne
4 *Keep you busy do they?* Prince Charles
5 *What's your job?* Prince Philip (at the reply, '*I'm a postman*', he will say, '*Oh, you're a postman, are you?*')
6 *Where have you come from?* The Queen
7 *Pay you enough, do they?* Prince Charles
8 *Have you done this sort of thing before?* Princess Anne

Seven subjects upon which Royal lips are sealed

1 The Royal proposal

No one has ever been told whether the Queen proposed to Prince Philip, as Queen Victoria had proposed to Prince Albert, or whether Prince Philip took the initiative.

2 Prince Charles's bedwear

Despite being asked by many journalists over the years, Prince Charles has never revealed what he wears in bed, if anything.

3 Royal wills

The contents of Royal wills are never made public.

4 The Queen's ring

No one knows the inscription that Prince Philip had engraved on the Queen's wedding ring.

5 Vital statistics

The vital statistics of the female members of the Royal Family have never been made public, though keen statisticians have hazarded guesses.

6 The Queen's fortune

The Queen has never revealed the full extent of her personal fortune, despite many requests from politicians. She is undoubtedly the richest woman in the world.

7 A private joke

When the Queen was getting ready to speak in front of Canadian television cameras in 1956 she was visibly shaking. Prince Philip asked a technician to '*Tell her to remember the wailing and gnashing of teeth.*' When these words were repeated to her, the Queen immediately cheered up. To this day, no one understands the meaning of this private joke.

4 Three stages in the Queen's temper – how to tell if you've said the wrong thing

1 She gives you a frozen stare and says nothing
2 She starts tapping her foot
3 She says, '*How amusing for you,*' and walks away

Eleven people who failed to recognise Royalty

1 Lady Diana Cooper

Chatting with the Queen at a party for Sir Robert Mayer, Lady Diana Cooper suddenly realised who she was talking to. *'Oh, I'm so sorry'*, she said, *'I didn't recognise you without your crown.'*

2 A wedding guest

At the reception for King George V and Queen Mary's wedding in 1893, a guest mistook George for the Tsarevich and asked him whether he had come to London to transact other business, or just to attend the wedding.

3 Dawson Damer

At the same reception, Dawson Damer, a little the worse for drink, rushed up to Queen Victoria and said, *'Gad, How glad I am to see you! How well you're looking! But, I say, do forgive me – your face is, of course, very familiar to me; but I can't for the life of me recall your name!'* The Queen smiled kindly and replied, *'Oh, never mind my name, Mr Damer, I'm very glad to see you. Sit down and tell me all about yourself.'*

4 A French seaman

Resting in a beach bar on her holiday island of Mustique, Princess Margaret was once approached by a drunken French skipper who obviously did not recognise the Princess out of formal dress. When he attempted to sit on her lap, he was led firmly away.

5 A cowherd's wife

When he was on the run, King Alfred the Great took refuge, anonymously, with a cowherd and his wife. The cowherd's wife left some loaves by a fire next to which King Alfred was sharpening his arrows. When the woman came back she saw the loaves burning and said in fury, *'You wretch, you're only too fond of them when they're nicely done; why can't you turn them when you see them burning?'*

6 President Truman's mother

When the Queen visited Washington DC in 1951, she was taken to meet President Truman's elderly mother, who had just heard the election results from England. *'I'm so glad your father's been re-elected!'* she crowed to the Queen, confusing the King with Winston Churchill.

7 A gatekeeper

In 1981, shortly before her wedding, Princess Diana was refused admission to the Royal Box at Ascot by a gatekeeper who failed to recognise her. After his mistake had been rectified, the embarrassed gatekeeper told reporters, *'I'll never make the same mistake again'.*

8 E M Forster

When he was an old man, the celebrated author attended a wedding at St James's Palace. He was asked if he would like to meet the Queen Mother, by a friend, who motioned in her direction. *'Oh, I thought that was the wedding cake,'* said Forster.

9 A housemaid

When Princess Diana was in Australia before the announcement of her engagement, Prince Charles had some difficulty in contacting her. He recalled later: *'I rang up on one occasion and I said, "Can I speak –" and they said: "No, we're not taking any calls." So I said: "It's the Prince of Wales speaking." '*

"How do I know it's the Prince of Wales?" *came back the reply. I said: "You don't. But I am" in a rage. And eventually . . . I mean, I got the number because they were staying somewhere else.'*

10 Various public officials

While at naval college, King George VI made friends with a fellow student who looked so like him that the shy George would often get him to stand in for him at minor public functions. On one occasion, even King George V was deceived.

11 A party guest

At a cocktail party, a guest was chatting to Princess Mary, the sister of King George VI, without being able to remember exactly who she was. *'And tell me,'* asked the guest, *'What's your brother doing these days?' 'He's still King,'* came the reply.

6 *Six people who were wrongly dressed in front of King Edward VII*

1 An admiral's daughter

When the daughter of a distinguished admiral arrived at a party given by King Edward VII clad in a dress which ended an inch above her ankles, the King said: *'I am afraid you must have made a mistake. This is a dinner, not a tennis, party.'*

2 Lord Harris

'Goin' rattin' Harris?' King Edward VII asked Lord Harris who had turned up at Ascot wearing a tweed suit.

3 The Earl of Rosebery

Arriving for an official ceremony at Windsor wearing plain clothes rather than dress uniform, the Earl of Rosebery was eyed up and down by the King. '*I presume you have come in the suite of the American Ambassador,*' he said.

4 Queen Alexandra

At a formal dinner, King Edward VII sent his wife back to her room to put her Garter Star on the correct side of her dress. He refused to listen to her protestations that it would clash with her other jewellery.

5 A Swedish diplomat

As he was shaking hands with a Swedish diplomat, King Edward VII whispered, '*Hunt and Roskell, 25 Old Bond Street.*' Bemused, the Swede went to the address and there he found the Court Jewellers. They informed him that his Orders were on the wrong way round.

6 A young guardsman

Though King Edward VII himself popularised the wearing of the dinner jacket on informal occasions, when a young Guardsman chose to wear one to the Marlborough Club, the King looked at him fiercely and then said, '*I suppose, my young friend, you are going to a costume ball?*'

Five tricks of the trade: how the Royal family keep things running smoothly 7

1 Concealed cards

All Ladies-in-Waiting and Equerries accompanying members of the Royal Family keep tiny timetables each of which accounts for every five minutes of each particular visit. The timetables are photographically reduced to pocket-size and contain the names and rank of all those to be met.

2 Memory tests

When King George V was training his ten-year-old son and heir, King Edward VIII, he took him into a room in which fifty guests were assembled and introduced him to each of them. Edward was then taken into an adjoining room, shown a sketch of where the guests had been standing, and was then required to repeat their names. This test was repeated regularly. After a few months he was able to remember thirty-five to forty names of guests.

3 Crown training
Before her Coronation, the Queen wore the 5lb St Edward's Crown around Buckingham Palace for a few days to get used to the weight. She even wore it while feeding the corgis.

4 Ending a conversation
When the Queen has a lot of people to meet, she ends a conversation by taking a half step backwards and smiling broadly.

5 Choreographic dinner
In the State Dining Room at Buckingham Palace, traffic-light devices are concealed in the vases of flowers at each corner. When the lights go amber, the footmen begin to serve, and when the lights go green they clear the plates away.

8   *Six everyday objects which have been specially adapted for the Queen's use*

1 Blotting paper
To prevent any private or state secrets from being revealed, the Queen uses special black blotting paper. Used blotting paper is destroyed daily.

2 Handbag
So that the Queen does not have to fish for her handbag at the end of state banquets, it is fitted with a special clip so that it can be secured to tables.

3 Kettles
The breakfast kettle at Buckingham Palace has a special swivel, designed by Prince Philip. He also adapted a Victorian silver kettle by adding an electric element; the Queen uses it to make the tea herself.

4 Television set
Television programmes are 'piped' to the Queen's set to avoid any interference.

5 Car mascot
A silver model of St George, naked with a dead dragon at his feet, is transferred to whichever car the Queen travels in.

6 Clock
The clock in Horse Guards' Parade is put forward or back as

needed to ensure that it strikes eleven exactly as the Queen enters the Parade Ground for Trooping the Colour at the Queen's Birthday Parade.

The Queen's car mascot

Six things altered by Royalty 9

1 The marital coat of arms
Princess Diana is the first Royal bride to include her family's motto ('*Dieu defend le droit*') on her marital coat of arms.
2 The spelling of a title
The Queen dropped the final 'k' from the title of 'Master of the Queen's Music(k)'.
3 The Parliamentary Declaration
King George V objected to the anti-Catholic sentiments in the Parliamentary Declaration, and refused to open Parliament until

they had been reworded. Previously, the King had to profess a belief that *'the Invocation or Adoration of the Virgin Mary or any other Saint, and the Sacrifice of the Mass as they are now used in the Church of Rome, are superstitious and idolatrous.'* The new Parliamentary Declaration asks the monarch to go no further than declare himself or herself 'a faithful Protestant'.

4 The Birthday Parade
The Queen changed the day of the Birthday Parade from Thursday to Saturday in 1959 to lessen traffic congestion.

5 A Rolls Royce
Before accepting delivery of a new Rolls Royce in 1972, Princess Margaret insisted on the following alterations: the indicators to be removed; the rear lights to be refitted in a cluster; the gloss woodwork to be replaced with matt. She retained the numberplate from her old car, 3 GXM.

6 The Investiture crown
The crown placed on Prince Charles's head at his Investiture proved too large for him in the dress rehearsals and kept slipping over his eyes. Though it had been altered by the time of the Investiture itself, the Queen later confessed to Noel Coward that she and Prince Charles had nearly burst out giggling in the middle of the ceremony at the recollection of it slipping.

10   *The Civil List*

1 The Queen – £3,541,300
2 The Queen Mother – £306,000
3 Prince Philip – £171,000
4 Princess Anne – £106,500
5 Prince Andrew – £20,000
6 Princess Margaret – £104,500
7 Princess Alice, Duchess of Gloucester – £42,000
8 The Duke of Gloucester – £83,900
9 The Duke of Kent – £113,000
10 Princess Alexandra – £107,800

> The total cost of the civil list is £4,710,000. All staff and household expenses, etc. are paid from this sum. The Prince and Princess of Wales receive nothing, but three-quarters of the revenue of the Duchy of Cornwall (£413,000) is theirs.

Six comparable costs to the Monarchy

In 1982, the total amount of money paid to the Royal Family was raised to £4,710,000. This seems a lot until it is compared with the following costs:

1 Failed Driving Tests, 1981: £13,000,000.
2 British Rail's loss, 1980: £76,900,000.
3 British Rail's Advertising, 1981: £4,774,100.
4 'Buzby' Telephone Advertising, 1981: £4,156,200.
5 British Airways loss, 1980: £145,000,000.
6 Paul McCartney's estimated earnings, 1981: £20,000,000.

Six things the Queen need not worry about

1 Income tax
No one, possibly including the Queen and her financial advisers, Baring Brothers, knows exactly what the extent of her private fortune is, but she does not have to pay income tax.

2 Death duties
The Queen does not pay Death Duties, although all the other members of her family must.

3 Dogs' licence
She is not required to apply for one.

4 Telephone bills
Paid by the Civil List.

5 Stamps
The Queen's post carries the Royal cipher and no stamp at all.

6 Subpoenas
The Queen is not obliged to give evidence in court and cannot be sued.

Seven things given up by Royalty in wartime

The First World War
1 Drink and good food

On the advice of Lloyd George, King George V banned all alcohol in the Royal households. Nevertheless, it was widely understood that when the King arose from the dinner table saying that he was going to his study *'to attend to a small matter of business'* the business would include a bottle of port. His guests, however, did not escape. The American Ambassador at the time recorded eating a dinner of one egg, a piece of bread and a glass of lemonade at the Palace.

2 Clean napkins

For the first time in her life, Queen Mary employed napkin rings, thus saving on laundry.

3 Shooting for pleasure

On his short holidays at Sandringham and Windsor (he never visited Balmoral during the war) King George V would only shoot game for the benefit of hospitals and local farmers.

The Second World War
4 Some Buckingham Palace railings

20 tons of metal were produced from a section of the Buckingham Palace railings.

5 Smart servants

In 1943, servants in the Royal homes changed their white ties and tails for battle dress, buttoned to the neck.

6 Deep baths

All the baths at Buckingham Palace were painted with a 5 inch line.

7 The Dean of Windsor's Flowers

In 1940, the Deanery Garden at Windsor was converted into a vegetable plot. The Dean's window boxes were seen to be sprouting lettuces.

1 Formal dinners

'*Life at Buckingham Palace isn't too bad, but too many formal dinners (Yuk!)*' Princess Diana in a letter to a friend shortly after her engagement. To her flatmates, she had said on leaving, '*For God's sake ring me up, I'm going to need you.*'

2 Lack of privacy

'*We princes are set as it were upon stages in the sight and view of all the world.*' Queen Elizabeth I.

'*I have as much privacy as a goldfish in a bowl.*' Princess Margaret.

3 Competition

'*Don't forget that nowadays we have to compete with Elizabeth Taylor and the Beatles.*' Princess Alexandra.

4 Proximity to work

'*We live above the shop.*' Prince Philip.

'*Ours is not a family, it's a firm.*' King George VI.

5 State visits

'*What rot, and a waste of time, money, and energy all these state visits are.*' King Edward VIII in his diary at Oxford.

6 Sycophants

'*The trouble is that very often the worst people come first and the really nice people hang back because they don't want to be accused of sucking up.*' Prince Charles.

7 Reticence

'*We sailors never smile when on duty.*' King George V.

'*I have been trained since childhood never to show emotion in public.*' The Queen.

8 Restraint

'*How would you like to make a thousand speeches and never once be allowed to say what you think yourself?*' King Edward VIII to Winston Churchill.

9 Tirelessness

When a young relation said he was tired while touring a hospital, Queen Mary replied, '*Stuff and nonsense! You are a member of the British Royal Family and we are **never** tired.*'

10 Public reaction

'*The pleased incredulity with which the public reacts to the elementary demonstrations on the part of Royalty that they are, after all, like other people is matched by the public's firm refusal to accept them as such.*' King Edward VIII, writing in the **New York Daily News**, 1966.

15 *Eight calamities which have occurred on Royal trips abroad*

1 The disappearing reception committee
When the Queen visited Dubrovnik in 1973 she was surprised to find no reception committee was there to greet her. They had all rushed off before she arrived, having been mistakenly informed that the Queen's plane had been diverted to Titograd.

2 The crushed hat
On an official trip to Australia in 1959, Princess Alexandra climbed into the back of the Governor's limousine and sat on top of his new silk top hat. She held it up to the crowd and shouted, *'Look what I've done now!'*

3 The incautious car
On the same trip, the pilot car in Princess Alexandra's procession knocked down an elderly lady. The Princess immediately ordered the cars to stop, delivered the lady to hospital, had her personal doctor examine her and had 30 official bouquets delivered to her.

4 The slothful host
Visiting Morocco in 1980, the Queen was visibly angry (tapping her foot) at being kept waiting in a tent in the desert for more than half an hour while her host King Hassan lounged in his air-conditioned caravan.

5 The over-enthusiastic cooler
The commercial refrigeration plant placed in the Queen's bedroom in Nigeria in 1956 in order to cool it down had the effect of freezing it. The room had then to be thawed before the Queen could make herself at home.

6 The collapsing dance floor
When Edward VII attended a ball at the Academy of Music in New York in 1860, the dance floor collapsed under the weight of the people assembled to greet him. Carpenters were called in. After three hours their work was completed, and the orchestra struck up a tune. This was interrupted by incessant hammering from underneath the floor. It emerged that one of the carpenters had been sealed in. At first the organisers thought it best to leave him there until the end of the party, but he kept banging so loudly that they eventually let him out.

7 The disappearing jewel case
In New Zealand, the Queen's jewel case was loaded onto a commercial flight and went off in an entirely different direction. It was later recovered.

8 The outbreak of hats

A rumour spread through Lagos just before the Queen's visit to Nigeria in 1956 that headgear should be removed in the presence of Royalty. The natives in their hundreds and thousands bought hats for the purpose of taking them off.

Fifteen things which have been refused to Royalty

1 Companionship

Twenty-one year old Kim Deas refused to visit Prince Andrew at Buckingham Palace after he had pleaded for her presence in a midnight phone call in 1981. The Prince started off by ordering Miss Deas and later went on to say that he was *'bored'* and *'lonely'*. But still she did not relent.

2 A photograph

In 1868, Queen Victoria asked for a photograph of Lewis Carroll, author of *Alice in Wonderland*. He refused her one, and later explained to a young friend, Margaret Cunnynghame, why he had done so: *'I was obliged to answer: "Mr Dodgson presents his compliments to Her Majesty, and regrets to say that his rule is never to give his photograph except to **young** ladies." I am told she was annoyed about it, and said, "I'm not so old as all that comes to!" and one doesn't like to annoy Queens.'*

3 A trip across the Niagara Falls

On his trip to America in 1860, King Edward VII had to be restrained from accepting an offer to be conveyed across the Niagara Falls in a wheelbarrow by the tight rope walker Charles Blondin.

4 Entrance

In 1964, Princess Margaret was refused entrance to a Roman Catholic basilica in Padua because she was wearing a sleeveless dress.

In 1980, Prince Andrew was refused entrance to Annabel's night club because he was not wearing a tie. Eventually, the management found a tie for him and he was allowed in.

5 A title

The day of the Duchess of Windsor's marriage, she was informed by a telegram from Buckingham Palace that she would not be allowed (in the face of all precedent) to use the title 'Her Royal Highness.'

6 A club membership
When Prince Charles was at Cambridge, he was refused
permission to join the University Labour Club by Lord Butler,
the Master of his college.

7 A jump
At a cross-country event in Cheshire in 1979, Prince Charles's
horse *St David* refused to jump no less than twelve times.

8 Service in Exile
When King Edward VIII abdicated, he told his valet, Crisp, that
he would be going to France with him. Crisp refused. '*He gave up
his job, I gave up mine*', he was reported as saying later. He was
taken on by King George VI instead.

9 An historical romance
After Jane Austen sent the Prince Regent a copy of her novel
Emma in 1816, she received a reply thanking her and suggesting
that '*any historical romance, illustrative of the history of the august
House of Coburg, would just now be very interesting.*'

   She replied: '*I could not sit seriously down to write a serious romance
under any other motive than to save my life; and if it were indispensable
for me to keep it up and never relax into laughing at myself or other
people, I am sure I should be hung before I had finished the first
chapter . . . .*'

10 Marriage
The Queen Mother refused two proposals of marriage from King
George VI before finally accepting his third offer. Of her
acceptance, she later said, '*I'm not sure my reply wasn't more of a
surprise to me than it was to him.*' King William IV had to be even
more patient. He was refused by Miss Catherine Tylney-Long,
the Dowager Lady Downshire, Miss Margaret Mercer
Elphinstone, Lady Berkeley, the youngest daughter of the King of
Denmark, the daughter of the Elector of Hesse-Cassel and The
Duchess of Oldenburg (who found him '*definitely unpleasant*'). At
last he was accepted by Adelaide of Saxe-Meiningen, and the
marriage was very happy.

11 Permission to write a letter
In 1939, Neville Chamberlain twice refused to allow King George
VI to write a personal letter to Adolf Hitler, '*one ex-serviceman to
another*', in an attempt to avert the war.

12 A church wedding
In 1978, the Pope refused to allow Prince and Princess Michael of
Kent to be married in a Catholic church. They had earlier
announced that their children would be raised in the Church of
England.

13 Entrance

After a furious row with his wife, Prince Albert locked himself into his room. Equally livid, Queen Victoria knocked on the door. '*Who is there?*' asked Prince Albert.

'*The Queen of England*', replied Queen Victoria.

Albert made no reply, and did not open the door. Again there was a hail of knocks. '*Who is there?*' asked Prince Albert once more.

'*The Queen of England*', replied Queen Victoria.

The question and the answer were repeated many times. But then came a gentler knocking. '*Who is there?*' asked Prince Albert.

'*Your wife Victoria, Albert*' came the reply.

Immediately, the door was opened.

14 A rejection

When King Edward VIII started seeing Mrs Simpson, he stopped seeing his old girlfriend, Lady Furness, and asked his equerry, Trotter, to do the same. '*Sir,*' replied Trotter, '*I made friends with Thelma at your request. I don't sack my friends.*' The King then dismissed him.

15 Cocktails

When King Edward VIII took a liking to American-style cocktails, his butler, Finch, refused to mix them for him. Eventually Finch was persuaded to mix the cocktails, but he put his foot down at the inclusion of ice.

Six common misconceptions about Royalty corrected 17

1 **Misconception:** The Royal Family cannot vote.
   Correction: Only the Queen is not allowed to vote. The other members of the Royal Family could vote, but choose to demonstrate their Royal disinterest in politics.

2 **Misconception:** The Investiture of the Prince of Wales is an ancient ceremony.
   Correction: It is not. It was invented by Lloyd George for the future King Edward VIII in 1911 as a vote catcher.

3 **Misconception:** The Black Prince (son of Edward III) was famed throughout Europe in the fourteenth century by this name.
   Correction: This Edward, Prince of Wales was a success on the battlefield during the Hundred Years' War and was the first

Prince of Wales to use the three ostrich feathers as his crest and the motto *Ich dien*. But he was not known as The Black Prince until 200 years after his death. The name refers to the black armour in which he was buried.

4 **Misconception:** The Duke of Edinburgh has been known as Prince Philip since the Queen and he were married.
Correction: He ceased to be Prince Philip of Greece and Denmark on 28 February 1947 when he became a British subject (as Philip Mountbatten). On the day before his wedding to Princess Elizabeth he was granted the style of 'Royal Highness' and on the wedding day itself he was created Duke of Edinburgh by which style he was known until he was granted the titular dignity of Prince on 22 February 1957.

5 **Misconception:** The Labour Party has declared itself anti-Monarchist.
Correction: Despite many backbench requests, the issue of the Monarch has never been raised for debate at the Annual Labour Party Conference.

6 **Misconception:** Richard III was a hunchback.
Correction: No contemporary evidence suggests this to be true. The elderly Countess of Desmond remembered King Richard III as *'the handsomest man in the room, except for his brother Edward . . . (he) was very well made.'*

18   *Ten things the Queen could do with Royal prerogative*

1 Dismiss the government
2 Declare war
3 Disband the army
4 Sell all the ships in the Navy
5 Dismiss the Civil Service
6 Give territory away to a foreign power
7 Make everyone a peer
8 Declare a State of Emergency. (The Queen has once done this, on 31 May 1955, as the result of the Railway Strike.)
9 Pardon all offenders
10 Make every parish in the United Kingdom a university

Four articles in the Queen's daily use with Her Royal cipher upon them

1 Her personal kettle
2 The butter pats served to her for breakfast
3 Her cheques
4 Her milkbottles. The Queen has said that she first felt that she was really Queen when she saw her own monogram on the bottles at Windsor.

Five compensations for the burdens of Royalty

1 Expert execution
A specially expert swordsman was imported from France to behead Anne Boleyn. He was paid £23 to reduce her suffering to the minimum.

2 Sexual credibility
Princess Anne was the only female competitor in the 1976 Montreal Olympics not to be given a sex test.

3 The exclusive use of scarlet livery
At the coronations, those peers whose family livery includes scarlet have to change for the occasion to a darker shade known as '*murrey*' in heraldry. (Murrey is a late Medieval word for mulberry.)

4 Large areas of the sky
Five nautical miles on either side of a route from London to Marsham in Norfolk (for Sandringham); London to Aberdeen (for Balmoral); London to Caithness (Castle of Mey) are designated Purple Air Ways. These areas must be avoided for one half hour before the Royal Family will pass through them on the Queen's Flight.

5 Tax-free drink in exile
The Duke of Windsor, who was resident in France for most of his life after the Abdication, enjoyed Diplomatic Status until his death. His house was leased from the French Government for a token sum, and he paid no income tax. He bought all of his drink, petrol, motorcars, television sets and household appliances duty free in the British Embassy shop and Military Commissary.

Ten Royal collections

1 Stamps
King George V made a collection of 325 stamp albums, now in the possession of the Queen. It is reputed to be the most valuable of its sort in the world. He and Queen Mary also collected snuff boxes.

2 Books
The son of King George III, Augustus, Duke of Sussex, collected over 50,000 books and 5,000 bibles.

3 Loo seats
Prince Charles says he has collected 100 seats. Further contributions are welcome.

4 Meissen pugs
The Duke and Duchess of Windsor had a large collection of china dogs.

5 Cartoons of themselves
Prince Philip's large collection of contemporary cartoons about him are hung in the lavatory at Sandringham; Prince Charles hangs his own in a corridor.

6 Fine paintings and French furniture
It is said of King George IV that his penchant for very expensive paintings and furniture very nearly turned England into a republic. His expenditure was legendary and his debts prodigious. But the collection is now considered one of the finest in the world.

7 Death-bed photographs
Queen Victoria solicited photographs and sketches of her friends and servants (and indeed anyone with whom she was connected who had died) from their relations immediately she had heard of the death.

8 Models of her children's hands and her husband's ear
Queen Victoria had Prince Albert's '*sweet little ear*' modelled in marble in his lifetime and treasured it after his death. She had all her children's hands sculpted in marble too, and always kept them by her.

9 Objets d'art
Queen Mary amassed an enormous collection of jade figurines, china and tea caddies and family portraits and miniatures. Her collection was not just famous for its extent, but for the method she was reputed to use. Extortion would be too strong a word, but the Queen's visits to large houses were sometimes wisely preceded by a diplomatic tucking-away of family *objets d'art*.

10 Trolls

Until the advent of Princess Diana, Prince Charles used to sport a collection of trolls around the mantelpieces of his private apartments. Since his marriage, the trolls have been packed away.

Eleven Royal extravagances 22

1 King Henry VI's Coronation banquet
The extensive menu included red soup in which white lions were swimming, golden leopards immersed in custard and the head of a leopard crowned with ostrich feathers.

2 King Edward VII's larder
As King Edward VII and his guests were killing more than 30,000 game birds a year on the Sandringham estate, he ordered the largest larder in the world to be built in the house to accommodate them.

3 Princess Diana's hair
Princess Diana has an average of three shampoos a week, with conditioner. Her hairdresser is Kevin of '*Headlines*' in South Kensington.

4 The Royal basins
At Buckingham Palace and Windsor Castle there are three basins in a row, marked, '*Hands*,' '*Teeth*,' and '*Face*'. They were installed by King Edward VII.

5 Queen Victoria's breakfast
Queen Victoria used to breakfast in the garden at Osborne under a green fringed parasol tent, surrounded by her Indian servants. Every object on the table, except her cup and saucer, but including her egg cup, was made of solid gold.

6 Queen Elizabeth I's wardrobe
It included over 2,000 dresses.

7 The Duchess of Windsor's face
The Duchess of Windsor hired a professional make-up artist from Elizabeth Arden in Paris to visit her every morning.

8 Anne Boleyn's head
King Henry VIII brought a swordsman all the way from France for the execution of his wife, Anne Boleyn.

9 The Duchess of Windsor's travelling wardrobe
In 1954, the Duchess of Windsor arrived in England with 35 pieces of luggage. Her secretary explained that the Duchess had 'just an ordinary wardrobe for a week's stay.'

10 King Edward VII's christening
The bill for King Edward VII's christening came to £200,000.
11 King Edward VII's model farm
In 1907, King Edward VII commissioned Fabergé to model the farm animals at Sandringham, including pigs, chickens, ducks, shire horses and his prize Short Horn bull. He commissioned him further to model his dog, Caesar, Queen Mary's pekingese, and his Derby winner, Persimmon.

23 Fourteen money-saving hints from the Royal family

1 Keep detailed accounts
As a child, the Queen kept detailed accounts of her shilling-a-week pocket money.
2 Cut your employees' beer allowances
To their disgust, King Edward VIII cut the Palace staff's beer allowances. The staff affected included those who unloaded and carted the King's crates of champagne.
3 Let your house
Princess Margaret lets her house in Mustique, Les Jolies Eaux, for £750 a week.
4 Save paper
Queen Mary would always re-use old tissue paper and wrapping paper, envelopes and half-used writing paper.
5 Never abandon a cigar
After his abdication, King Edward VIII habitually saved his half-smoked Havanas, relighting them the next day.
6 Demolish some rooms
In 1977, the Queen demolished 91 of Sandringham's 361 rooms. She had been planning to demolish a few more, but the cost of demolition became prohibitive.
7 Make full use of welfare facilities
Shortly after Prince Charles was born, a Palace official went to Westminster Food Office to collect the baby's ration book for free cod-liver oil and orange juice.
8 Recycle your sequins
The Queen has the sequins and beads removed from her old evening dresses and attached to new ones.
9 Abandon your train
In 1964, bowing to the new Socialist government, the Queen

announced that she would be giving up the use of the 8 coach Royal Train, including the children's coach that had been built for Prince Charles and Princess Anne in 1955. For ever after the Royal coaches would be tacked onto an ordinary train.

10 Cut down on lavatory paper
On a visit to Windsor Castle in 1892, the courtiers of King Edward VII were surprised to find that Queen Victoria had ordered newspapers to be placed in the lavatories, with a function that was not primarily informative.

11 Drive an 11-year-old car
The Queen's personal car is a 1971 dark green 3.5 litre Rover, which she intends to drive until it wears out completely.

12 Have your hats re-trimmed
The Queen Mother instructs her milliner to salvage any hats that can be used again, and has them re-trimmed to match new dresses.

13 Charge for performances
During rehearsals for their 1941 Christmas pantomime, 'Cinderella', the Queen disagreed with Princess Margaret over whether the specially invited audience should be made to pay. 'No one will pay to see us', said the Queen.
'Nonsense', replied Princess Margaret, 'They'll pay anything to see us.' In the end, a charge of 7s 6d a head was levied.

14 Look after the pennies
As a child, Prince Charles once mislaid a dog lead at Sandringham, to the annoyance of the Queen, who sent him back to look for it. 'Dog leads cost money', she explained.

Princess Margaret's Christmas present list   24

(Compiled by the Queen to help her write her Thank You letters when the Queen was ten and Princess Margaret was six.)

Present	Given by
See-saw	Mummie
Dolls with dresses	"
Umbrella	Papa
Teniquoit	"
Brooch	Mummie
Calendar	Grannie

Silver Coffee Pot	*Lilibet*
Clock	*to*
Puzzle	*Margaret*
Pen and Pencil	Equerry
China Field Mice	M.E.
Bag and Cricket set	Boforts
Electric Stove	David B.L.
China lamb	Linda

25 *Four unusual personal possessions of Royalty*

1 The smallest watch in the world
This watch, measuring only five-sixteenths of an inch in diameter, was presented to the Queen on a State Visit to France. Unfortunately she lost it when out for a walk, but she was given another one on her next State Visit to France.

2 Two miniature chastity belts
Prince Charles ordered them from a Halstead firm in 1974, swearing that he was intending to use them as loo paper holders.

3 A dead leg
Henry VII's most treasured possession was St George's left leg.

4 A racecourse commentary system
This system, known as The Blower, was installed in Clarence House in 1965 for the benefit of the Queen Mother. 'She cannot always get to the races' said a spokesman, 'and she does like to follow her horses' progress.'

26 *Four Royal personages who kept dwarves*

1 Princess Augusta
The mother of King George III kept the last Court Dwarf in England, Coppernin.

2 Charles I
The king eventually knighted his 3' 9" dwarf, Sir Jeffrey Hudson, for his usefulness in Court intrigues and diplomacy.

3 Edward VI

The constant attendant of this king was his dwarf called Xit.

4 Queen Mary I

The tiniest dwarf in Royal service was Queen Mary's two foot Page of Honour, John Jarvis.

Seven odd belongings of Prince Charles 27

1 The Oval Cricket Ground
2 Dartmoor Prison
3 The right to an annual tithe of 300 puffins from the inhabitants of the Scilly Isles.
4 The cargo of any Cornish shipwreck
5 The village of Daglingworth in Gloucestershire.
6 The worldly goods of any Cornishman who dies intestate and without next of kin.
7 Any whale or porpoise washed up on Cornish beaches.

Prince Philip's six most cherished souvenirs 28

1 His father's signet ring
2 A pennant from the destroyer *Whelp*
3 His Coronation programme
4 A Greek lucky medallion
5 His certificate as a Qualified Boiler Trimmer (gained after a series of six-hour shifts in tropical conditions, necessitated after the Chinese stokers had deserted en masse).
6 The receipted bill for his wife's wedding bouquet.

Eighteen gifts given by the Royal Family to each other

1 A pink wooden rocking elephant
Given by Prince Charles to Prince Andrew for his second birthday. Prince Charles made it in the woodwork shop at Cheam.

2 Chelsea china
Given each year by King George VI to the Queen Mother.

3 Miniature gardening tools
Given by Queen Mary to the Queen for her seventh birthday.

4 A bowl and a pot
Given by Prince Andrew to the Queen Mother in 1978. He made them himself at Gordonstoun.

The Queen and Prince Philip watch 6-year-old Ian Heggie demonstrating the James Bond car they will be giving to Prince Andrew

5 A miniature Aston Martin

Given by his parents to Prince Andrew when he was six years old. It cost an estimated £4,000 to build, and like the real James Bond car, it came complete with artificial machine guns concealed in the sidelights and a smoke-screen system.

6 Three titles

Given by King George VI to Prince Philip before his marriage. They were Baron Greenwich, Earl of Merioneth and Duke of Edinburgh. 'It is a great deal to give a man all at once,' wrote King George VI to Queen Mary, 'but I know Philip understands his new responsibilities on his marriage to Lilibet.'

7 A silver gilt cup

Given by Queen Mary to Prince Charles for his christening. King George III had given it as a christening present to a godson in 1780 – 'so that I gave a present from my great grandfather to my great grandson 168 years later', wrote Queen Mary.

8 A pair of leather gun cases

Given by Prince Charles to Mark Phillips as a wedding present.

9 A clockwork monkey

Given by Queen Mary to the Queen for her third birthday.

10 A miniature polo mallet

Given by Prince Philip to Prince Charles for his thirteenth birthday.

11 A cartoon

Given by Prince Charles to Prince Philip in 1962. Drawn by Prince Charles himself it showed Prince Philip standing on a ten gallon jar of hair restorer.

12 A picnic set

Given by Princess Margaret to the Queen as a wedding present.

13 Three brace of grouse

Sent by King George VI from hospital to his brother, the Duke of Windsor, shortly before he died in 1952.

14 White flowers

Prince Philip gives bouquets of white flowers, each year bigger than the one before, to the Queen on their wedding anniversary.

15 A complete cinema

Given by Lord Mountbatten to the Queen and Prince Philip as a wedding present.

16 A gold soup bowl

Given by Edward VIII to George V for Christmas in 1912, at his own suggestion. Queen Mary wrote to her son: 'It costs £150 but he is most anxious to have it.'

17 Musical Coronation mugs
Given by Queen Mary to the Queen and Princess Margaret in 1937.
18 One dozen chair covers
Made by King George VI in *petit point* (in which he was expert) and presented to the Queen Mother for Royal Lodge.

30   *Ten gifts to Royalty from commoners*

1 A crocodile
In 1961, the people of the village of Berending in Gambia gave the Queen a two-year-old crocodile in a pierced silver biscuit box as a present for Prince Andrew. The Queen's Private Secretary Sir Martin Charteris had to keep it in his bath for the rest of the trip. The next year, on a visit to Liberia, the Queen was presented with two hippos, also for Prince Andrew.
2 A miniature Sherlock Holmes story
Sir Arthur Conan Doyle gave Queen Mary a special Sherlock Holmes story for inclusion in miniature in her Doll's House.
3 32,000 food parcels
Married in an age of post-war austerity, the Queen and Prince Philip received 32,000 food parcels as wedding presents from well-wishing Americans.
4 £500,000
An eccentric miser, John Neild, left Queen Victoria a half a million pounds in 1852. Queen Victoria spent some of the money on buying Balmoral for Albert.
5 A gold chainmail pinafore
The Queen was presented with a gold chainmail pinafore on her 1979 tour of the Arabian gulf. It is not known whether she wears it about the house.
6 One-and-a-half tons of nappies
At the announcement of the birth of Prince Charles, the people of America sent the Queen one-and-a-half tons of nappies.
7 A solid silver inkstand
One of King Edward VII's most treasured possessions was a solid silver inkstand sent to him anonymously. It was inscribed, '*To the Prince of Wales from one who saw him conduct a blind beggar across the streets. In memory of a kind Christian action.*'

8 £20,000

Aged twelve, Princess Margaret was left £20,000 by a friend of the family, Mrs Ronnie Greville.

9 A piece of cloth woven from thread spun by Mahatma Gandhi

This personal wedding present from Gandhi to the Queen was much distrusted by Queen Mary, who suspected that it was a loin cloth. Princess Margaret cautiously hid it under some of the one-and-a-half thousand other wedding presents on display so that her grandmother would not be rendered furious when she saw it.

10 A wastepaper basket

The Queen's Dresser, Bobo Macdonald, gave the Queen and Prince Philip a waste paper basket as a wedding present.

Four odd Royal souvenirs 31

1 A bullet

After an assassin had narrowly missed him in Brussels in 1900, King Edward VII asked for the assassin's bullet to be dislodged, and he kept it for the rest of his life.

2 A flag

King George VI specially asked for the last of the Union Jacks to have flown above the British Residency at Lucknow since the siege of 1857, when India became independent in 1947. He then hung the flag above Windsor Castle.

3 A numberplate

The Queen has always kept the numberplate from the first car her father gave her for her eighteenth birthday. Its registration number is JGY 280.

4 A pen

The Queen still writes with the pen which belonged to her father, King George VI.

32   *Three favourite Royal riddles*

1 '*How do I like my tea?*'
'*In a cup.*'
King George VI
2 '*How do you tell the head of a worm from the tail?*'
'*Put it in flour and wait till it coughs.*'
Prince Charles
3 '*What is it that being born without life, head, lip or eye, yet doth run roaring through the world til it die?*'
'*A fart*'
King Henry VIII

33   *Eleven naughty members of the Royal Family*

1 Prince Charles

As a young boy, Prince Charles put an icecube down a footman's neck.
Later in life, he threw the Moderator of the Church of Scotland into the fountain at Balmoral.

2 Princess Margaret

As a young girl, Princess Margaret enjoyed putting acorns in any shoes or gumboots left outdoors.

3 King Edward VII

The young King Edward VII would make faces, spit and throw stones at his stern tutor, Mr Gibbs. (His German tutor was forced to report that 'it isn't only that he is inattentive, but when I scold him he just pulls my beard.') On a walking tour, he drove a flock of sheep into Lake Windermere.

4 Prince Andrew

The young Prince Andrew was once caught using a silver tray as a toboggan down the stairs at Buckingham Palace. He has also been known to tie the bootlaces of a sentry together and to pour bubble bath into the fountain at Windsor. By 1981, his naughtiness had become more sophisticated: Commander Shallow at the Royal Navy Air Station at Culdrose was forced to pin up a notice forbidding Prince Andrew and his fellow officers from watching blue movies on the Mess video.

5 King George VI
The young King George VI would seize every opportunity with his brother, King Edward VIII, to rush out of the schoolroom at Sandringham and quickly climb a tree. They would be closely followed by their tutor, Mr Hansell, searching and calling for them.

6 Princess Anne
On discovering that the Buckingham Palace sentries had to present arms every time she walked past them, Princess Anne used to rush backwards and forwards in front of them. She was eventually discovered and ordered to stop.

7 Prince Philip
Prince Philip liberated a pigsty and set the animals stampeding into the Landgravine of Hesse's tea party when he was 5.

8 The Queen
Once when she was frustrated with the grind of her French lessons, the Queen poured ink from an ornamental silver inkpot all over her own head. After the Queen as a child had been particularly naughty, her Governess refused to speak to her. For a time the Queen sat in a frustrated silence, and then she said, 'You *must* answer. It's royalty speaking!' For this, she was given a sound ticking-off by the Queen Mother.

9 King Edward VIII
When the young King Edward VIII was eating a meal with his grandfather, King Edward VII, he butted into the conversation. His grandfather told him to keep quiet until he was given permission to speak. Once permission had been given, he said, 'It's too late now, Grandpa. It was a caterpillar on your lettuce, but you've eaten it.'

10 Princess Marina
When Princess Marina was rude to her nanny she was punished by being made to eat her porridge from a china bowl, and not from her usual silver bowl which had been given to her for her christening by Queen Alexandra.

11 Princess Diana
When her stepmother, Raine, refused the sixteen-year-old Princess Diana use of her stereo record player, Princess Diana got her own back by disconnecting the wiring.

Eight members of the Royal Family who have cracked jokes

1 Princess Anne

Sick of bogus pre-wedding stories about her in the French press, Princess Anne asked a French visitor soon after her wedding, 'Am I divorced yet?'

2 Prince Arthur

In 1501, on the morning after his marriage to Catherine of Aragon, Arthur, Prince of Wales, joked: 'I have been deep into Spain this night.'

3 Prince Andrew

In his first public speech, to the Oxford and Cambridge Centenary Varsity rugby teams in 1981, Prince Andrew told of a cannibal father and son who saw an attractive girl in the jungle. 'The son, not well up on the facts of life at all said: "Look at her father, why don't we take her home for dinner?" The father said: "I have a better idea. We will take her home . . . and eat your mother." '

4 Prince Philip

In 1950, Prince Philip in HMS *Magpie* escorted the Queen in HMS *Surprise* into Malta Harbour. The two ships exchanged signals:
Surprise to *Magpie*. 'Princess full of beans.'
Magpie to *Surprise*: 'Is that the best you can give her for breakfast?'

5 King George VI

Knighting his surgeon, Professor James Learmonth, in 1949, King George VI said, 'You used a knife on me. Now I'm going to use one on you.'

6 The Queen Mother

Once, when caught up in a crowd which was pressing too close, the Queen Mother murmured, 'Please don't touch the exhibits.'

7 The Queen

The Queen opened her speech on the anniversary of her Silver Wedding by saying, 'I think that everyone will concede that on this of all days I should begin my speech with the words, "My husband and I".'

When the Dutch Ambassador told the Queen in 1981 that he was planning to retire to England, the Queen asked him to which county he was going. 'South Gloucestershire, Ma'am', he replied. Thinking of all the members of her family who lived there, the Queen said, 'Oh, how common!'

On another occasion, driving away from Buckingham Palace, a lady-in-waiting made fun of a young man who used to wait by the gates every time the Queen drove out. 'Don't laugh', said the Queen, 'You are talking about my only loyal subject.'

8 Mark Phillips

The attempted kidnap of Princess Anne in 1974 came at a time when she and Mark Phillips were expected for dinner with an old schoolfriend of hers. At half past nine, Mark Phillips rang her up. 'Oh,' said the schoolfriend, 'Have you been held up?' 'Well, you could say that', quipped Mark Phillips.

Two uses Prince Philip has made of a top hat   35

1 Receptacle

Visiting Athens for the first time since his infancy for the State reinterment of his relations who had died in exile from Greece, the fifteen-year-old Prince Philip was suddenly overcome with nausea and vomited into his new top hat.

2 Camouflage

Since he lacks the Queen's enthusiasm for horseracing, Prince Philip has been known to conceal a transistor radio in his top hat at Ascot so that he can listen to the cricket results.

Twenty-two objects employed in Royal practical jokes   36

1 Dead birds

Regularly concealed in guests' beds by King Edward VII.

2 A tadpole sandwich

Fed by King Edward VIII to his French tutor, M. Hua.

3 A whoopee cushion

Placed on the Bishop of Norwich's chair at Sandringham by Prince Charles.

4 Queen Victoria's apron strings

Tied together by Princess Beatrice around her mother's chair.

5 'Just married' balloons

Attached by Prince Andrew and Prince Edward to Prince Charles and Princess Diana's leaving carriage after their wedding.

6 Frogs

Placed by King James I down the Earl of Pembroke's neck. But as Pembroke hated frogs, so King James hated pigs, and Pembroke had his revenge by depositing a pig in the King's bedroom.

7 Invisible ink

Poured by Prince Michael of Kent aged 12 all over a carpet at Coppins, his family home. Alas, someone had switched the bottles and the ink did not disappear. The carpet had to be cleaned and was never the same again.

8 Salt and pepper cocktails

Mixed by King George VI and Edward VIII as children for their grandmother, Queen Alexandra. Though she often saw them pour salt and pepper into her glass of water, she would always humour them by drinking it.

9 A live lobster

Placed in a friend's bed by King Edward VII.

10 Disintegrating tea spoons

Given to King George VI by his Maths tutor at Osborne, and tried out on his father, King George V. He later reported that the joke was 'not greatly appreciated'.

11 Exploding cigars

Handed around by Prince Charles at Dartmouth one night after dinner.

12 Bed linen

Rearranged to form apple pie beds by Princess Diana for her guests in Scotland in 1979.

13 Dracula fangs

Worn by Prince Philip to chase the Queen around the Royal Train early in their marriage.

14 Sticky pear drops

Placed by King Edward VII in the pockets of his friends' evening clothes.

15 A toy snake

Produced from a can labelled 'Mixed Nuts' given to the Queen by Prince Philip.

16 The gardener's broom

Frequently hidden by the young Princess Margaret. She would hide and chortle as he tried to find it.

17 Dried peas

Placed in friends' beds by King Edward VII. ('If anyone caught his foot on a mat, or nearly fell into the fire or out of a window, the mirth of the whole Royal Family knew no bounds', wrote Mary Bulteel at the time.)

18 A rotor arm

Removed by King George VI from the distributor of the engine on which his daughter Elizabeth was working at her ATS camp during the war. He came back some time later and remarked to his perfectionist daughter, 'What, not got it going yet?'

19 Knives and forks

Removed from a dining room table in Buckingham Palace by the young Prince Andrew as a footman was laying them. Prince Andrew had concealed himself under the table.

20 False beards

Worn by the Queen, and her ladies-in-waiting to greet Prince Philip on return from a trip on which he had grown a real beard in the South Pacific in 1957.

21 Shoes

Conned off his fellow officers by Prince Charles at the Cranwell RAF college in 1971. He made a broadcast over the Tannoy saying that 'because of a basic design fault in the heel, the shoe firm were withdrawing all shoes.' Over half the college delivered their shoes to the porter's lodge.

22 A Candle

Applied to the last page of a speech Harry Secombe was delivering in his capacity as president of the Lord's Taverners to introduce Prince Philip. As he did, his speech went up in flames. Prince Philip had waggishly set fire to it with a candle.

Nine reasons for Royal tears   37

1 A horse dying

Princess Diana cried in public when Prince Charles's horse *Allibar* died in 1981.

Princess Anne cried when her horse *Doublet* had to be put down after it had broken a leg on Smith's Lawn in 1974. Her tears may have arisen from guilt as much as sadness – two different vets had advised the Princess that *Doublet* was unfit to be ridden.

2 An engagement announced

Queen Mary cried when she heard that her son wished to marry Mrs Simpson. She ate little, and had many sleepless nights.

The Queen Mother cried as she told her Household that Princess Margaret and Peter Townsend intended to marry.

3 A future husband introduced

When Henrietta Maria of France first met her intended husband, Charles I, she burst into tears.

Mary cried when she first met William of Orange.

4 A grandmother

Perhaps overawed by her Indian servants, George VI and Edward VIII would frequently burst into tears in front of Queen Victoria. 'What have I done wrong now?', the old lady would ask.

5 Daughters acting

In December 1940, King George VI wept through a Nativity play which starred his two daughters. 'It is such a wonderful story', he said.

6 A fiancé abdicating

In her memoirs, the Duchess of Windsor describes listening to Edward VIII's Abdication speech on the radio: 'I was lying on the sofa with my hands over my eyes, trying to hide my tears.'

7 A melancholy wedding

When the flatulent forty-year old Prince Frederick of Württemberg married Princess Charlotte, the daughter of King George III, in 1797, the King, the bride and her sisters cried all the way through the service. The groom was the only person in the Chapel Royal to remain dry-eyed.

8 A rival despatched

Queen Elizabeth I wept at Greenwich in 1587 when she heard that Mary, Queen of Scots had been executed before an invited audience at Fotheringay. She herself had reluctantly signed the death warrant.

9 Life revealing itself

On his seventeenth birthday, the future Edward VII wept when his father, Prince Albert, handed him a document which began: 'Life is composed of duties.'

38   *Ten Palaces and residences owned by the Queen*

1 Buckingham Palace
2 Windsor Castle
3 The Palace of Holyroodhouse, Edinburgh
4 The Palace of Westminster – still in theory the monarch's principal residence
5 The Tower of London

6 St James's Palace
7 Kensington Palace
8 Hampton Court Palace
9 Balmoral
10 Sandringham

The Queen's house calendar 39

1 Autumn – Buckingham Palace
2 Christmas – Windsor Castle
3 January, February – Sandringham
4 Easter – Windsor Castle
5 Early Summer – Holyroodhouse
6 Summer – Balmoral

Contradictory Royal views on three houses 40

1 Sandringham
King George V – 'The place I love better than anywhere in the world.'
King Edward VIII – 'Dickens in a Cartier setting.'
2 Windsor Castle
King Edward VI, aged twelve – 'Methinks I am in prison. Here be no galleries, nor gardens to walk in!'
Queen Mary – 'This dear glorious old castle so full of historical associations.'
3 Balmoral
Queen Victoria – 'A pretty little castle in the old Scotch style.'
King Edward VII – 'The Highland Barn of a 1,000 draughts.'

41 Seven Royal comments on Buckingham Palace

1 *'Everything is so straggly, such distances and so fatiguing.'* Queen Victoria
2 *'A Sepulchre.'* King Edward VII
3 *'An Icebox.'* King George VI
4 *'It has a dank musty smell.'* King Edward VIII
5 *'This isn't ours. It's a tied cottage.'* Prince Philip
6 *'A very cosy house.'* Princess Margaret
7 *'I don't feel as relaxed at Buckingham Palace as I do in my own home – but then I don't expect anyone does when they visit their mother-in-law.'* Mark Phillips.

42 Three things that lurk under Buckingham Palace

1 A sewer
Buckingham Palace was built on top of a sewer.
2 An underground line
A (nearly) secret branch of London's Underground Train system links Buckingham Palace to Heathrow airport. It would be used as an escape route in the event of an emergency.
3 A corpse
It is almost certain that when the Shah of Persia stayed at Buckingham Palace he ordered one of his staff to be executed with a bowstring and buried somewhere in the Palace grounds.

43 Four intruders in Royal homes

1 An army deserter
At Buckingham Palace during the war, an army deserter, whose family had all been killed in an air raid, leapt from behind the curtains and threw himself at the Queen Mother's feet when she was alone in her bedroom. 'For a moment my heart stood still', she later commented. She talked to him gently, edging slowly back to the alarm bell on the wall. 'Poor man' she said after help had come, 'I felt so sorry for him'.

2 A timid assassin

In 1584, William Parry, a Welsh spy, stole into Queen Elizabeth I's garden at Richmond, intent on killing her. But when he set eyes on the Queen he was 'so daunted with the majesty of her presence' that he could not do it.

3 An over-enthusiastic monarchist

A fortnight after the birth of the Princess Royal, an intruder, the seventeen-year-old son of a tailor, was discovered hiding under a sofa in the room adjoining the bedroom of Queen Victoria. He had been in Buckingham Palace for three days, living off any food he saw lying about. He had seen Queen Victoria, heard the baby Princess cry and even sat on the throne. Two years previously he had entered the Palace disguised as a chimney sweep. The Boy Jones, as he came to be known, was sent for three months to a house of correction. At the end of the three months, he returned once more to the Palace, where he was discovered and sent back for three more months. On his release he refused an offer of £4 to appear on stage, preferring to pay another visit to Buckingham Palace. This time he was shipped off to sea. A year later, after his ship had docked at Portsmouth, he was arrested making his way back to the Palace. For a final time he was put to sea, but he soon disappeared from his ship, never to be seen or heard of again.

4 Two German tourists

In the summer of 1981, police at Buckingham Palace discovered two young German tourists asleep in the gardens. They had scaled the wall the night before thinking that it was a park.

Six additional security aids of members of the Royal Family   44

1 The Queen

The Queen's bedroom door is always guarded by a uniformed policeman.

2 Queen Mary

During the war, Queen Mary kept three suitcases packed in case the Germans invaded. A fourth was ready on standby to be filled with her precious jewels.

3 The Duchess of Windsor

The Duchess of Windsor constantly kept her husband's pistol by the side of her bed after he died.

4 King James I
King James I had a terror of being stabbed, and wore such heavily quilted and padded clothes for protection that his walk was often compared to that of a duck.
5 King George VI
King George VI learnt to use a pistol and a sten gun during the war; he took the sten gun with him everywhere.
6 The Queen Mother
The Queen Mother was taught to use a revolver in 1940. 'Now I shall not go down like all the others,' she commented.

45 *Five things thrown at Royalty*

1 A large wooden chair
Visiting the South East London Juvenile Court in the 1960s, Princess Alexandra flinched when she was nearly hit by a large wooden chair thrown a full fifteen feet by a boy who had just been sentenced to a term in Wormwood Scrubs for stealing a pewter mug from a tramp.
2 A stone
In 1875, Queen Alexandra was struck by a splinter of glass when a stone smashed the window of her railway carriage as she passed Eton. Though the headmaster of Eton felt confident that it was the work of a local hooligan, and not a boy from the college, he promised a full inquiry. If it was discovered to be one of his pupils 'they will be flogged with the utmost severity and then expelled.' No such culprit was found.
3 A lemonade bottle
Prince Charles's car windscreen was shattered when a man threw a lemonade bottle at him in Newcastle, 1978.
4 A loaded revolver
While presenting new colours to the Brigade of Guards in 1935, King George V had a loaded gun thrown at him by a deranged Irish journalist called George McMahon (real name: Jerome Bannigan). The gun hit the near hind leg of the King's horse. 'We'll know in a moment if it's a bomb', said the King to his son, the future George VI. McMahon was sentenced to 12 months' hard labour, charged with 'intent of alarming His Majesty'.
5 A block of concrete
In Belfast in 1966, a seventeen-year-old youth, John Morgan, threw a block of concrete at the Queen's car. It missed.

Eight members of the Royal Family who have survived attacks

1 Queen Victoria

During the course of Queen Victoria's reign, there were no less than seven attempts on her life, all except one of them from adolescents with unloaded guns.

2 Queen Elizabeth II

In 1981, the Queen narrowly escaped death when she walked within 200 yards of the place where, later in the day, 7lbs of gelignite exploded. She was opening an oil terminal at Sullom Voe in Scotland. Earlier that same year a seventeen-year-old called Marcus Sarjeant fired six blank shots at the Queen during the Trooping of the Colour. He was charged under the Treason Act of 1842. 'Life must go on' was the Queen's comment later.

3 King Edward VII and Queen Alexandra

In 1900, while the Royal Train had stopped for a short while at Brussels on its way to Copenhagen, a sixteen-year-old tinsmith's apprentice, Baptiste Sipido, rushed from the crowd, put a revolver through the window of the Royal carriage, fired at point–blank range and somehow missed. Sipido, who gave sympathy for the Boers as his motive, was released on parole and shortly afterwards disappeared. 'The poor fool' was Edward's comment.

4 Queen Elizabeth I

When a shot fired from the shore wounded one of her bargemen, Queen Elizabeth I gave him her handkerchief saying, 'Be of good cheer, for you will never want. For the bullet was meant for me.'

5 Princess Anne

In 1974, travelling back from the première of a film about the Riding for the Disabled organisation, Princess Anne was attacked by a man who had swerved his car in front of hers in the Mall. The assailant, Ian Ball, was charged with attempting to murder the two policemen who had stood in his way, and wounding two others. Following this incident, the Queen appointed Princess Anne a Dame Grand Cross of the Royal Victorian Order, and Mark Phillips, who had also been present, a Commander of the same order. For his bravery in beating off the attacker, Inspector Beaton was given the George Cross. Ball had planned to hold Princess Anne for a ransom of £3 million, at the same time wishing to draw attention to the lack of facilities for mental illness on the National Health Service.

6 Prince Charles

In 1974, while he was stationed at the Royal Navy barracks at

Portland in Dorset, Prince Charles was woken up at two o'clock one morning by a noise in his sitting room. When he opened the connecting door he was jumped on by an armed assailant. Woken by the sound of the struggle, Detective-Chief Inspector Paul Officer rushed in just in time to prevent the assailant, a deranged lieutenant at the Navy base, from bringing a chair down on Charles's head.

7 Princess Diana's portrait

Shortly after it was put on exhibit at the National Portrait Gallery, in August 1981, Bryan Organ's portrait of Lady Diana Spencer was viciously slashed with a knife by an eighteen-year-old who caused more than £1,000 worth of damage to the picture and gravely shocked the Royal Family. He said his attack was a protest against the death on hunger strike of Bobby Sands, a member of the IRA. All Royal portraits at the Gallery have since been protected by plastic shields.

8 King Edward VIII

In 1925, at Melton Races, the future King Edward VIII was attacked by a shawled woman wielding a hatpin. She drew blood, but he took it in his stride, saying that very often a woman might stick a pin in him or punch him with all her might. 'They could get no satisfaction from kicking the Houses of Parliament, whereas I am both handy and responsive.'

9 King George III

In 1786 a housemaid called Margaret Nicholson attempted to stab King George III as he rode in his carriage. She was swiftly overpowered, but as the crowd began to attack her, the King shouted, 'The poor creature is mad! Do not hurt her! She has not hurt me!' Margaret Nicholson was later declared insane and was sent to an asylum.

47 *Nine objects stolen from Royalty*

1 An exercise book

One of Prince Charles's exercise books was stolen from a classroom when he was fifteen years old. It contained essays on democracy, the monarchy and publicity. It was eventually retrieved, but only after copies had been made of it and offered to various continental publishers. The German magazine *Stern* reputedly paid £1,000 for the right to publish extracts.

2 A motorcar

Soon after her marriage, Princess Margaret's black convertible

Nash Metropolitan motorcar was stolen from outside a house in which she was lunching. After a long police chase, a fourteen-year-old boy was arrested.

3 Two sheepskin coats
In 1968, Prince Michael of Kent had two sheepskin coats stolen from the MG 1100 that he had parked outside the Kensington Odeon.

4 Two suitcases
In 1957, Princess Alexandra had two suitcases taken from the back of her parked car. A few days later, the suitcases were located in a left luggage office at London Bridge station, and the two thieves fell into a trap laid by the police. 'If I had known who the cases belonged to, I wouldn't have touched them', commented one of the thieves. 'I knew every policemen in England would be looking for me.' He was then led away to begin a six-month jail sentence.

5 Jewellery
When the Duchess of Windsor was staying with the Earl of Dudley in 1946, a thief broke in and stole £20,000 worth of jewellery which had been given to her by her husband.

6 A bottle of vodka
In 1978, a bottle of rare vodka was stolen from a party given in Kensington Palace by Princess Margaret. The next morning the Princess telephoned every guest and, by a process of elimination, unmasked the culprit.

7 Wedding presents
In 1963, as Princess Alexandra lay pregnant in Thatched House Lodge in Richmond Park, a burglar climbed into the next door room. The Princess screamed when she saw him, and he rushed away with a number of her wedding presents.

8 The Royal Standard
On the Queen's first visit to Australia in 1954, the Royal Standard, which flies from the wing of her car, was taken so often by someone in a throng that replacements had to be sent for from England.

9 Small change
When he was a student at Cambridge, Prince Charles once complained to a stallholder in the vegetable market that he had been shortchanged.

And one object stolen by Royalty . . . **A Persian Carpet**
Aged nine, Prince Philip removed one of his family's best Persian carpets and imitating the thriving Athens street-hawkers, attempted to sell it to passers-by. His parents caught him in time.

Eleven appropriate names for Royal servants

1 Hurl

The chauffeur who once stopped so suddenly that the Queen Mother fell from her seat.

2 Crisp

The valet of Edward VIII, and later George VI

3 Trotter

Brigadier-General Trotter, the equerry to the young Edward VIII.

4 Footer

Victor Footer, of the 3rd Battalion Coldstream Guards, was sentenced to ten days confinement to barracks in 1959 after an American tourist had complained that while guarding Buckingham Palace he had marched forward and stepped on her foot. Later the same year it was decided to retreat the Guards behind the railings.

John Brown, Queen Victoria's familiar ghillie

5 Prince

William Prince, the Registrar for Westminster, whose job it once was to register Prince Andrew's birth.

6 Sharp and Officer

Two Royal detectives

7 Reeks

Mr Robin Reeks, the farm manager at Windsor until 1979.

8 Green

Donald Green, Prince Charles's detective at Gordonstoun, who made the mistake of leaving Charles unattended in Oban, causing him to seek refuge from the crowd in a bar where he ordered a Cherry Brandy, though he was under age, and was noticed by a journalist.

9 Checketts

Squadron Leader Checketts, Personal Secretary to Prince Charles.

10 Innocent

Queen Victoria's monthly nurse was called Mrs Innocent.

And one assailant . . .

11 Pate

Robert Pate was transported in 1850 for injuring Queen Victoria by hitting her over the head with a cane.

Twelve rude Royal servants 49

1 Princess Margaret's butler

In 1960, soon after Princess Margaret's marriage, her butler, Mr Cronin, handed in his notice following a disagreement with Lord Snowdon. He then told the *Sunday People* why. 'I was mortified by the strange standards imposed on me,' he said. 'There was a difference of opinion – a clash of personalities. It led to a climax and I have taken the only step open to me.'

2 Queen Mary I's headmaster

Queen Mary I selected Nicholas Udall for the headmastership of Westminster School – a strange choice, as he had been dismissed from the headmastership of Eton College for molesting his pupils and for stealing a college plate.

3 Queen Victoria's ghillie

Queen Victoria's coarse-grained manservant John Brown was once heard criticising her choice of clothes. 'Whit are ye daeing with that auld black dress on ye agin?' he asked. The Queen obediently went in and changed.

4 King Edward VIII's nurse

King George V and Queen Mary took three years to discover that the nurse they had employed to look after their children was entirely unsuitable. Her first desire was to turn the royal parents against their children. To this end, she would pinch the children before they went in to see their parents. They would then cry and be sent upstairs in disgrace.

5 Marie of Mecklenberg-Strelitz

In 1897, Marie was impregnated by Hecht, a palace servant. He was immediately dismissed. Thereupon he pioneered the tradition of 'kiss and tell' by selling his story to the newspapers. The baby was farmed out, and the family refused to mention Marie's name (a rebuff that Queen Victoria considered 'wicked'). Various members of the family entertained theories to how Hecht had managed to achieve his devilish ends. The Grand Duchess Augusta thought he had terrorised her, Queen Victoria thought he had drugged her, and both the Duke of York and the German Emperor favoured hypnotism.

6 The Queen's Defence Minister

In 1977 the Labour Defence Minister, Mr Fred Mulley, fell fast asleep in the chair next to the Queen while they were both supposed to be watching a Royal Air Force review.

7 Prince Philip's valet

In 1954, Prince Philip's valet of two years published his memoirs in the *Sunday Pictorial*. The palace complained to the Press Council, saying that the *Sunday Pictorial* had aided and abetted a breach of trust. Nowadays, all royal servants must sign an undertaking never to speak to the Press.

8 Princess Margaret's footman

David Payne, a former footman of Princess Margaret, changed his sex in Cannes during the summer of 1969.

9 King George V's stalker

Deerstalking near Balmoral, King George V once missed a very easy shot and said to his Scottish stalker, 'Take this damned rifle away. Never let me see it again'. To which the stalker replied, 'Yer Majesty, dinna waste yer breath damning the rifle. It was a verra bad shot'.

10 The Queen Mother's portrait painter

Commissioned to paint a portrait of the Queen Mother, Augustus John failed to turn up for the first session. The waiting Queen Mother was eventually delivered a telegram from the artist apologising for his absence, and saying he was suffering 'from the influence'. But he was present at subsequent sittings, sustained by numerous bottles of sherry and brandy placed in a cupboard adjoining his easel by the Palace staff.

11 King Henry VIII's footmen
King Henry VIII once had to warn his servants against wiping their greasy fingers on his tapestries.

12 Queen Charlotte's maid
Sarah Wilson, a servant of one of the Ladies-in-Waiting to Queen Charlotte, the wife of King George III, was caught trying on the Queen's jewels. Banished for life to America, she took with her a small selection of the jewels and one of the Queen's dresses. She wore her booty in America, pretending she was Princess Susanna Carolina Matilda, a sister of the Queen. For eighteen months, she was a leading figure in American society until she was discovered, arrested and sent back into service.

The Queen's ten Ladies-in-Waiting 50

1 The Duchess of Grafton: *Mistress of the Robes*
2 The Marchioness of Abergavenny: *Lady of the Bedchamber*
3 The Countess of Airlie: *Lady of the Bedchamber*
4 The Countess of Cromer: *Extra Lady of the Bedchamber*
5 Hon. Mary Morrison: *Woman of the Bedchamber*
6 Lady Susan Hussey: *Woman of the Bedchamber*
7 Lady Abel Smith: *Woman of the Bedchamber*
8 Mrs John Dugdale: *Woman of the Bedchamber*
9 Mrs John Woodroffe: *Extra Woman of the Bedchamber*
10 Lady Rose Baring: *Extra Woman of the Bedchamber*

Eight victims of Royal bad manners 51

1 The Archbishop of Canterbury
When Michael Ramsey, the then Archbishop of Canterbury, was giving the address at Prince Charles's confirmation, he was irritated to see Prince Philip reading a book rather than paying attention. 'Bloody rude, that's what I call it', he remarked later to the Dean of Windsor.

2 The Bald Eagle
When they were both touring America in 1970, Prince Charles asked an official why the Bald Eagle was chosen as America's

45

national symbol. Before the official could reply, Princess Anne butted in that it was 'rather a bad choice'.

3 Margaret Trudeau
'He looked long and hard down my cleavage,' the former wife of the Prime Minister of Canada complained after sitting next to Prince Charles at dinner.

4 A Dutch chauffeur
While he was being driven from Amsterdam airport in 1968 by a bi-lingual Dutch chauffeur, Prince Philip looked out of the car window and said to his detective, 'What a po-faced lot these Dutch are. Look at them.' The Dutch chauffeur became so irate at this remark that only the well-practised excuses of the Prince's detective encouraged him to keep driving.

5 A fat person
As a child, Princess Margaret prodded a fat visitor to Buckingham Palace with her finger and asked, 'Is that *all* you?'

6 Queen Catherine of Aragon
When it was announced to him that his wife, Queen Catherine of Aragon, was dead, King Henry VIII threw up his arms and said, 'God be praised. The old harridan is dead!'

7 The chairman of a reception committee
Having just descended the steps of his aeroplane, Prince Philip was asked by the chairman of a reception committee, 'How was your flight?'
'Have you ever flown in a plane', asked Prince Philip in reply.
'Yes, your Royal Highness, often.'
'Well, it was just like that.'

8 Mrs Freda Dudley Ward
After 14 years as the mistress of King Edward VIII she was told by the switchboard at St James's Palace, 'I don't know how to say it – I have orders not to put you through.'

52 · *Fourteen people who have insulted Royalty*

1 H G Wells
H G Wells once wrote that the royal family was 'uninspiring and alien'. King George V retorted to friends, 'I may be uninspiring but I'm everlastingly damned if I'm alien.'

2 Lord Northcliffe
Lord Northcliffe once described King Edward VII as 'the best monarch we've ever had – on a racecourse.'

Mr Fred Mulley snoozing

3 John Lennon
In 1969, John Lennon announced that he was returning his MBE
to the Queen. 'It was an embarrassment to me. It was a
humiliation. I don't believe in Royalty and titles', he explained.
4 A Brazilian general
At a state banquet in 1968 in Brasilia, Prince Philip asked a
Brazilian General where he had got all his medals from. The
General replied that he had earned them in the war. 'The war?'
replied Prince Philip. 'I didn't know Brazil was in the war that
long.'

'At least, sir,' came the reply, 'I didn't get them for marrying
my wife.'
5 Beau Brummell
When King George IV cut Beau Brummell at a ball in the Argyle
rooms, Brummell riposted by asking Lord Alvanley, 'Alvanley,
who is your fat friend?' Brummell was immediately banished
from court, but he was unrepentant: 'I made him what he is', he
would tell his friends, 'And I can unmake him.'
6 Prudence Glynn
In 1981, Prudence Glynn, the then Fashion Editor of *The Times*,
wrote an article in the *International Herald Tribune* describing
Princess Diana as 'a fashion disaster in her own right' and

47

criticising a strapless dress she had worn for making her look as if she was sitting in a hip bath.

7 Sir Frederick Johnstone
In the closing hours of an evening party, King Edward VII said to Sir Frederick Johnstone, 'Freddy, you're very drunk.' To which Sir Frederick replied, 'Tum-tum, you're very fat.'

8 An old peasant woman
When Queen Victoria showed an old Scottish peasant woman some of her own, rather poor, knitting, the woman looked at it in disgust and said that she pitied Queen Victoria's 'gude mon' if he had not better stockings to wear than that.

9 Angus Ogilvy
After Angus Ogilvy had been implicated in the Lonrho affair, the Duke of Edinburgh said, 'You've landed us in it this time.' To which Angus Ogilvy replied, 'Well, at least I don't have a sister-in-law who's shacking up with a hippy.'

10 The Duchess of Montrose and Lady Sarah Ingestre
After the Flora Hastings affair, in which the young Queen Victoria had wrongly suspected a dying lady-in-waiting of being illicitly pregnant, the Duchess of Montrose and Lady Sarah Ingestre hissed the Queen as she entered the Royal box at Ascot. 'Those two abominable women ought to be flogged', the Queen commented later.

11 Lord Hervey
After seeing the baby born to the Princess of Wales in 1737, Lord Hervey described her as 'a little rat of a girl, about the bigness of a large toothpick case'.

12 Miss Mary Blomfield
At a Court presentation, while a young suffragette, Miss Mary Blomfield, the daughter of a knight, was still in her curtsey to King George V she screamed out, 'For God's sake, Your Majesty, stop persecuting women!' The King said that he did not know what things were coming to.

13 A *Times* obituary writer
On the death of King George IV in 1830, *The Times* said, 'There never was an individual less regretted by his fellow-creatures than this deceased King.'

14 The Stock Market
At the death of Queen Anne, the Stock Exchange index rose by 3 per cent.

. . . And one rude mynah bird
At a Sandringham flower show a nine-year-old mynah bird asked the Queen Mother, 'Can your mother skin a rabbit?' The Queen Mother laughed and said, 'I can't answer that one.' To which the bird replied, 'Well, clear off!'

Eight people who have been honoured with Royal graciousness

1 An Indian prince
When an Indian prince began throwing asparagus stalks over his shoulder at an official dinner, King Edward VII obliged by doing the same.

2 A Boer
When the Queen Mother visited South Africa after the war, one of her Boer hosts said that he could never forgive the English for having conquered his country. 'I understand', replied the Queen Mother, 'We feel much the same in Scotland.'

3 Mrs Keppel
When her husband King Edward VII was on his deathbed, Queen Alexandra sent for his mistress, Alice Keppel, and led her to the King by the hand.

4 The President of Chile
In 1968, the President of Chile, Eduardo Frei Montalva, wrote to the Queen inviting her to come and stay, addressing her as 'Good and big friend'. The Queen accepted his invitation, signing herself, 'Your good friend, Elizabeth R'.

5 John Brown
Once when strolling with Queen Victoria, her brawny manservant John Brown fell to the ground in a drunken stupor. The Queen overlooked the real reason for his fall, saying that she had been distinctly aware of a slight earthquake shock herself.

6 The Labour Cabinet
King George V received the Ministers of the first ever Socialist Government in 1924 wearing a tie in the Labour Party colour, red.

7 A Quaker
When the Quaker William Penn didn't remove his hat in the presence of King Charles II, the King took his own hat off. 'Friend Charles', asked the Quaker, 'why dost thou not keep on thy hat?'
'Tis the custom of this house for only one person to remain covered at a time', came the reply.

8 Anne Boleyn's fellow guests
Though Anne Boleyn was greatly given to vomiting during meals, she would always bring along a noblewoman who she employed specially to hold up a sheet when the urge came upon her. She first developed this method at her Coronation banquet.

54 Four charities of which Princess Diana is patron

1 The Royal School for the Blind
2 The Welsh National Opera
3 The Malcolm Sargent Cancer Fund for Children
4 The Pre-School Playgroups Association

55 Four sacrifices made by the Royal Family

1 Smoking
Prince Philip gave up smoking the night before his wedding.
2 India
'The first time Bertie wrote me a letter with the I for Emperor left out, very sad.'
Written by Queen Mary on the back of the envelope, dated 18 August 1947.
3 Ears
Before her Coronation, the Queen Mother had her ears pierced to accommodate the royal jewels.
4 Digestion
Taking a spoonful of Curried Snake Meat towards his mouth at a Gurkha Survival School in Hong Kong, Prince Charles was heard to remark, 'Boy, the things I do for England!'
On a visit to Fiji, the Queen swallowed in one draught, as etiquette demanded, the national soap-like Yaqona drink. The Queen Mother had not been able to bring herself to do this on two previous visits.

Three acts of kindness of the Queen to Princess Margaret when they were very young

1 When Prince Margaret was too young to join the Girl Guides but desperately keen, the Queen said to the Guide leader, 'She is very strong you know. And she loves getting dirty, don't you, Margaret?'
2 During the war, the Queen interrupted her parents: 'I don't think we ought to talk about battles in front of Margaret. We don't want to upset her.'
3 Looking at the Welsh gold that had been sent for her wedding ring, The Queen said, 'There is enough for two rings. We can save a piece for Margaret.'

Fifteen things given up for Royalty

1 A tooth
To show Queen Elizabeth I the ease with which her own rotten tooth could be removed the Bishop of London had one of his own teeth extracted.

2 Manhood
Before Princess Margaret's tour of HMS *Eastbourne* in 1969, Lt Commander Stephen Meberton of Plymouth checked that the Princess would be able to negotiate the steep ladders and narrow hatchway by going around the same course himself wearing a tight skirt.

3 £75
In January 1982, showjumper Harvey Smith was fined £75 for hitting a man in a restaurant he had overheard making abusive remarks about the Royal Family.

4 Hair
When George III discovered a louse on his plate at dinner in 1787 he ordered all his kitchen staff to shave their heads.

5 Dignity
Quite apart from allowing himself to fall into financial ruin through excessive entertainment of King Edward VII, Christopher Sykes would also allow the King to humiliate him for fun. Sykes was once dressed by the King in a suit of armour and then locked out, to clank about in the suit in public. One of the King's

favourite tricks was to pour brandy over Sykes's head at the end of dinner. 'As your Majesty pleases', he would say, to the raucous laughter of his guests.

6 Food
As the two greyhounds belonging to the British Embassy in Brazil were well known for their incessant farting, they were both starved for several days before the Queen visited in 1968.

7 Sleep
When Queen Elizabeth I visited Sir Thomas Gresham's new house at Osterley in Middlesex, she happened to mention that she thought the courtyard was too large and would look better with a dividing wall. Sir Thomas immediately sent to London for workmen and by the time the Queen woke up the next morning, there was the wall.

8 A strike
In 1953, Southampton dockers broke their strike to load the Queen Mother's luggage onto an ocean liner in defiance of the national dock strike. 'She is the nicest lady in the world', said a union official.

9 Comfort
Even when Queen Victoria's Prime Minister Gladstone, was in his eighties, he stood up throughout his meetings with her.

10 Consciousness
Before toastmaster Ivor Spencer was due to introduce Prince Charles to a Press Club dinner in February 1982, he popped into the Royal lavatory. Wishing to dry his hands, he pulled the Towelmaster, which collapsed on him and knocked him out.

11 A pain-free bottom
Whenever King Edward VI did badly at his lessons, his whipping boy, Barnaby Fitzpatrick, was smacked.

12 Smoking
J D Jamieson, the Bond Street chemist in charge of making the holy oil for the Queen's Coronation, gave up smoking for the occasion to improve his sense of smell.

13 Writing
Lord Palmerston once made this report to Queen Victoria: 'Your Majesty may perhaps have heard that Ibrahim Pasha (the ruler of Egypt) learned to write his name while your Majesty's messenger was waiting for the Queen's Album; and that when he had written his name in the book, he threw away the pen, saying that as the first time in his life he had written his name had been for the Queen of England, so it should be the last, for he would never write it again for anyone else.'

14 Undergraduate lives

When Queen Elizabeth I was watching a play performed by undergraduates at Christchurch, the stage collapsed. Though three students were killed and another five injured, the play carried on, and the Queen later thanked the author of the play 'for his great pains'.

15 Home

Lisa Evans and Patricia Moore, both aged fourteen, from Hayle in Cornwall, ran away from home for ten days in order to see the Royal Wedding in 1981. Unfortunately, when the big day arrived they couldn't see anything because of the crowds.

Six memorable curtseys   58

1 The Queen's last curtsey

Before the Queen was two years old, it was revealed that she had learnt to curtsey. Her last ever curtsey was to her father's body at his funeral in St George's Chapel, Windsor.

2 Princess Alexandra to Queen Mary

Aged three, Princess Alexandra ran up to Queen Mary and said, 'Look! I can curtsey!'

3 Princess Margaret to Basil Charles

After she had performed a duet of *Walk on By* with Basil Charles, the barman on Mustique, Princess Margaret curtsied to him. He in turn hugged her.

4 Prince Philip to King George VI

Shortly after his marriage, Prince Philip spent Christmas at Sandringham. Embarrassed that the kilt he was wearing (which had once belonged to George V) was too short, he greeted King George VI with a curtsey, saying as he did so, 'Don't I look beautiful?' The King roared at him in language only ever tested by the Royal Family in private.

5 Mary Quant to the Queen

On the announcement that she had been awarded the OBE, Mary Quant exclaimed, 'I can hardly believe it. But what's it going to be like curtseying in a mini-skirt?'

6 The first curtsey to Princess Diana

The first public curtsey to Princess Diana was performed by the wife of the Governor of Gibraltar when the Royal couple briefly visited that place in August 1981.

59 The six Maids-of-Honour at the Queen's Coronation

1 Lady Jane Vane-Tempest-Stewart
2 Lady Mary Baillie-Hamilton
3 Lady Jane Heathcote-Drummond-Willoughby
4 Lady Anne Coke
5 Lady Moyra Hamilton
6 Lady Rosemary Spencer-Churchill

60 Thirty-two unroyal aspects of Royalty

1 Prince Philip was born on the dining room table of his parents' home, which was called 'Mon Repos', on the island of Corfu.
2 At the moment the Queen acceded to the Throne she was wearing russet-coloured slacks, with a yellow shirt and cardigan.
3 Prince Philip, who hates racing, has been known to visit Ascot wearing a radio in his top hat so that he can hear the cricket commentaries.
4 Prince Charles as a child enjoyed collecting the plastic gifts from cereal packets. He would sometimes get cross when the butler refused to open more than one packet at a time.
5 'They are both over the moon', said Princess Diana's sister Sarah when the Royal engagement was announced, 'He met Miss Right and she met Mr Right. They just clicked.'
6 Princess Anne pronounces 'either' 'eether'. She also says 'at this moment in time' instead of 'now'.
7 'Well, Mr Baldwin, this is a pretty kettle of fish' was Queen Mary's comment to Stanley Baldwin on the Abdication crisis. She had picked up her cockney from her brothers.
8 Edward VIII pronounced many words with a cockney accent. For 'lady' he would say 'lidy'. This was a constant source of irritation to his father.
9 A keen barbecuer, Prince Philip went through a stage of taking his enthusiasm indoors. For a time he insisted on cooking his sausages at the breakfast table in a special electric pan. Exasperated by the smell of the sausages still hanging around the room at lunch time, the Queen persuaded her husband to refrain.

10 Aged five, Prince Charles pressed a half-sucked sweet into the Queen's hand in public.

11 At the announcement of Mark Phillip's engagement to Princess Anne, his grandmother, Mrs John Tiarks, commented, 'It's quite a feather in the family's cap to have a member become engaged to a Royal.'

12 King Edward VII installed an American bowling alley at Sandringham.

13 Queen Victoria liked to wear an apron about the house.

14 King Edward VIII refers to children as 'kids' throughout his book, *Family Album*.

15 In 1939, the Queen bought her Christmas presents from Woolworth in Aberdeen.

16 All the way through a square-dancing evening in Canada in 1951, Prince Philip was observed dancing in jeans with a price tag still on.

17 As a child, Princess Alexandra, liked to be known as 'Sandra'.

18 Princess Anne's car numberplate, 1420 H, presented to her by the 14th/20th King's Hussars was bought by them off a United Dairies Milk Float in Ealing.

19 At his first meeting with President Truman in 1945, King

Prince Philip and The Queen barn-dance in Ottawa

George VI asked for the president's autograph, 'for my wife and daughters'.

20 The Duke of Windsor, Edward VIII used to say, 'Will you come to dinner with the Duchess and *I* tonight?' a rare fault in his grammar. He would also always use his wife's pronunciation of his title, calling himself, 'The Dook'.

21 Princess Diana's favourite television programme is the soap opera, *Crossroads*.

22 Princess Anne refers to her family as 'royals'.

23 At school, when Princess Alexandra once spilt some ink and was told to mop it up, she muttered, 'Meet the new char, Mrs Kent'.

24 If he thought he would like to see more of any dancing partner, King Edward VIII would stop in the middle of the dance floor, take out a little gold pencil, and write the woman's telephone number on his shirt cuff.

25 Names in the Queen Mother's ancestry include Smith, Browne, Tucker, Webb and Carpenter.

26 Queen Victoria was known to enjoy writing the initials 'V R I' in the dust on the dining-room table at Windsor Castle.

27 When King Edward VIII's court went into mourning for King George V, Mrs Simpson remarked to friends that she had not worn black stockings since giving up the can-can.

28 When a nephew of the Queen Mother produced a cocktail swizzle-stick, King George VI said, 'We don't think that would do at all in smart society, but it's all right here of course.'

29 At the end of Palace balls, King George VI liked to lead a lengthy conga line of guests up and down the staircases and corridors.

30 Talking to Cilla Black before switching on the Christmas lights in Regent Street in November 1981, Princess Diana said, 'I see you've brought your other half with you. I've left mine at home watching telly.'

31 On a private visit to Jamaica in 1966, the Queen and Prince Philip were given beach huts called 'Kosy Korna' and 'Memories' at the Silver Sands Beach Club.

32 The Queen is a keen enthusiast of racing pigeons. Her 250 racers, each with a leg ring stamped E R, are kept in a pigeon loft in their trainer's semi-detached house in King's Lynn, where the Queen inspects them.

Ten places you could have been served by Royalty

1 Private dinner parties in London in 1979

Princess Diana cooked and served for private dinner parties when she studied the culinary arts with Elizabeth Russell in Wimbledon.

2 Mr Pratt's grocery shop in 1953

Prince Michael of Kent used to slice the bacon as a child in this small shop in Iver, Bucks.

3 The Savoy Hotel in 1946

Angus Ogilvy was a waiter at the Savoy Hotel as a young man until he was dismissed for dropping an omelette at the feet of an important customer.

4 The Coppins milk round 1958

In 1958, Prince Michael of Kent had a milk round serving the tenants of his mother's estate, Coppins.

5 A dress shop in Australia in the 1960s

Princess Michael of Kent served in her mother's dress shop in Sydney.

6 An antiques emporium in Paris in the 1930s

Princess Marina, the mother of Princess Alexandra, helped Prince Philip's mother in her Paris shop which sold Greek antiques to benefit charity in the 1930s.

7 A Red Cross canteen in the Bahamas during the war

The Duchess of Windsor cooked an estimated 40,000 eggs at the Red Cross canteen when the Duke was Governor-General of the Bahamas during the war.

8 A Brighton restaurant in the 1950s

Lord Snowdon was a waiter in a restaurant in Brighton (and worked for a while as a £2.00 a week tout for a London bedsitter agency).

9 A newsagents in Oban in the 1980s

Princess Diana's mother owns a small newsagents shop in this small coastal town and has often served there.

10 A church fête in Scotland in the 1950s

At a fête organised by the Queen Mother at Crathie Church near Balmoral, the Queen presided at the Royal Stall and all the members of the Royal Family sold goods during the afternoon.

Three old flatmates of Princess Diana and their jobs

1 Anne Bolton
Works for Savills, the estate agents
2 Virginia Pitman
Restores antique china
3 Carolyn Pride
Studies at the Royal College of Music, specialising in singing.

Four trends set by Royalty

1 Limping
After Queen Alexandra had developed a limp following an attack of rheumatic fever, fashionable ladies began to walk with 'the Alexandra Limp'.
2 Hooting
Great noise and confusion was caused by hundreds of motorists who fitted copies of Queen Mary's very distinctive warning hooter to their cars.
3 Shaking
King Edward VII set a fashion for shaking hands with the elbow kept stiffly in at the side, though his reason for starting it was dictated by necessity: he had suffered rheumatism in his arm.
4 Fondling
Fashionable Edwardian ladies abandoned the practice of carrying their little dogs in their laps while riding in their coaches, and following the example of Queen Alexandra, instead substituted their children.

Seven occupations the Royal family might have chosen

1 Long distance lorry driver
Princess Anne – she said this profession would have appealed to her in an interview in 1979.
2 Ballet dancer
Princess Diana – but by the age of 13 she was already too tall.

3 Bareback rider in a circus
Princess Alexandra's childhood ambition.

4 An engine driver
King Edward VIII – 'because they get so lovely and dirty', he said when he was a child.

5 A schoolmaster
Prince Charles – 'He would have made a very good schoolmaster', said one of his tutors at Cambridge.

6 An astronaut
Prince Edward – he mentioned this ambition to Neil Armstrong when he visited Buckingham Palace.

7 A lady living in the country
The Queen – as a child she told her riding teacher, Horace Smith, that she would like to be a lady living in the country with lots of horses and dogs.

Nine abandoned Royal plans 65

1 George I's turnips
George I once talked of planting turnips in St James's Park, but the idea was never taken up.

2 Prince Andrew's beard
In 1981, stationed at the Culdrose Naval Base, Prince Andrew attempted to grow a beard. In the allowed three week period, the beard never fully developed, leaving Lieutenant Commander David Warren no choice but to order the Prince to remove it. On receiving the order, Prince Andrew was said to have sulked 'all afternoon'.

3 Edward VIII's revenge
'You wait until I am King. I'll chop your head off', Edward VIII once said to his brother George VI when they were both children. This he never did.

4 Henry VII's final crusade
Towards the end of his life, Henry VII planned a crusade against the Turks. He abandoned the idea when a whip-round at court raised only eleven guineas.

5 Queen Victoria's emigration
In 1859, Queen Victoria wrote to her daughter, the Princess Royal, 'I am sick of all this horrid business of politics, and Europe in general, and think you will hear of me going with the children to live in Australia, and to think of Europe as the Moon!' But she remained in Britain.

6 The Queen's laws for horses

As a child aged 5, the Queen said, 'If I am ever Queen I shall make a law that there must be no riding on Sundays. Horses should have a rest too. And I shan't let anyone dock their pony's tail'. No such legislation has since been proposed.

7 The Queen Mother's marriage

As a child, the Queen Mother pointed a handsome footman out to a friend, saying, 'That's James. I'm going to marry him when I'm older.' Instead, she married George VI.

8 George VI's book

George VI had been planning to write a book on the history of Royal Lodge, Windsor, but on becoming King could find no time for it.

9 King Edward VIII's emigration

In 1926, Edward, fed up with his father's ceaseless criticism, sent a letter to him from South America threatening to renounce his rights to the throne and settle in one of the dominions. Only a slackening of King George's V's severity prevented him from so doing.

Sir Winston Churchill welcomes The Queen to Number Ten

Five pioneering actions of the Queen

1 Flying the Atlantic
Accompanied by Prince Philip, the Queen flew across the Atlantic to Canada in a BOAC airliner in 1951, in defiance of many who said that flying was still too dangerous.

2 Going out to have her hair done
Staying in Malta with Prince Philip who was stationed there, the Queen became the first member of the Royal Family to leave her own house to get her hair done. She is said to have found the experience 'exhilarating'.

3 Being born in a private, numbered house
She was born at 17, Bruton Street, London W.1 on 21 April, 1926.

4 Entering 10 Downing Street
Winston Churchill entertained The Queen and Prince Philip to dinner at 10 Downing Street on the eve of his resignation in 1955. The Prime Minister was visibly moved when the Queen proposed his health.

5 Visiting a leper colony
The Queen and Prince Philip visited the Oji River Settlement in Africa on 9 February, 1956. There they adopted several leper children, and have paid for their medical and other needs ever since. One child, Edau, is the same age as Prince Charles. The Queen Mother has also adopted a leper child.

Five ways in which Prince Charles has broken new ground

He is the first Heir to the Throne to have:

1 gone to school
2 taken a university degree
3 married an English woman (the first for 300 years)
4 parachuted ('the heir to the throne is thrown to the air' a wit commented at the time)
5 ridden on the back of a killer whale (in Windsor Great Park in 1976)

Four left-handed Monarchs

1 King James I
2 King George II
3 King George IV
4 King George VI. (He was eventually trained to use his right hand.)

Twenty-one physical peculiarities of Royalty

1 Supernumerary breast
Anne Boleyn had three breasts (the third quite rudimentary). She also had an extra finger, which she always skilfully hid in her skirts. Henry VIII considered having her put away on the grounds of witchcraft but settled for simple repudiation.

2 Bulk
Queen Anne was extremely fat and very short indeed. Her coffin had to be made nearly twice as wide as it was long.

3 A tendency to shrink
Queen Mary's mental anguish during the Abdication caused her to lose 25 lbs. (Her hair turned entirely white during the First World War.)

4 Legendary strength
It was said that William the Conqueror was so strong that he could vault into the saddle clad in full armour.

5 Relative height
Queen Mary was 4 inches taller than her consort, William of Orange.

6 Apparent lack of arms
'I am often asked whether it is because of some genetic trait that I stand with my hands behind my back like my father. The answer is that we both have the same tailor. He makes our sleeves so tight that we can't get our hands in front' – Prince Charles's explanation for the rare appearance of his arms.

7 Hirsuteness
Catherine of Aragon wore her hair almost down to her feet, and let it flow loose at her wedding.

8 Supreme height
Edward IV is acknowledged to have been the tallest King of

Prince Charles's physical peculiarity

England, standing well over 6 feet tall, and his claim to be the handsomest has not so far been challenged.

9 A very large tongue

James I had a tongue which was much too large for his mouth; this caused a severe speech impediment. Combined with this unattractive feature 'his walk was ever circular, his fingers ever in that walk fiddling with his codpiece.'

10 A languid lid

A contemporary of King Henry III described him as having 'one of his eyelids hanging down and almost covering the black(part) of his eye.'

11 A notable bosom

The Times, reporting on one of Queen Victoria's portraits, wrote: 'The Queen's bosom has been deliciously handled and has been brought out by the artist in full rotundity.'

12 Dwarfishness

Queen Matilda, wife of William the Conqueror, attained a height of only 4 feet 2 inches. King Charles I stood only 4 feet 7 inches tall.

13 Tiny feet

The Queen Mother's shoe size is only three and a half.

14 Disproportionate arms

Though King Edward I's legs were remarkably short, his arms were over a yard long.

15 Obesity

Judging by his armour, King Henry VIII put on 17 inches to his waist in 5 years. He was so fat that machines with pulleys had to hoist him up into the saddle.

16 A petite bosom

'I've got tiny boobs and big shoulders.' – Princess Michael of Kent talking to Jean Rook, 1980.

17 A large bosom

When Patrick Lichfield developed his photographs of the Royal Family Group in 1972, he realised that his camera had distorted the extent of Princess Margaret's bosom. He specially apologised to the Princess.

18 A flat chest

'Flat as a board' is how Queen Victoria described Queen Alexandra's chest.

19 Pink eyes

King Edward the Confessor was an albino.

20 A hunchback

After marrying Prince William of Orange, who was a hunchback, the daughter of King George II told her father that she loved her husband so much that she would have married him if he were a baboon. When the King saw the Prince in his nightclothes, he said to the Princess, 'Well, then, there's baboon enough for you.'

21 Hunched shoulders

As a child, Prince Andrew always reminded Prince Philip's mother of Prince Philip. They would both hunch their shoulders about their ears when things excited or perplexed them.

Fourteen upsetting diseases suffered by English monarchs

1 Chalk stones in the fingers
Suffered by King William IV

2 Piles
Suffered by George II

3 Speech impediment
Suffered by William Rufus, King Charles I and King George VI
(who would always say 'Their Majesties' because he stuttered on
Ks and Qs).

4 Sinusitis
Suffered by the Queen.

5 Syphilis or gonorrhoea
Suffered by King Henry VIII, King Edward VI, Queen Mary I,
Queen Mary II, King James II, Queen Anne, and King William
IV. The doctors treating King Henry VIII thought that he caught
it when Cardinal Wolsey whispered in his ear.

6 Gout
Suffered by King Henry VII, King Henry VIII, King Charles II,
Queen Anne, King George I, King George II, King George III,
King George IV.

7 Knock knees
Suffered by King George VI.

8 Swollen hand
Suffered by King Edward VIII during a tour of Australia. The
vigorous handshakes of the Australians caused his hand to become
so swollen and sore that it had to be bandaged. For the rest of his
visit, he shook hands with his left hand.

9 Recurrent inflammation of the wrist
Suffered by Prince Philip, eventually forcing him to give up
playing polo.

10 Porphyria
Suffered by Queen Anne and King George III.

11 Migraine
Suffered by Princess Margaret and Queen Mary I.

12 Whooping cough
Suffered by the Queen Mother on her honeymoon.

13 Ivy rash
Suffered by the Queen when helping Queen Mary remove ivy
from the Sandringham walls.

14 Homesickness
Suffered to such an extent by Princess Diana at her finishing

school, Chateau D'Oex near Montreux, in 1978 that she returned home after only one term.

71   *Five peculiar cures adopted by Royalty*

1 A strong wind
The Queen Mother has long thought that 'a strong wind will blow the germs away'.

2 Scarlet cloth
When King Edward I caught smallpox, his doctor wrapped his body entirely in scarlet cloth. The King was cured.

3 Pigeons
When Prince Henry, eldest son of King James I, caught typhus his doctor prescribed a treatment of pigeons pecking at the bottoms of his feet. Prince Henry died, aged 18.

4 A straitjacket
King George III suffered from what is now recognised as porphyria, but was then considered madness. Symptoms include severe abdominal pain, dizziness and swelling of the glands. For this, he was shut away, encased in a straitjacket. He refused to sign any State papers until he was released.

5 A stag's bowels
King James I used to plunge his legs into the bowels of dead stags, swearing that it strengthened the sinews.

72   *Three homoeopathic remedies used by the Queen*

The Royal Family were introduced to homoeopathy in the 1920s by Sir John Weir, who was succeeded by Dr Margery Blackie, also a homoeopathic physician.
For her sinus trouble:
1 **Arsenic** to prevent sneezing
2 **Onions** to deal with a runny nose
3 **Deadly nightshade** for the Queen's sore throat

Eight things which have caused Royalty to fall

1 A washing line
As a child, Princess Anne fell from her horse when she failed to spot a washing line in the grounds of Balmoral.

2 Thin ice
Prince Albert fell into the lake at Buckingham Palace while skating on thin ice.

3 Ducks
The Queen as a child fell into the same lake while looking for duck's eggs.

4 Stairs
In 1958, Prince Charles fell down a flight of stairs at Cheam School. His leg was put in plaster.

In 1898 King Edward VII fell down a spiral staircase at Waddesdon Manor and broke a kneecap.

In January 1982, Princess Diana fell down a staircase at Sandringham. She was immediately taken to bed, where the local doctor and the Princess's own doctor examined her. She was then declared to be fine.

5 An uneven path
On his first public engagement as a pageboy at the wedding of his father's sister Sarah, Peter Phillips fell on a gravel path leading to the church. He picked himself up without crying and carried on.

As a child, Prince Andrew fell on a garden path and began to cry. Princess Anne was so upset at the sight that she started crying too.

6 A favourite chair
When King George V sat on his favourite wicker armchair at Sandringham to deliver his first Christmas broadcast, the seat fell through and he collapsed on the ground. 'God bless my soul!' he exclaimed.

7 Spurs
At a ball held in Windsor Castle, the first ball there for half a century, Prince Adolphus of Teck and Princess Victoria fell flat on their backs when the Prince's spurs caught in a long gown of the King's mistress, Mrs Keppel.

8 A slippery carpet
As a page at the Queen's wedding, Prince Michael of Kent tripped and fell as he was carrying the Queen's train. He quickly picked himself up and carried on.

Eight members of the Royal Family who nearly ran out of money

1 The Queen Mother

When the Queen Mother was a young girl, she ran so short of money that she was reduced to sending her father this simple message: 'S.O.S., L.S.D., R.S.V.P.'

2 Princess Margaret

After the announcement of Roddy Llewellyn's engagement to Tania Soskin, Princess Margaret was reported as saying, 'I'm very happy for him – and anyway I couldn't have afforded him much longer.'

3 Queen Mary's mother

Princess Mary Adelaide was rarely out of debt. One of her chief creditors was Mr John Barker, the Kensington grocer, who had contributed to a new church hall that Princess Mary Adelaide was required to open. People were startled when towards the end of her speech, she said, 'And now I must propose a special vote of thanks to Mr Barker, to whom we all owe so much.' Towards the end of her life her debts to tradesmen totalled £70,000.

4 King George IV

When he was the Prince of Wales, King George IV was menaced by bailiffs when he was staying with Mrs Fitzherbert. They allowed him twenty-four hours to collect the £2,000 he owed. He managed this only by pawning quantities of jewellery.

5 Mark Phillips

In March 1980, Mark Phillips told reporters, 'We are just a young couple and we've just started farming. We've a mortgage like everyone else . . . The pot is only so big.'

6 King Edward VII

In the Spring of 1881 so many papers carried news of King Edward VII's large debts that the Hotel Bristol in Paris, where the King was staying, was besieged by money lenders' agents. The only way the Prefect of Police managed to disperse the crowd was by threatening to arrest everybody as vagrants.

7 Prince Philip

In 1969 Prince Philip told American television viewers that the Royal Family would 'go into the red next year', adding that there was a possibility that they would have to leave Buckingham Palace. 'We've had to sell a small yacht and I shall have to give up polo fairly soon – things like that.'

8 King Charles II

King Charles II once asked Dr Stillingfleet why he read his

sermons when he was in front of the King when he didn't at any other time. Dr Stillingfleet replied that he was overawed by the Royal presence, and then he asked the King why *he* read his speeches, when he had no-one who could possibly overawe him. 'I have asked my subjects so often for money that I am ashamed to look them in the face', replied the King.

Four members of the Royal Family who have been thrown from a horse 75

1 King Edward VIII
King Edward VIII was injured when he fell off his horse during a practice gallop while staying with Lord Dalmeny at Mentmore Towers. 'I'm afraid your collar bone must be broken, Sir', said his equerry, Fruity Metcalfe. 'I believe it is', he replied. It was. A month later, he was knocked unconscious when he fell at an army point-to-point near Wokingham.

2 Prince Charles
In 1981, Prince Charles fell off his horse twice at Sandown Park and again at Cheltenham five days later. The *Daily Express* sent no less than five photographers to Cheltenham to cover the event.

3 King George V
In 1915, while inspecting his troops on the Western Front, King George V fell and fractured his pelvis when his horse took fright and reared. The King returned to England in agony.

4 Princess Diana
Princess Diana fell off her horse Romany aged 10 and broke her arm. She later confessed that this had caused her to lose her riding nerve.

Five causes of Royal mishaps 76

1 A little dog
In 1924, King George VI played a game of golf with Frank Hodges of the Miners' Federation and Evan Williams of the Mining Association. All went well for the King until the very last hole, when a little dog whipped out from nowhere and stole the King's golfball.

2 A lift

Soon after Lord Mountbatten had moved in to his thirty-room flat – London's first penthouse – he invited Queen Mary to see it. Before she reached the correct floor, Queen Mary became stuck when the modern express lift jammed.

3 Another lift

On their way to a Royal Film Performance in 1960, Prince Philip, Princess Alexandra and the Duchess of Kent were trapped in a Buckingham Palace lift. Cliff Richard was kept waiting for twenty-five minutes in the cinema foyer.

4 A wet flag

During a solemn moment in the Jubilee Review in Horse Guards' Parade in 1954, Prince Philip was slapped across the face by a wet flag hanging too low from the dais. A smile was seen to light up the Queen's ceremonial face.

5 A funny joke

Convalescing from a serious operation King George V welcomed his humorous friend Mr J. H. Thomas. But Thomas told such a funny story that the King's laughter damaged his lung so thoroughly that he had to have a second operation.

77 *Three racing colours of the sport's most popular monarchs*

1 King Edward VII
Purple, gold braid and scarlet sleeves
2 The Queen Mother
Buff and pale blue stripes, black cap and gold tassel
3 The Queen
Red and blue

78 *Six first ponies of members of the Royal Family*

1 Tiny Wee
Mark Phillip's first Shetland pony
2 Mr Dinkum
Prince Andrew's first pony

Master Peter Phillips on Smokey

3 Bandit
Princess Anne's first pony, which she had to share with Prince Charles.
4 High Jinks
Princess Anne's first pony of her own, a present for her twelfth birthday.
5 Fum
Prince Charles's first Shetland pony
6 Smokey
Peter Phillip's first Shetland pony

A selection of Royal pets 79

1 Charlotte
George V's pet parrot, which was allowed to help itself to anything on the breakfast table.
2 Satan and Emma
The Queen Mother's childhood pet pigs.
3 Disraeli, Trooper, Imp and Davy Crocket
The four pugs which the Duke and Duchess of Windsor dressed alike in little wing collars and bow ties.

4 Harvey
Prince Charles's childhood rabbit
5 A Skye terrier
The faithful pet of Mary Tudor, it was found hiding under her skirts after her execution.
6 A tame fox
Charles II kept a tame fox which frightened the Queen by jumping onto her bed. (He also gave his name to the King Charles Spaniel, he had troops of them, which followed him everywhere.)
7 Susan
The Queen's favourite corgi, her first, and the great-grandmother of the present tribe. Susan accompanied the Queen on her honeymoon tucked into the travelling rug along with four hot-water bottles.
8 William and Greensleeves
Prince Charles and Princess Anne's favourite horses when they were children. William once walked into the schoolroom and shared their tea.
9 Caesar
Edward VII's dog, who attended the King's funeral, trotting behind his coffin.
10 Florence, Harvey and Francis
A cocker spaniel, and two labradors, belonging to Princess Anne, Prince Charles and Prince Andrew, respectively.
11 Dashy
Queen Victoria's favourite spaniel
12 Charlton
A horse the Queen named after Bobby and Jackie Charlton, the two footballing brothers who helped take England to victory in the 1966 World Cup.

80 *How to keep your corgis content: the Queen's routine advice*

1 Always keep a bowl of clean water on the sitting-room floor.
2 Keep a pile of white towels by the steps to your Private Apartments. Use them for drying the corgis if they have been out in the rain.
3 Have a footman enter with a silver tray each afternoon. On it

should be: a jug of gravy, a plate of dog biscuits, a bowl of dog food and three spoons.

4 Mix the food according to the taste of each corgi.
5 Serve the corgis' meals on a large white cloth spread over the carpet.
6 Clear up the dishes, food and utensils yourself.
7 Personally remove any fleas you may detect on your corgis.
8 At Christmas each year give each corgi a stocking. HINT: Chocolate Drops always go down well.

The Queen with her very first corgi, Susan

Two Royal pardons to sheep

1 Queen Alexandra and the sheep

On a trip up the Nile, Queen Alexandra was shown the sheep she was to be served for dinner. Instead of having it killed, she insisted upon it being sent home to England, to pass its remaining years in peace.

2 The Queen and the lambs

As a young child, the Queen made a firm rule concerning her garden plot. 'No more mint sauce from my garden,' she told her family, 'It means deading the lambs.'

Six shy members of the Royal Family

1 The Duke of Gloucester

The dust-jacket of one of the Duke of Gloucester's architectural books describes its author thus: 'Richard Gloucester is a 29-year-old architect and photographer who lives in London.'

2 Queen Victoria

When Queen Victoria met Dickens in her old age, she gave him a copy of her book *More Leaves from a Journal of a Life in the Highlands* inscribed, 'From the humblest of writers to one of the greatest'.

3 Princess Alexandra

As a child, Princess Alexandra was painfully shy. 'It's no good saying that they're not looking at me', she said aged 8 in a car on the way to Crathie church, 'I know they *are* and it's awful.' She cried when she realised that the film of the Queen's wedding was to be shown at Heathfield. She did not want all her schoolmates to see her as a bridesmaid. The Headmistress allowed her to lie on her bed instead of watching it with them.

4 Queen Mary

Attending a performance of *No, No, Nanette* in 1925, Queen Mary turned her head away when the chorus came on stage in bathing costumes.

5 King George V

King George V's hands shook from nervousness so much when he opened Parliament that he had all his speeches printed in very large type. As the years went by, the type grew even larger.

6 King George VI

King George VI's shyness was at its most acute when he was a child. Once he sat in the dark in a sitting room rather than ask a servant to light the gas.

Eleven Royal communication problems

1 George IV's greatest enemy

In 1821, a courtier came to King George IV with news of Napoleon's death, saying, 'Your greatest enemy is dead, sir.' To which the King replied, 'By God, is she?'

2 The Queen's apology

When the Queen was sitting beside an African ruler in a horse-drawn carriage, one of the horses farted. 'I'm so sorry', said the Queen. 'Oh, don't worry', replied the African ruler, 'If you hadn't apologised, I'd have thought it was the horse.'

3 King George V's foolishness

In 1904 King George V was telephoned by Sir Arthur Davidson. 'Did you happen to see in the papers that some damned fool has given as much as £1,400 for one stamp?' asked Sir Arthur. 'I was that damned fool', replied the King.

4 King Edward VII's garter

King Edward VII, a great stickler for correct costume, once sent the painter Benjamin Constant a Garter ribbon to show that the colour he had painted it in a portrait of Queen Victoria was the wrong shade of blue. Seeing the ribbon, Constant thought that he had been made a Knight of the Garter. When he discovered that he had not, he 'absolutely refused' to change the picture.

5 King Edward VIII's message

At the very beginning of his attachment to Freda Dudley Ward, King Edward VIII sent a card to the house in which she lived with her mother-in-law. He addressed it 'Mrs Dudley Ward' and asked if he might come to tea. The elderly mother-in-law sent everyone out of the house and entertained Edward alone, assuming that the note had been intended for her.

6 King Edward VII's guest

Reluctantly giving a dinner for the launch of the *Dictionary of National Biography* at Marlborough House in 1882, King Edward VII pointed to Canon Ainger, who had written on Charles and

Mary Lamb, and asked Sir Sidney Lee, 'Why is he here? He is not a writer.'

'He is a very great authority on Lamb', replied Lee.

Dumbfounded that some sort of specialist butcher had been invited, the King threw down his knife and fork. 'On lamb!!!' he exclaimed.

7 Queen Victoria's inquiry

Queen Victoria once asked the aged Admiral Foley to lunch to report on the sinking of the *Eurydice*. 'After she had exhausted this melancholy subject', wrote the Queen's grandson, William, 'my grandmother, in order to give the conversation a more cheerful turn, inquired after his sister, whom she knew well, whereon the Admiral, who was hard of hearing and still pursuing his train of thought about the *Eurydice*, replied in his stentorian voice: "Well, Ma'am, I am going to have her turned over and take a good look at her bottom and have it well scraped." The effect of his answer was stupendous. My grandmother put down her knife and fork, hid her face in her handkerchief and shook and heaved with laughter till the tears rolled down her face.'

8 Princess Margaret's farewell

Princess Margaret's meaning had to be explained to the Governor of Kenya, Sir Stanley Baring, when his leave-taking bow to the Princess produced the assurance: 'See you later, alligator.'

9 Queen Victoria's request

Queen Victoria so adored *Alice in Wonderland* when it was first published that she wrote to Lewis Carroll sending her compliments and adding that she would be greatly pleased to receive any other book of his. The author was greatly flattered and sent her a copy of his *Syllabus of Plane Algebraical Geometry*.

10 King George III's diplomacy

Once during the time when King George III's madness was severe, he approached an oak in Windsor Great Park, shook hands with it and addressed it on continental politics thinking that it was the King of Prussia.

11 King Edward VII's trip

Being shown around HMS *Victory*, King Edward VII's attention was drawn to a plaque on the deck. 'This is where Nelson fell, Your Majesty', said his guide. 'I'm not surprised', replied the King, 'I nearly tripped over the damn thing myself.'

Nine memorable Royal vehicle accidents

1 Prince Philip's MG
Four weeks before his wedding Prince Philip crashed his MG into a tree while travelling from Buckingham Palace to a naval college in Corsham. He travelled the rest of the way by thumbing lifts.

2 Queen Mary's Daimler
In May 1939, Queen Mary's Daimler was hit by a heavy lorry carrying steel tubing. Queen Mary had been pointing out to her fellow passenger, Lord Claud Hamilton, that he had a caterpillar on his trousers when the accident occurred. The car overturned, and Queen Mary was thrown to the floor, breaking her umbrella on the way. But she emerged from the wreckage with not a curl out of place. 'No fuss,' she said, 'I am quite all right.'

3 The Duchess of Cambridge's brougham
Almost seventy years to the day before Queen Mary's accident, her grandmother, Augusta, Duchess of Cambridge had been travelling in her brougham when a hansom cab crashed into it. The brougham overturned, and the Duchess escaped with minor bruising.

4 Queen Victoria's carriage
In 1863, a drunken coachman managed to overturn Queen Victoria's carriage. 'We were all precipitated to the ground', the Queen wrote later. She described the coachman as 'utterly confused and bewildered'. She sustained a black eye. On another occasion, an overturned carriage preceded another mishap: 'Dear Frankie Clark lifted me out of the carriage and, would you believe it, all my petticoats came undone!'

5 King Edward VIII's railway carriage
When King Edward VIII was touring western Australia in 1920, his train was derailed on a sharp curve where the track had been weakened by heavy rains. He emerged from his upturned carriage unscathed.

6 Prince Philip's Lagonda
After he had delivered a successful speech on road safety to a luncheon meeting in 1957, Prince Philip drove his Lagonda into a car which emerged suddenly from a side street.

7 The Duke of Gloucester's Rolls Royce
Driving back from Sir Winston Churchill's funeral in 1965, the Duke of Gloucester suddenly ordered his chauffeur to hand over the wheel, much against the wishes of the Duchess. Before long the Rolls Royce was in a field and the Duchess was in hospital

with a broken arm. When the Duke visited the hospital, the furious Duchess refused to see him.

8 Princess Alexandra's Mini

In 1962, Princess Alexandra ran her Mini into a lorry in Kensington High Street. She admitted later that she had been driving a bit too fast.

9 The Duke of Kent's shooting brake

In 1954, a year after passing his driving test, the Duke of Kent collided his shooting brake into an estate car on the road from Sandhurst and was taken to hospital unconscious. In the next eighteen months he had two more crashes.

85   *Five narrow escapes in the air by Royalty*

1 Mark Phillips in a helicopter

In September 1977, Mark Phillips's helicopter had to make an emergency landing on its way between Leeds and Harrogate: 'My old ticker started fluttering a bit but the pilot was first class', he commented.

2 Prince Charles in a Basset

In 1970, co-piloting a Basset with his father, Prince Charles avoided a collision with a Piper Aztec over the Sussex Downs by three seconds.

3 Princess Diana in a Boeing 737

In May 1981, Princess Diana's Boeing 737 was hit by lightning six miles out of Heathrow on its way to Aberdeen. There was a flash and a thud before normal service was resumed.

4 Prince Philip in a Royal Andover

In November 1981, Prince Philip narrowly missed a jumbo jet on its way to Miami when he flew a Royal Andover 600 feet too low. A secret inquiry cleared air traffic control, but refused to blame Prince Philip because though he was piloting he was not the commander of the plane.

5 Prince Charles in a parachute

In 1971, on his first-ever parachute jump over Studland Bay, Prince Charles got his feet caught in the rigging. He quickly managed to free them but, he commented later, 'it was a rather hairy experience.'

Three sets of injuries sustained by Princess Anne

1 Broken nose
Sustained while riding with the Oxford University draghounds, 1965.
2 Bruised shoulder and thigh
Sustained while riding in the European Championships at Kiev, 1973.
3 Cracked vertebra and concussion
Sustained during riding trials at Durweston in Dorset, 1976.

Three accidents to Royal animals

1 The Queen Mother's racehorse
In 1956, the Queen Mother's horse *Devon Loch* collapsed and died within inches of the winning post of the Grand National. Her first remark was 'I must go down and comfort those poor people' and she went immediately to the jockey, Dick Francis, the trainer, and the stable lads. The Duke of Devonshire, who was accompanying her, said of her response, 'I hope the Russians saw it. It was the most perfect display of dignity that I have ever witnessed.'
2 The Queen's favourite corgi
When the Queen was still a teenager, her favourite corgi, Jane, was run over by one of the gardeners at Windsor. Hearing that the gardener was very upset, the Queen wrote him a letter assuring him that it wasn't his fault.
3 The Duchess of Windsor's cairn terrier
Two months before her wedding to King Edward VIII, the Duchess of Windsor's cairn terrier 'Slipper' died from an adder bite, an event which made headline news.
. . . And one Royal animal which bit back. In 1954 it was revealed that a Buckingham Palace sentry was receiving treatment for a septic leg wound after being bitten by one of the Royal corgis. Though the case against her was never proven conclusively, Susan, the Queen's favourite, came under strong suspicion.

Eight areas in which Royalty has failed

1 Football
As Captain of the 1st Eleven at his prep school, Cheam, Prince Charles lost all his games of the term. Over the season, the total of goals scored by Cheam's opponents was 82. Cheam's own total was 4.

2 Domestic science
'Cook, Needlewoman and Child Nurse (badges) are holding me up a bit', the Queen wrote to her Guide Captain aged fifteen.

3 Silk farming
In 1609 King James I decided to produce silk for weaving. To this end, he planted 30,000 black mulberry trees on the ground where Buckingham Palace now stands. He had not been informed that silkworms only like eating the leaves of white mulberry trees. One of the original trees still stands, in the South West corner of the Palace gardens.

4 Music
At their respective schools, Prince Charles took up the trumpet and Princess Anne the oboe. Both were advised to give up shortly afterwards.

5 Maths O-Level
Prince Charles failed it twice.

6 Alchemy
Encouraged by the Dutchman Cornelius Lannoy's predictions that he could turn metal into gold, Queen Elizabeth I built a laboratory for him. When no gold was forthcoming, Mr Lannoy was sent to the Tower of London on a charge of deception.

7 Operating a ticket machine
Opening the new Victoria Line extension to the London Underground in 1968, the Queen was handed a sixpence by her equerry John Slater. The sixpence went straight through the machine. She was handed another, and the same thing happened again. Only on a third attempt did a ticket emerge.

8 Television
Mark Phillips is the only registered failure of Television Interview Training Consultancy, a company which trains people to put themselves over well on television. 'He was bloody hopeless', said his tutor in 1982. 'Eventually I told him just to keep quiet and keep smiling.'

Four words King George V found difficulty in spelling

1 Business
2 Mausoleum
3 Academy
4 Highbrow (he tended to spell it 'Eyebrow')

Five terrible puns by Prince Charles

1 'That just sleighed me.'
At the end of going sledging with Eskimoes
2 'I bet they're having a whale of a time.'
Passing a whaling ship
3 'I like to give myself Heirs.'
Leering at a pretty girl in a Cambridge revue
4 'I am not accustomed in any way to unveiling busts. . . . I now complete the process of allowing my father to expose himself.'
Unveiling a bust of his father
5 'I presume you've taken the pill this morning. Of course, I mean the seasick pill.'
Welcoming Miss Spotlight on board his ship

Nine unusual Royal gifts to commoners

1 A gold toothpick
King Charles I gave his gaoler, Colonel Matthew Thomlinson, his gold toothpick, before setting off to be executed.
2 The Queen's autograph
On the 16th of April, 1945, the Queen granted female Sergeant Pat Hayes's request for an autograph. 'But of course', she said, 'I'd love to. Where is your diary?' This is believed to be the only occasion on which the Queen has signed an autograph for a member of the public.

3 A carcass
When King Edward VII's Derby winner, *Persimmon*, died in 1908, the King presented him to the Natural History Museum.

4 An electric fan
Shocked at the perspiration of students at a training centre for domestic servants that she had visited, Queen Mary sent them an electric fan.

5 A cello
Prince Charles gave his 1804 cello, which had once belonged to King George IV, to the Royal Opera House. They sold it for £15,000.

6 A book
Queen Victoria gave a copy of her book, *Leaves from A Journal of Our Life in the Highlands* to Charles Dickens, whom she greatly admired. It was inscribed, 'To one of the greatest authors from one of the humblest.'

7 Brocade covered cupboards
In 1929, Queen Mary's Christmas gifts to her friends were strange brocade-covered 'cupboards' in which they were supposed to hide their telephones – instruments of unparalleled vulgarity, in her opinion.

8 A lace bonnet
At his request, Queen Victoria gave a visiting West African chief one of her widow's caps with long white streamers. 'I should like to be the only chief entitled to wear it. I will pass it on to my successors,' he said. One of Victoria's granddaughters has a photograph of him in full regalia, with the Queen's lace cap on his head, surmounted by a top hat.

9 A large carpet
Queen Mary spent eight years making a carpet measuring 108 feet by 78 feet. It contained over a million stitches. In 1950 she gave the carpet to a charity exhibition at the Victoria and Albert Museum, where 90,000 people each paid sixpence to see it. 'It is the Queen's view', reported her Lady-in-Waiting, 'That it is the duty of every individual to contribute something directly to help the country in its need for dollars.'

Twelve famous people who have said nice things about Royalty

1 Barbra Streisand on Prince Charles
'This real English Gentleman.'

2 Noel Coward on the Queen Mother
'She has an infinite grace of mind, charm, humour and deep down kindness.'

3 Will Rogers on the young King Edward VIII
'The Prince is a good kid. Too bad I can't afford to carry a guy like that around with me. I'd have a swell act if I could.'

4 Senator Joseph Macarthy on the Queen Mother
'She's sharp.'

5 General De Gaulle on King George VI and the Queen Mother
'The only two people who have always shown me humanity and understanding' (said on leaving Britain in 1944).

6 Sammy Cahn on Princess Margaret
'She sings well for a Princess!'

7 Winston Churchill on King George VI and the Queen Mother
'Your Majesties are more beloved by all classes and conditions than any of the princes of the past.'

8 Adolf Hitler on the Queen
'Ein fabelhaftes Kind' ('a marvellous child').

9 Gladstone on King Edward VII
'He knows everything except what is in books.'

10 Richard Crossman on the Queen
'She has a lovely laugh. She laughs with her whole face and she just can't assume a mere smile because she's a very spontaneous person.'

11 Keir Hardie on Queen Mary
'When that woman laughs, she does laugh, and not make a contortion like so many royalties.'

12 Oscar Wilde on Queen Victoria
'The three women I have admired most are Queen Victoria, Sarah Bernhardt and Lily Langtry – I would have married any one of them with pleasure' (said shortly before he died).

93 *Five men of God who said the wrong thing to Royalty*

1 A consoling clergyman

Trying to console Queen Victoria after the death of Prince Albert, a clergyman suggested that henceforth she regard herself as married to Christ. 'That is what I call twaddle', replied the Queen.

2 Thomas à Becket

'Who will rid me of this turbulent priest?' asked King Henry II, after his Archbishop of Canterbury had taken a contrary view in an argument about the legal jurisdiction over clergymen. There was no shortage of volunteers, and Thomas à Becket was killed in Canterbury Cathedral in 1170.

3 A Presbyterian minister

A Presbyterian minister was interrupted in mid-sermon by King James I shouting out, 'I give not a turd for your preaching.'

4 An Anglican bishop

When a bishop was giving a sermon on the sinful vanity of decking one's body with finery, the extravagantly dressed Queen Elizabeth I brought him to a halt and ordered him to change the subject.

5 John Stubbs

When the extreme puritan John Stubbs suggested that Queen Elizabeth I was too old to marry, the Queen ordered his right hand to be cut off. Just as the axe was coming down on his right hand, the good-natured Stubbs lifted up his hat with his left hand and yelled, 'God Save the Queen!'

94 *Eight members of the Royal Family and their religious inclinations*

1 King Charles II

On his death bed, he was converted to Catholicism. During his life, he had been used to receiving Holy Communion with three bishops on one side of him and his three illegitimate sons by three different mistresses on the other.

2 Princess Andrew

Prince Philip's mother, Princess Andrew, founded The Christian Sisterhood of Martha and Mary in 1948. She lived as a nun in the

Prince Philip escorting his mother, Princess Andrew, to a wedding in 1957

habit of the Russian Orthodox Church, spending the last two years of her life in Buckingham Palace, where she died aged 84 in 1969.

3 Edward the Confessor

Edward the Confessor was canonised by Pope Alexander III in 1161.

4 King George III

The private prayer book of King George III reveals in his own hand the obliteration of the words 'our most religious and gracious king' and, in their place, 'a most miserable sinner'.

5 The Duchess of Edinburgh

Queen Mary's aunt, the Duchess of Edinburgh, kept a Russian priest and two chanters with her wherever she went.

6 The Queen

A preacher who visited Glamis Castle when the Queen was a child told her that he would send her a book as a present. 'Not about God', requested the Queen, 'I know all about him already.'

7 King James I

Known as 'the wisest fool in Christendom', James I instigated the Authorised Version of the Bible in 1604, a translation which makes all others seem *parvenu*.

8 King Henry VII

Before he died, King Henry VII arranged for no less than 10,000 masses to be said for the repose of his soul.

95 *Seven causes of Royal embarrassment*

1 A fat mother

As a child, Queen Mary dreaded her mother coming to watch her at Taglioni's dancing lessons. Whereas all the other children's mothers needed only one chair each to sit on, the 17 stone Duchess of Teck needed two, a cause of much classroom mirth.

2 A running dye

On holiday in Le Touquet in 1934, King Edward VIII took on the appearance of a Red Indian when the dye in his bathing costume ran.

3 A naughty photograph

After the announcement of Mark Phillips's engagement to Princess Anne, the press visited him at his barracks and managed to persuade him to pose with his legs astride the barrel of a tank and his hands clutching that barrel. For some time afterwards the photograph circulated amongst journalists, but it was never printed.

4 A true Scot

At a levee in St James' Palace, George III blushed deeply when a bowing Scottish colonel's kilt rode up. The King screamed out, 'Keep the ladies at the back! Keep the ladies at the back!'

5 An indiscreet duchess

At a large lunch party in Biarritz attended by King Edward VII, a Portuguese duchess picked up the place card of the man next to her and said, 'Kep-pel . . . Kep-pel . . . How very odd of you to have the same name as the King's mistress.' She was in fact speaking to the King's mistress's husband.

6 An inanimate dog

When a guest at a Balmoral house party farted, King George V politely kicked the dog near his heel and said, 'Filthy brute!' Unfortunately, the dog was china and was smashed into little bits.

7 A cinematic kiss

Queen Mary's aunt, Augusta, was embarrassed to have been filmed kissing her niece in 1912: 'Fancy our going *kissing* all over the world' she later wrote, 'but it is impossible to stop those horrid Kino-men.'

Three members of the Royal Family who had to buy back their own letters

1 The Duke of York

After she had publicly admitted taking bribes from officers who wished for promotion, Mrs Clarke was repudiated by her lover, the Duke of York, son of King George III. In a fit of pique and commerce, Mrs Clarke threatened to publish the Duke's love letters to her. The money she exacted from the anxious Duke allowed Mrs Clarke to live in Paris happily ever after.

2 King Edward VII

On the death in 1871 of King Edward VII's mistress Madame Giulia Barucci, who had once described herself as 'the greatest whore in the world', her brother, Pirro Benini, wrote to the King from Florence demanding £1,500 for the return of his love letters to her. After much discussion and intrigue, Benini agreed to sell the letters for a mere £240.

3 The Queen

In 1963, a relation of the Queen's childhood music teacher offered for sale in New York two letters written by the Queen and Princess Margaret. They were purchased by the British Ambassador and returned to the Queen.

Two Royal experts who wrote articles ahead of their times

1 Marion Crawford

After Marion Crawford, a former Governess to the Queen and Princess Margaret, had earned Royal opprobrium for writing a best-selling book entitled *The Little Princesses*, she was

commissioned by *Woman's Own* magazine to write an article on
'The Social Season'. On 15 June 1955, detailed descriptions of that
year's racing at Ascot and The Trooping of The Colour appeared.
Alas, both events had been cancelled due to a rail strike, making
remarks like 'The Queen has never looked lovelier' seem a little
out of place.

2 A peer's daughter

An exclusive article in a monthly magazine containing a full
description of 'How I saw The Coronation By A Peer's Daughter'
appeared on London newstands shortly after King Edward VII's
Coronation had been postponed because the King had
appendicitis. To save face, the magazine went to great expense to
buy up its own copies from newsagents all over the country.

98 *Five rhymes about Royalty*

1 *King Charles I walked and talked*
   Half an hour after his head was cut off
              From 'Peter Puzzlewell, A Choice Collection of
              Riddles, Charades and Rebuses

2 *George the Third*
   Ought never to have occurred
   One can only wonder
   At so grotesque a blunder.
              By Eric Clerihew Bentley

3 *George the First was always reckoned*
   Vile, but viler George the Second;
   And what mortal ever heard
   Any good of George the Third?
   When from earth the Fourth descended
   God be praised, the Georges ended.
              By Walter Savage Landor

4 *Here lies poor Fred, who was alive and is dead.*
   We had rather it had been his Father,
   Had it been his brother, better'n any other,
   Had it been his sister no one would have missed her,
   Had it been the whole generation, all the better for the nation,

But as it's just poor Fred, who was alive and is dead,
There's no more to be said.

> Jacobite jingle on the death of King George II's son
> Frederick.

5 *Here lies our Sovereign lord, the King*
Whose promise none relies on;
Who never said a foolish thing,
Nor ever did a wise one.

> By John Wilmot, Earl of Rochester. Surprisingly, King
> Charles II, its subject, seemed to approve of the rhyme.
> 'This is very true' he said, 'for my words are my own,
> and my actions are my ministers!'

Twenty-six rumours which have circulated about the Royal Family

1 Prince Philip and the Profumo scandal

In June 1963, there was much speculation that Prince Philip was in some way involved in the Profumo affair. The only basis for these rumours seems to have been that he once gave a private sitting to ringleader Stephen Ward, who was a portrait painter.

2 The Royal babies and deformities

There is a long tradition of rumours springing up before a Royal baby is seen in public. The strongest have been when Princess Margaret was rumoured to be deaf and dumb, when Prince Charles was rumoured to have a club foot and when Prince Andrew was rumoured to be mentally defective.

3 Mark Phillips and a television personality

In 1981, Mark Phillips strongly denied rumours that he was having an affair with Angela Rippon, a television personality with whom he was writing a book about horses. Of his relationship with his wife, he commented, 'There has been no harm done between us but, at the same time, when you read something like that, it sows seeds. It puts a thought there that was not there before. It does not help anybody.'

4 Queen Victoria's mourning

Three years after Prince Albert's death, there were rumours that Queen Victoria was going out of mourning for him. In 1864, the Queen wrote a letter to *The Times* saying, 'This idea cannot be too explicitly contradicted.' She remained in mourning for the rest of her life.

5 The evacuation of the Little Princesses

During the war, there were frequent rumours that the Queen and Princess Margaret had been evacuated to Canada. For their safety, these rumours were never denied. 'The children won't leave without me; I won't leave without the King; and the King will never leave' was the Queen Mother's way of setting out the true position.

6 The Duke of Cumberland's child

In the eighteenth century, it was rumoured that King George III's son Ernest, Duke of Cumberland, had fathered his sister Sophia's child.

7 Prince Andrew's way with women

When 16-year-old Clio Nathaniels ran away from Gordonstoun there were press rumours that she had had a row with Prince Andrew. Her father denied it. 'Nonsense', he said.

8 Prince Philip and a childhood love

There was much speculation in the late 1940s and early 1950s about Prince Philip's relationship with his childhood friend Hélène Cordet. He gave her away at her wedding, and was godfather to both her children. Inevitably, some said that they were his own. She was not invited to the Royal Wedding in 1947, even though her mother attended. She later became the hostess of an early television show, *Hotel Continental*.

9 King George V and an earlier wife

For nearly twenty years, rumours abounded that King George V had married the daughter of an English admiral in Malta in 1890. This would have invalidated his marriage to Queen Mary. Finally, in 1910, the rumour was quashed when a journalist called Mylius was successfully prosecuted for printing the story in the Paris newspaper, *The Liberator*. Queen Mary was delighted. 'The story is now doomed', she wrote in her diary.

10 Mrs Simpson's phantom pregnancy

Soon after the Abdication, a doctor joined Mrs Simpson's houseparty in France. Immediately, rumours went around that she was pregnant.

11 Lord Snowdon and Princess Margaret

As early as 1967, Lord Snowdon was denying rumours that his marriage was on the rocks. After a trip to Tokyo, he rebuked a press conference. 'How do these things get started?', he asked. 'When I'm away, and I'm away quite a lot for my paper, I write home and I telephone like other husbands in love with their wives.'

12 The Queen Mother's pregnancy

Even though she was aged 51 when her husband King George VI died, there were rumours that she was pregnant. If this had been true, and she had had a son, then the Queen would have been deprived of the throne. But it was not.

13 Prince Albert's arrest

Shortly before England entered into the Crimean War in 1854, press reports that Prince Albert had been arrested as a traitor were so strong that crowds gathered outside the Tower of London to watch him being brought in in chains.

14 Princess Margaret's reunion

Two and a half years after they had parted, Princess Margaret and Peter Townsend met for three hours in Clarence House. This gave rise to such speculation that Buckingham Palace issued a statement that nothing had changed since the Princess's original statement in 1955.

15 Queen Elizabeth I's suitor

Rumour was so strong that Robert Dudley, Earl of Leicester had killed his wife so that he could marry Queen Elizabeth I that he was eventually banished from court. Though he claimed that his wife had fallen downstairs, the hood on the head of her corpse was completely undisturbed, suggesting that it had been arranged to look like an accident. Mary, Queen of Scots was among the unconvinced. 'So the Queen of England is to marry her horse-keeper, who has killed his wife to make room for her', she remarked bluntly.

16 Queen Mary's last wish

It is rumoured within Buckingham Palace that Queen Mary's last wish, to see her granddaughter wearing the Monarch's crown, was fulfilled, even though she died ten weeks before the Coronation. Queen Elizabeth II is said to have sent for the crown and worn it in Marlborough House in front of her dying grandmother.

17 Prince Albert's father

Among many rumours against Prince Albert was one that his father was a Jewish Court Chamberlain who had had an affair with his mother.

18 Prince Charles's liaison

Shortly before the announcement of Prince Charles's engagement to Lady Diana Spencer, it was announced in the *Sunday Mirror* that they had conducted a liaison in the Royal Train, stationed in a siding. Though the *Sunday Mirror's* editor, Mr Robert Edwards, failed to come up with any evidence to support his newspaper's claim, he refused a request from Buckingham Palace that the allegation be withdrawn.

19 The Queen Mother's governorships

Just as there are frequent rumours that Prince Charles is to be appointed the Governor of one country or another, so there were similar rumours about the Queen Mother in the 1950s. In 1952, she was rumoured to be the next Governor General of Australia, and in 1957 there were further rumours that she would be the next Governor General of Canada. 'What a novel idea', said the Queen when asked about it by Canadian reporters, 'I'm afraid we would miss her too much.'

20 King Edward VII's war talk

In 1907, rumours of war abounded. These came to a peak in August, when a photograph of King Edward VII in conversation with Campbell-Bannerman in Austria was printed with the dramatic caption, 'Is it Peace or War?' In fact the King had been asking Campbell-Bannerman whether he thought halibut tasted better boiled or baked.

21 King George VI's ambition

In 1928, the Duke of York (later George VI) wrote to his elder brother the Prince of Wales, who was in Africa: 'There is a lovely story going about that the reason of your rushing home is that in the event of anything happening to Papa I am going to bag the Throne in your absence!!! Just like the Middle Ages!' In the event, he was devastated by his brother's Abdication and felt unequal to the job of replacing him.

22 Prince Philip's rift

When Prince Philip took a lengthy trip in the South Atlantic with his friend Michael Parker in 1956, rumours circulated that he had had a huge row with the Queen, and that he and Parker were attending 'wild parties'. Buckingham Palace issued an official denial of rumours of a rift. Prince Philip's reunion with the Queen in Lisbon received heavy publicity.

23 The Queen Mother's second marriage

In the 1950s American newspapers frequently rumoured that the Queen Mother was planning to marry her Treasurer, Sir Arthur Penn.

24 King Edward VII's wage claim

When an anonymous article appeared in *The Times* in 1874 denying that King Edward VII was in debt but adding that he deserved more money, it was strongly rumoured to have been written by Edward himself.

25 Charles II's burglary

When Captain Blood, an Irishman who had been apprehended attempting to steal the Crown Jewels from the Tower of London in 1671, was pardoned, released, given £500 and had his Irish estates restored to him, credible rumours abounded that King Charles II, who was on hard times, had organised the entire burglary.

26 The Queen and her pregnancies

In 1972 the French newspaper *France Dimanche* looked through its cuttings files on the Queen for the previous 14 years, and saw that there had been published in different newspapers in France: 63 stories on the Queen's 'imminent' Abdication; 73 telling of her likely divorce from Prince Philip; 115 accounts of quarrels with Lord Snowdon; 17 reports of rudeness to other monarchs (such as Princess Grace of Monaco); and 92 scoops about the Queen being pregnant. Two of these were correct.

Four events which contradicted Royal denials

100

1 Princess Anne's engagement

'There is no romance and no grounds for these rumours of a romance': Princess Anne. Six months later her engagement to Mark Phillips was announced.

2 The Queen's engagement

During 1946 and the first half of 1947, Buckingham Palace issued four official denials of any engagement between the Queen and Prince Philip. In July 1947, their engagement was announced.

3 The Duchess of Kent's engagement

'The Duke and my daughter are just good friends. A romance? Good gracious I don't think so': Sir William Worsley, father of the future Duchess of Kent, 1957.

4 Princess Diana's holiday

'Diana is not here and is not coming', said Mrs Shand-Kydd from her farm in Australia in February 1981. Weeks later, it emerged that her daughter *had* been there, enjoying her last days of freedom before the announcement of her engagement to Prince Charles.

Thirteen democratic gestures of Royalty

1 Queen Mary and the threepenny lunch

In 1939, Queen Mary sat down with 264 children who had been evacuated from London to Chichester for a threepenny lunch consisting of stewed steak, potatoes and jam-tart. Liquid refreshment was afforded from a bakelite mug filled with water *ad lib*. 'This is all very good', she remarked.

2 King Edward VII and King Kalakaua

When the Germans objected to King Kalakaua of the Hawaiian Islands taking precedence over the Crown Prince of Germany at an official dinner, King Edward VII retorted, 'Either the brute is a king or else he is an ordinary black nigger, and if he is not a king, why is he here at all?'

3 King George III and the stable lad

On an early morning stroll around Windsor Castle, King George III bumped into a boy in the stables. He asked him what job he did. The boy replied that he worked in the stables. 'And how much do they pay you?', asked the King. 'They only give me victuals and clothes,' replied the boy. 'Be content', said the King, 'I have no more.'

4 Princess Anne and the Brownies

A Buckingham Palace pack of Brownies was formed in 1959 for the sake of Princess Anne. The nine-year-old Princess's fellow Brownies included the daughter of a London taxi driver and the daughter of a hotel maintenance engineer.

5 King George VI and the people of Malta

'You have made the people of Malta very happy today, Sir', said the Lieutenant-Governor of Malta when King George VI paid the war-torn island a surprise visit in 1943. 'But I have been the happiest man in Malta today', replied the King.

6 Princess Marina and the war widows

When her husband, The Duke of Kent, was killed in an aircrash in 1941, Princess Marina said bravely, 'I must pull myself together. I am just one among thousands of war widows.'

7 The Queen and the hot dogs

At an Afternoon Party for the American Bar Association in the summer of 1957, the Queen forsook the traditional Palace fare of cucumber sandwiches and strawberries for the American snack, 'Hot Dogs'. She remarked in passing that her mother and father had much enjoyed the hot dogs that President Roosevelt had laid on for them on their visit to America in 1939.

8 Angus Ogilvy and the free cigarettes

At the close of a charity reception in 1974, the pop group Mud, famous for their hit *Tiger Feet*, were surprised to notice Angus Ogilvy overtake them on their dash for the free cigarettes. They were even more startled when he turned around and offered this advice: 'Steam in there, sons, or the waiters will get 'em.'

9 William IV and his mates

Upon joining his ship, the young man who would be William IV announced to the other boys: 'I am entered as Prince William Henry but my father's name is Guelph and therefore if you please you may call me William Guelph for I am nothing more than a sailor like yourselves.'

10 The Queen and the Labour Exchange

The Queen registered at the Windsor Labour Exchange on her sixteenth birthday, as required by law.

11 King George V and the Socialists

King George V put on a red tie for the first time in his life to demonstrate a spirit of co-operation when he met his first socialist Government in 1923.

12 King George VI and his people

When King George VI was visiting the East End after a heavy bombing, a voice from the crowd shouted, 'Thank God for a good King!' to which King George VI shouted back, 'Thank God for a good people.'

13 The Queen and the Underground

On 15 May 1939, the Queen and Princess Margaret went for their first ride on the London Underground System. They sat next to Mrs Simmons, a charlady from Muswell Hill.

Eight social blunders by Royalty

1 Mark Phillips and the mud

Late for a class at Cirencester Agricultural College, Mark Phillips parked his car on a strictly prohibited area of grass next to his classroom. A downpour during the class ensured that his car got stuck in the mud. His classmates ignored all his pleas to help push. Eventually, Mark Phillips stomped off, abandoning the sunken car.

2 King George V and the butlers

In Delhi in 1911, King George V was introduced to the two distinguished brothers, Sir Montagu and Sir Harcourt Butler.

'These are the two Butlers, sir', said his equerry.

'Yes, but what are their names?' inquired the King.

3 Princess Alexandra and the communion wafer

In 1976, at the service of canonisation of her husband's ancestor, The Blessed John Ogilvy, in Rome, Princess Alexandra took the Roman Catholic communion. For this she later apologised, saying that she had not realised that it was exclusive to members of the Roman Catholic faith.

4 Prince Philip, his mother, and the Queen's engagement ring

So enthusiastic was Prince Philip's mother, Princess Andrew, at the sight of her son's designs for the Queen's engagement ring that she went with them to a jeweller before a proper measurement had been organised. The resulting ring, laden with Prince Philip's family jewels, was far too big for the Queen's finger. 'We won't have to wait till it's right, will we?' was the Queen's anxious comment.

5 Queen Mary and the park

Opening a park in Glasgow, Queen Mary commented to a city councillor, 'It's a beautiful park, but what a shame about all the houses around it.'

6 The Queen Mother and the Zulu

On the Royal visit to South Africa after the Second World War, a giant Zulu charged through the police cordon and rushed at the Royal party. Straightaway the Queen Mother started beating him off with her umbrella. Then she realised that he was offering Princess Elizabeth a ten shilling note as a twenty-first birthday present. 'It was the worst mistake of my life,' the Queen Mother commented later.

7 Queen Mary and John Buchan

When King George V met John Buchan in 1935, he said to him 'I don't get much time for reading, but when I do I enjoy your books, *The Thirty Nine Steps* and so on. Now, before you go, the Queen would like to have a word with you.' Buchan then had a private word with Queen Mary, who said: 'The King does not get much time for reading and when he does I'm afraid he reads the most awful rubbish.'

8 The Queen and a detour

At an agricultural show in New Zealand the Queen and Prince Philip made an unwitting detour off the official red carpet and went down another, laid at an angle to it by an enterprising exhibitor. They sauntered amiably down the 40 yards of maverick carpet and ended up inspecting a 2-room holiday chalet which had not been listed in their schedule.

Eight groups of people who have been outraged by remarks of Prince Philip 103

1 The Greeks

In 1963, to the Sydney press, Prince Philip claimed that though he was born in Greece he wasn't a Greek. The next day the Greek press was packed with photographs of Prince Philip aged nine wearing Evzone's uniform.

2 The Australians

In 1968, replying to a speech in Australia by Chief Justice Sir Garfield Barwick, Prince Philip said, 'When he was on the subject of Australia being wedded to democracy, I had to laugh at that.' He went on to attack the notion that there were few religious divisions and no racism in Australia. An editorial in the *Melbourne Herald* commented, 'Someone back home should tell the Prince it's about time he grew up.'

2 The Canadians

'The monarchy exists not for its own benefit, but for that of the country. We don't come here for our health. We can think of better ways of enjoying ourselves.' From a speech by Prince Philip in Ottawa in 1969. A few weeks later the Queen's portrait was removed from some Canadian banknotes and replaced with pictures of past Canadian premiers.

4 The Spanish

'We're fed up with the story of Gibraltar, and it is very expensive at that': Prince Philip to King Juan Carlos of Spain, October 1977.

5 The French

'Isn't it a pity that Louis XVI was sent to the scaffold?', Prince Philip to a French politician.

6 The Tom Jones Fan Club

At a Small Businessman's Association lunch in 1969 Prince Philip answered someone who had said that no one could make a fortune in Britain any more. 'What about Tom Jones? He's made a million and he's a bloody awful singer.' The night before, Tom Jones had sung before the Prince in the Royal Variety Show. 'I was singing for charity – not auditioning for Prince Philip,' the singer retorted later.

7 British liberals

In 1969, Prince Philip remarked to General Alfredo Stroessner, the Dictator of Paraguay that it was 'a pleasant change to be in a country that isn't ruled by its people.' After much outcry from the British press came an explanation from the Palace – that he was referring only to minor nuisances in Britain, like the Lord's Day Observance Society.

8 The unemployed

On the Jimmy Young radio show in June 1981, Prince Philip said, 'A few years ago everybody was saying we must have much more leisure, everybody is working too much. Now that everybody has got so much leisure – it may be involuntary, but they have got it – they are complaining they are unemployed. People do not seem to be able to make up their mind what they want, do they?' Twenty Labour MPs tabled a Commons motion protesting at the Prince's 'ill-informed comments'. He later apologised.

104   *Three alternatives to 'My Husband and I' that have been tried by the Queen*

1 We
2 I and my husband
3 Me and my husband
   (Prince Philip prefers 'My husband and I')

Five famous people's opinions of   105
Prince Philip

1 James Callaghan
'I think Philip is a very fine fellow.'
2 Clive Jenkins
'He's the best argument for republicanism since George III.'
3 Michael Parker, an equerry to Philip
'No one has a kinder heart, or takes more trouble to conceal it.'
4 Frank Sinatra
'I have found him always terribly kind, most interesting, and highly intelligent. He has what I consider to be the most important attribute in a man – a great sense of humour.'
5 An anonymous British ambassador
'If anyone asks me, "Is it true that Prince Philip said, or did, such and such a thing?" I immediately answer, "Yes, yes, yes, of course it is." '

Three humble statements by Prince   106
Philip

1 'Constitutionally I don't exist.'
2 'I'm a discredited Balkan prince of no particular merit or distinction.'
3 'My only tangible contribution to British life has been to improve the rear lights on lorries.'

Seven members of the Royal Family   107
who gambled

1 King George II
Though King George II was every bit a gambling man, it made him uneasy to learn that his subjects were betting that he would die within a year at 10 to 1. Overcoming his disquiet, he himself placed a bet of 50 guineas. A year later he said that he'd never won 500 guineas with greater pleasure. (Nowadays, reputable bookmakers refuse bets on Royal misfortune.)

2 King George IV

When he lost a four-in-hand race with his coachman, King George IV knighted him.

3 King Henry VIII

King Henry VIII was such a gambling enthusiast that he spent over £3,000 on it in only three years.

4 King Edward VII

King Edward VII's favourite game was Baccarat for which he had his own ivory chips with the Prince of Wales feathers. After his involvement in the Tranby Croft scandal, his mother, Queen Victoria, wrote to him telling him to give the game up. He wrote back saying that unless she promised never to mention giving it up again he would cease to visit her at Windsor. She never mentioned it again.

5 The Duchess of Windsor

The Duchess of Windsor loved poker. She got her taste for it in China, where at her first game ever she won $225, which was exactly equal to her month's allowance from her estranged husband. Her host, Herman Rogers, thereafter gave her a stake of $50 every night so that she could win the next day's shopping money.

6 King George V

A good part of King George V's stamp collection is the product of his skill at gambling on horses.

7 Queen Victoria

Queen Victoria loved playing cards for money. All who lost to her were required to pay her in newly minted coins, of which her Ladies and Gentlemen-in-Waiting kept large stores.

108 Three occasions on which Mark Phillips has enjoyed himself a little too much

1 At his stag party

Two days before his wedding to Princess Anne, Mark Phillips hired a private room at Julie's restaurant in Holland Park to entertain his men friends to dinner. Towards the end of dinner, he challenged his Best Man, Captain Eric Grounds, to a champagne drinking contest. Perhaps emboldened by his skill in the first contest, Mark Phillips set himself a second – to juggle with a casserole dish. This resulted in wide-ranging casserole stains on his shirt and dinner jacket. When complaints about the noise began coming from other areas of the restaurant, Captain Eric Grounds was sent down to apologise.

2 At an hotel in Hamburg
In August 1976, there were reports in German newspapers that Princess Anne had locked Mark Phillips out of their bedroom in the Hotel Heidschnucke in Hamburg. Her complaints against her husband were said to include that he had drunk too much and that he had ignored her all evening.

3 Aboard a ferry
In June 1981, crew members of the St Edmund Sealink Ferry complained that on the crossing from Holland to Harwich Mark Phillips and other members of the British Equestrian team had acted 'like upper-class hooligans' during a midnight champagne party. Mark Phillips had sprayed champagne across the full length of the lounge bar and had also at one stage flicked water at two women grooms, driving the bar steward to ask of him, 'What would your mother-in-law say if she knew about this?'

Seven members of the Royal Family 109 who have been spanked

1 Prince Charles
On different occasions, Prince Charles has been spanked for sticking his tongue out at a crowd, for slipping an ice-cube down a footman's neck and, at Cheam, for switching schoolcaps around on pegs. For the latter offence, the Headmaster, Mr Beck, whacked him with a cricket bat.

2 King George VI
As a cadet at Dartmouth, King George VI received six of the best for letting off fireworks on Guy Fawkes Night. Sixteen other cadets received similar punishment. For a long time afterwards he claimed that the punishment had been unfair, as on the fourth stroke the cane had broken, and, he maintained, the remaining two whacks should not have been distributed.

3 Prince Michael of Kent
As a boy at Mr Chamier's house at Eton College, Prince Michael of Kent was caned by his House Captain for mobbing in the corridors.

4 Princess Anne

Prince Philip once had to smack Princess Anne when she disobeyed her nanny's order to put her sweater on.

5 The Queen

When the young Princess Elizabeth started poking about in a toolbag belonging to Mr Albert Tippele, a telephone repair man, Mr Tippele smacked her on the bottom. 'She ran away and her mother seemed pleased', Mr Tippele commented later.

6 Queen Mary I

Anne Boleyn so loathed Mary, the daughter of King Henry VIII's first wife, that she once sent her governess Lady Shelton a letter asking her to give Mary a box on the ear now and then, 'for the cursed bastard she is.'

7 Prince William of Denmark

The day after her arrival in England, Queen Alexandra used the scroll of the civic address delivered to her by a mayor to pound her brother William over the head.

110   *Five unsuitable friends of Royalty*

1 Harry Hastings

Harry Hastings was one of King Edward VII's more flamboyant friends at Oxford University. He breakfasted each morning on mackerel fried in gin, caviare on toast and a bottle of claret.

2 Sporting Joe

'Sporting Joe' was the nickname given to another of King Edward VII's friends, Lord Aylesford. When he was bored he would order his carriage to be driven at a gallop through the streets of London. He would perch on the roof throwing bags of flour at pedestrians and howling with laughter.

3 Fiona Watson

Soon after the Honourable Fiona Watson had been photographed in the company of Prince Charles, a former boyfriend revealed that she had once posed naked for *Penthouse* magazine.

4 Alice Perrers

Not only did King Edward III's mistress, Alice Perrers, pass on to the King the gonorrhoea that caused him to die: on his deathbed she removed all the rings from his fingers and kept them for herself.

5 Piers Gaveston

Piers Gaveston was the homosexual friend of King Edward II. He had a vicious wit, inventing malicious nicknames for much of the aristocracy. One man who had been served with a nickname 'The Black Hound of Arden', Guy Beauchamp of Warwick, eventually became so incensed that he murdered Gaveston in 1312.

Four scandals involving King Edward VII

1 The Baker Scandal

In June 1875, a Miss Rebecca Dickenson alleged in court that when she was travelling on a train from Petersfield to Waterloo, Colonel Valentine Baker, a close friend of King Edward VII had entered her carriage. From Liphook to Woking all went well, but when the train pulled out of Woking, Colonel Baker began asking 'insulting questions'. He then put his arm around her and 'forcibly' kissed her. Miss Dickenson attempted to grab a communication cord, but found that there was not one in the carriage. When Colonel Baker attempted to pull her clothes up she opened the window and screamed. This provoked no response, so she opened the carriage door and climbed onto the footboard 'determined to perish rather than re-enter the carriage.' After 6 miles of open-air travel her plight was noticed and the driver stopped the train at Esher. Baker was placed in a carriage with two other men, who noticed that a number of his buttons were undone. A Reverend Baldwin Brown rode the rest of the journey with Miss Dickenson. Though Colonel Baker was sentenced to 12 months in jail and fined £500, a large proportion of the general public thought that his high connections had got him off lightly. Public feeling against Colonel Baker and King Edward VII was further inflamed by a pamphlet that was hawked around before the trial, called, 'Alleged Disgusting and Indecent Outrages by Colonel Baker in a Railway Carriage; with a Narrative of the Courageous Conduct of Miss Dickenson.'

2 The Beresford scandal

In 1892, Lady Brooke wrote to her lover, Lord Charles Beresford, denouncing him as unfaithful and threatening vengeance because his wife, Mina, was expecting a baby. Unfortunately for Lady Brooke, Lord Charles Beresford was away at sea, and his wife opened the letter. She immediately took it to her solicitor, who kept it. In Lady Brooke's struggle to retrieve her letter she sought the aid of the Prince of Wales. Edward was quickly enraptured by

Lady Brooke. He went to Mina Beresford who was a friend of his, and asked her to return the letter. She refused, causing both Beresfords to be dropped from Edward's circle. When Edward started walking out with Lady Brooke, Lord Charles Beresford, dropped by a friend and rejected by a lover, threatened to go to the press with the whole story if the King did not write a letter of apology to his wife. After some deliberation, including a man-to-man fight, the King wrote the apology, the letter was returned to Lady Brooke, and Lord Charles and his wife were reinstated in society.

3 The Mordaunt scandal

In 1868 Lady Mordaunt had become sufficiently friendly with the Prince of Wales to make Sir Charles Mordaunt forbid her from exchanging letters and flirting with him. Early in 1869 Harriett was prematurely delivered of a child with an eye infection. Terrified that the child would go blind and deranged by the premature birth, Harriett confessed to her husband that she had been intimate with Lord Cole, the father of the child, and also with Sir Frederick Johnstone and the Prince of Wales. Sir Charles forced open her desk and discovered a handkerchief, a Valentine card and letters from Edward. There were also letters from Cole and Johnstone, later characterised in the court as damning. Sir Charles sued his wife for divorce on the grounds of her adultery with Cole and Johnstone. Lady Mordaunt's father entered a plea of insanity. In court in 1870, Edward was asked, 'Has there ever been any improper familiarity or criminal act between yourself and Lady Mordaunt?' To which he replied, 'There has not.' He was hissed in the street and later in the theatre and at Ascot. Lady Mordaunt was declared 'utterly unfit' to answer her own defence.

4 The Tranby Croft scandal

In 1880, King Edward VII stayed for Doncaster races at Tranby Croft, the home of Arthur Wilson. Among the guests was Sir William Gordon-Cumming, a member of four London clubs, a veteran of the Zulu war and a lieutenant-colonel in the Scots Guards. For two nights running, Gordon-Cumming was observed cheating at Baccarat by other members of the house party, though not by King Edward VII himself. After some consultation with Edward, the household confronted Gordon-Cumming with the accusation and he was made to sign a statement that he would never play cards again in his life. The statement was also signed by the others, pledging secrecy. But the secret got out, and, finding himself scorned and in danger of being court-martialled, Gordon-Cumming sued five of the household for slander. Though Edward was not a defendant, he was called as a witness. The jury found in favour of the defendants to the sound of much hissing from the public gallery. Again, Edward was booed at Ascot; Sir William retired to his Scottish estate at Gordonstoun.

Eleven times Royalty has sworn 112

1 'I can't see in this bloody wind'
Princess Anne aged 13 to the Queen at a Sydney showground.

2 'The damned things aren't working!'
King George VI rehearsing a speech into microphones in Wembley Stadium. The microphones were in fact working and the remark boomed out loud and clear.

3 'Christmas!'
Princess Margaret, on catching her dress on a nail in a box at Covent Garden.

4 'What a damnable wedding present!'
King Edward VIII on receiving news from the palace that neither his new wife nor any descendants could have the title HRH.

5 'Take it off. It looks damned silly and damned sloppy.'
King George VI to King Peter of Yugoslavia, who was wearing a watch chain over his Royal Yugoslav Air Force uniform.

6 'I hope to God that he breaks his bloody neck.'
Prince Philip, in 1961, when a press photographer in India fell from a tree.

7 'Damn it, you mean to let them into Parliament?!'
King George IV in 1829, having read of the plans for Catholic emancipation.

8 'I'll fix those bloody clocks!'
King Edward VIII, shortly after the death of his father, who had kept all the clocks in Sandringham half an hour early.

9 'God damn it, why don't you drink wine?'
King William IV to King Leopold of the Belgians, who had said that he would only like to drink water. 'I never let anybody drink water at my table.'

10 'What the hell comes next?'
Prince Charles, on forgetting his lines at the dress rehearsal of a Cambridge revue.

11 'Not bloody likely. That's the side that hurts.'
Princess Anne, asked by a radiologist to lie on her right side, after she had fallen from her horse in Kiev, 1973.

Fourteen reports on members of the Royal Family

1 Lord Snowdon's prep school report
'Armstrong-Jones may be good at something, but it's nothing we teach here.'

2 Prince Charles's football report
'At half-back Prince Charles seldom drove himself as hard as his ability and position demanded' (from the *Cheam School Chronicle*).

3 Princess Alexandra's final report from Heathfield
'. . . all the lovable qualities of quick sympathy, affection and generosity, laughter and total honesty are still there in abundance.'

4 Noel Coward's report on Princess Margaret's piano playing
'Surprisingly good, she has an impeccable ear, her piano playing is simple but has perfect rhythm and her method of singing is really very funny' (1948).

5 King Edward VII's German report
'He takes everything that is at hand and throws it with the greatest violence against the wall or window, without thinking the least of the consequences of what he is doing; or he stands in the corner stamping with his legs and screaming in the most dreadful manner' (report delivered to Queen Victoria and Prince Albert by his German tutor, Dr Becker).

6 Angus Ogilvy's Department of Trade report
After the Lonrho scandal of 1976, a Department of Trade report described Angus Ogilvy, who was a company director, as 'a weak man' and concluded that he was negligent in his duties. Angus Ogilvy maintained that the report was unfair.

7 Prince Andrew's report after a French trip from Gordonstoun
'He was a bit of a handful'

8 Prince Michael of Kent's Eton report
'He is in fact rather withdrawn and reserved. Possibly the other boys find him a bit unco-operative. His French is good and his German coming along nicely' (written by his housemaster, Cyril Chamier, in 1958).

9 King George VI's tutor's report
'I am very sorry to say that Prince Albert has caused two painful scenes in his bedroom this week. On the second occasion I understand that he narrowly escaped giving his brother a very severe kick, it being absolutely unprovoked' (delivered by Mr Hansell to King George V, 1904).

10 King Edward VIII's Oxford report
'Bookish he will never be.'
11 Prince Philip's final report from Gordonstoun
'Prince Philip is a born leader, but will need the exacting demands of a great service to do justice to himself. His best is outstanding; his second best is not good enough.'
12 King Edward VI's tutor's report
'Every day (he) readeth a portion of Solomon's Proverbs, wherein he delighteth much; and learneth there . . . to beware of strange and wanton women.'
13 Prince Charles's acting report
'Prince Charles played the traditional Gloucester with competence and depth; he had a good voice and excellent elocution, and very well conveyed the ambition and bitterness of the twisted hunchback' (from the *Cheam School Chronicle*).

Seven parental complaints about King Edward VII 114

1 'Oh! Bertie, alas! Alas! That is too sad a subject to enter on!' *Queen Victoria*
2 'His intellect is of no more use than a pistol packed in the bottom of a trunk if one were attacked in the robber-infested Apennines!' *Prince Albert*
3 'Handsome I cannot think him, with that painfully small and narrow head, those immense features and total want of chin.' *Queen Victoria*
4 'A thoroughgoing lazybones!' *Prince Albert*
5 'Dull and ignorant!' *Queen Victoria*
6 'I never can or shall look at him without a shudder.'
Queen Victoria
7 . . . and King Edward VII's comment on Queen Victoria
'I never left her presence without a sigh of relief.'

Six examples of Queen Victoria's sexiness

1 Searching through forgotten drawers in Buckingham Palace, Compton Mackenzie discovered a nude painting of the goddess Artemis with a note beneath it saying that it had been one of Queen Victoria's wedding presents to Prince Albert.
2 From her journal during the time of her engagement: '*We kissed each other again and again.*'
3 From her honeymoon journal: '*Albert's excessive love and affection gave me feelings of heavenly love and happiness.*'
4 From her everyday journal: '*Got up at 20 m. to 9. My dearest Albert put on my stockings for me. I went in and saw him shave, a great delight for me.*'
5 On Albert wearing a black jacket open at the neck: '*More beautiful than I can say*'.
6 '*Oh, doctor, can I have no more fun in bed?*' Queen Victoria asked her doctor when she was told her childbearing days were over.

Four Royal flirtations

1 Princess Margaret and a sailor
Aged seventeen, Princess Margaret brought a blush to a young sailor's cheek. Before she launched a ship in Belfast, the sailor presented her with a bouquet. She plucked out one of the roses and gave it to him.

2 Queen Victoria and a soldier
Aged seventy, Queen Victoria loved to tell the story of how at Windsor Castle one starlit night she had opened her bedroom window to look outside when a sentry, mistaking her for a young housemaid, began to flirt with her. The Queen swiftly drew the curtains, but was thrilled at what had happened.

3 Prince Philip and a 'lovely young thing'
Staying with his Aunt Aspasia in Venice aged seventeen, Prince Philip was allowed only twenty minutes to see home a girl whom his aunt later described as 'a lovely young thing in tulle or organdy'. Soon the sound of the motor launch became unaccountably silent, and the Prince was very late back. 'We had trouble with the sparking plugs' was his explanation.

4 Queen Elizabeth I and the Earl of Leicester
During a ceremony to bestow on her beloved Leicester the collar
of an earl, Queen Elizabeth I shocked several foreign envoys when
she was clearly observed tickling his neck.

Five places which have witnessed 117
kisses in public by Princess Diana

1 Waterloo Station
Princess Diana kissed Lord Maclean, the Lord Chamberlain, and
his henchman Sir John Johnston on Waterloo Station after her
wedding.
2 Egypt
Princess Diana blew a kiss to President and Mrs Sadat from the
steps of her plane as she prepared to leave Egypt at the end of her
honeymoon.
3 The Buckingham Palace forecourt
After some persuasion from his brothers, Prince Charles kissed
Princess Diana on the Buckingham Palace balcony after their
wedding.

Nicholas Hardy kisses the hand of his future Queen

4 The garden of Highgrove

Photographers with telephoto lenses turned a private kiss between Prince Charles and Princess Diana soon after they had moved into Highgrove, into a public one.

5 Dean Close School

'*May I kiss the hand of my future Queen?*' asked Nicholas Hardy, a pupil at Dean Close School, of Princess Diana. '*Yes, you may*', replied the Princess, adding. '*You will never live this down.*' Nicholas Hardy was later expelled as a boarder when he was caught smoking in his dormitory.

118 *Sixteen kings who had illegitimate children*

1 Henry I

21 known illegitimate children, including Robert, Earl of Gloucester, and Sybilla, wife of Alexander I, King of Scots.

2 Stephen

Gervase, Abbot of Westminster, and two other children.

3 Henry II

2 acknowledged illegitimate sons

4 Richard I

1 known illegitimate son

5 John

8 authenticated illegitimate children

6 Edward I

1 illegitimate son

7 Edward II

1 illegitimate son

8 Edward III

1 illegitimate son

9 Edward IV

2 known illegitimate children, including Arthur Plantagenet, Viscount Lisle

10 Henry VIII

1 acknowledged illegitimate son, Henry FitzRoy, Duke of Richmond

11 Charles II

14 or 15 illegitimate children, including: James, Duke of Monmouth, Henry FitzRoy, Duke of Grafton, Charles Beauclerk, Duke of St Albans, Charles Lennox, Duke of Richmond and Lennox

12 James II
6 known illegitimate children including: James FitzJames, Duke of Berwick (by Arabella Churchill, sister of the Duke of Marlborough), Henrietta FitzJames, also by Arabella Churchill.

13 George I
1 son and 3 daughters, never publicly acknowledged

14 George II
1 probable illegitimate son

15 George IV
2 illegitimate sons privately acknowledged, and possibly four other children

16 William IV
1 son by an unknown mother and 10 children by Mrs Jordan, the actress, including George FitzClarence, Earl of Munster.

Seven celebrated mistresses of kings

1 Nell Gwynne
She began her career as an orange seller at the Theatre Royal in Drury Lane, where she was noticed by King Charles II. One of her sons by the King was created Duke of St Albans. The King called her 'Nelly'; her name for him was 'Charles III', since her previous lovers, Buckhurst and Hart, had both been called Charles.

2 Louise de Kéroualle
A beautiful, witty and aristocratic Frenchwoman in the Court of Charles II, she had actually been sent as a spy by Louis XIV with orders to become the King's mistress, which she managed successfully. The King created her Duchess of Portsmouth and made one of her sons by him the Duke of Richmond. She was a Catholic, which prompted Nell Gwyn's celebrated crowd-control tactic when once confronted by a mob: 'Pray good people desist – I am the PROTESTANT whore!'

3 Madame Kielmansegge and Madame Schulenburg
Due to their distinctive appearance, these middle-aged ladies who came over from Hanover with King George I when he assumed the Throne were known as 'The Elephant and The Maypole'. They coexisted amiably.

4 Perdita
This was the stage name of an actress called Mary Robinson with whom the future King George IV became utterly infatuated. She

was his first love and he wrote her ardent love letters signed 'Florizel'. The actress, a good few years older than the Prince cannily extracted a bond for £20,000 from him, to be paid when he came of age – by which time he was tired of her but honoured the debt.

5 Lady Hertford and Lady Conyngham
The massive middle-aged marchionesses with whom King George IV consoled himself in later life.

6 Mrs Jordan
Mrs Jordan was a very successful actress of the time who lived with (and frequently supported) the future King William IV for 20 years. The couple produced 10 children who were well provided for when William acceded to the Throne. But his accession cost him their mother, for he was forced to repudiate her and marry Queen Adelaide in the hope of producing an heir to the Throne. Mrs Jordan died sad, alone and penniless in France six years after the King married.

7 Mrs Keppel
A gracious and tactful courtier who was admired not only by King Edward VII but appreciated by Queen Alexandra, who personally led Alice Keppel to the King's deathbed for a farewell. Commenting in later years on the Abdication of Edward VIII she said: 'We did it better in *my* day.' She is famous for her remark 'A royal mistress should curtsey first – and then jump into bed.'

120 *Five ancestors of Princess Diana who were mistresses of kings*

1 Lucy Walter *(mistress of King Charles II)*.
2 Barbara Palmer, Duchess of Cleveland *(mistress of King Charles II)*.
3 Louise de Kéroualle, Duchess of Portsmouth *(mistress of King Charles II)*.
4 Arabella Churchill *(mistress of King James II)*.
5 Frances, Countess of Jersey *(mistress of King George IV)*.

1 Queen Mary sees a Guards officer

Walking around Windsor Castle on a hot night, Queen Mary flung open a door to be confronted by a Guards officer lying naked on his bed. At a reception a few weeks later, the Guards officer was presented to Queen Mary. *'Ah, I believe we have met before'*, she remarked.

2 King Henry VI sees young ladies

King Henry VI, though young, was exceptionally puritanical. Blacman, his first biographer tells how 'at Christmas time a certain great lord brought before him a dance or show of young ladies with bared bosoms who were to dance in that guise before the King, . . . who very angrily averted his eyes, turned his back upon them, and went out to his chamber, saying: "Fy, fy, for shame, forsoothe ye be to blame!"

3 The Queen sees Roddy Llewellyn

The first time the Queen ever met her sister's boyfriend, Roddy Llewellyn was on a Saturday evening at Royal Lodge. The Queen was talking to a nanny in the nursery when Mr Llewellyn burst in wearing only a shirt and underpants, hoping to have buttons sewn on. *'Please forgive me, Ma'am, I look awful'*, he said. *'Don't worry, I don't look too good myself'*, replied the Queen.

The next day they were formally introduced after both had attended chapel at Windor.

4 Queen Victoria sees Lord Claud Hamilton

Staying at Balmoral, Queen Victoria was much displeased at the recurrent sight of the ten-year-old Lord Claud Hamilton turning frequent somersaults to prove that Highlanders wear nothing underneath their kilts.

5 King George III sees a Scots colonel

At a levee in St James's Palace, a low-bowing Scots colonel's kilt rode up his back. King George III was horrified. *'Keep the ladies at the back!'* he shouted, *'Keep the ladies at the back!'*

6 And one Queen who provided nudity . . .

In her old age, Queen Elizabeth I was in the curious habit of regularly opening the front of her robe, revealing the whole of her bare bosom to the assembled courtiers and ambassadors who surrounded her.

Six homosexual kings

1 William II
2 Richard I
3 Edward II
4 Richard II
5 James I
6 William III

Six fashion hints from Royalty

1 'A woman can never be too rich or too thin.'
The Duchess of Windsor

2 'A good suit goes on forever.'
Priness Anne

3 'These days girls simply don't have a hat.'
The Queen as a young lady, chiding the Queen Mother for
suggesting that a lady-in-waiting should wear a hat and not a
scarf.

4 'You should wear what you like.'
Princess Diana, talking to twenty-year-old Suzanne Long in
March 1982 at the Gateshead Music Centre. Miss Long, who was
sporting spikey hair, bright lipstick and a studded leather coat
covered in badges, had admitted to the Princess that she had
defied her grandmother's orders to wear something normal.

5 'I don't believe in fashion, full stop.'
Prince Charles

6 'Rings on each finger improve an ugly hand.'
Queen Victoria. Her plump hands embarrassed her, so she wore
rings on every finger when attending any grand event. This made
it particularly difficult for her to eat with a knife and fork, and
donning and removing gloves became a major operation.

1 A sprig of holly
It was placed at the throat of Queen Victoria as a child at mealtimes to encourage her to keep her chin up.

2 Bands
The Queen wore bands on her teeth at the age of thirteen. Around the same age, Prince Edward wore them for eighteen months.

3 Splints
As a boy George VI was made to wear splints at night to correct his knock-knees.

4 Contact lenses
They are worn by Mark Phillips and by Prince Philip. Andrew wears glasses, but never in public.

5 Shortened seats
The mobile seats used by Princess Margaret on royal planes have been specially adapted for her shortness. Before the backs of the seats were lowered she suffered from her hats falling off when she rested her head.

6 A tattoo
Aged sixteen George V employed a Japanese practitioner to tattoo a large blue and red dragon on his right arm.

7 High collars
Queen Alexandra used to wear high collars or many rows of pearls to conceal a scar on her neck.

8 Make-up
George VI wore tan make-up on official occasions in order to hide his pallid complexion.

9 Plastic surgery
When he was three years old, Viscount Linley had his ears adjusted by a plastic surgeon at Great Ormond Street Hospital for Children.

10 Cotton
After losing her teeth, Queen Elizabeth I never appeared in public without first padding out her mouth with wads of cotton.

11 Bleeding
To correct his too-florid complexion, George IV had himself bled to a more suitable pastel shade when he wanted to look his best.

12 Peroxide and eyelash dye
Princess Diana dyes her eyelashes and has her hair streaked blonde.

13 Poppy seeds and lead

Elizabeth I whitened her skin with a mixture of egg, powdered eggshell, poppy seeds, lead, borax and alum. When her hair began to thin, she wore a huge spangled red wig.

14 A corset

George IV wore a corset in middle age so that he could squeeze himself into his spendid clothes.

15 A soapbox

To give the impression of superior height to his bride, Prince Charles posed for the photographs from which the commemorative stamps were produced standing on a soapbox. For the engagement photograph, Princess Diana stood on a lower step.

16 Artificial hair

Queen Mary wore a fringe of artificial hair on her forehead, 'Just like a sponge' in the opinion of her father-in-law's court.

17 Discreet hair tint

After an experimental exposure of her greying temples, the Queen reverted to using a little brown dye on the silver strands.

18 Tapestry scissors

Princess Diana has admitted that she sometimes cuts Prince Charles's hair with her tapestry scissors.

125 *Four fancy dress costumes worn by the Queen*

1 Lord Bathtub

When the Queen and Princess Margaret were children they presented themselves to The Queen Mother dressed in a mixture of tablecloths and Red Indian feathers. '*And whom have I the pleasure of receiving?*' asked the Queen Mother. '*Lord Bathtub and Lady Plug*', replied the Queen.

2 A maid

In the first year of their marriage, the Queen and Prince Philip went to a Fancy Dress ball given by the American ambassador dressed up as a maid and a waiter.

3 The Spanish Infanta

When the Queen was pregnant with Prince Charles, she went to a Fancy Dress ball at Coppins dressed up as the Spanish Infanta. Prince Philip was a policeman.

116

4 A beatnik
In 1962, the Queen dressed up as a beatnik for a Come-As-A-Beatnik ball at Balmoral.

Six members of the Royal Family and the clothes they made fashionable

1 The Queen
Aged three, she was pictured on the cover of *Time* magazine, wearing yellow. This started a fashion trend for yellow.

2 King Edward VII
The most influential of all Royal fashion-setters, he introduced the dinner jacket (previously tails had been worn), and the unbuttoning of the last button of the waistcoat, and he popularised the Norfolk Jacket, the Homburg, knickerbockers and the sideways crease in trousers.

3 Princess Marina
When Princess Marina arrived in England in 1934 to marry the Duke of Kent she was wearing a fez-like hat and clothes in a shade of soft blue. The colour became known as 'Marina Blue' and was much copied; within two weeks the hat was in the shops as 'The Marina Pillbox', selling at two shillings and eleven pence.

4 Princess Diana
Her hairstyle has made Princess Diana the most copied member of the Royal Family in modern times, so much so that when Prince Charles visited New Zealand soon after the announcement of his engagement, he was confronted by a dozen 'Lady Diana lookalikes'. '*Not as good as the real thing*', he quipped. For a short time her pie-crust collars were also fashionable.

5 King Edward VIII
Even as a student at Oxford he was able to set fashions, popularizing plus fours, loud tweeds and trouser turnups. He introduced the bowler hat to America and brought about the convention of wearing a grey top hat instead of the black silk one.

6 Queen Victoria
Knowing her power to influence fashion, Queen Victoria wore Honiton lace for her wedding, to encourage the waning Devon lace industry.

127 *Three places to go if you want to dress like Prince Charles*

1 Turnbull & Asser of Jermyn Street for your shirts
2 Hawes & Curtis of Dover Street for your suits
3 Truefitt & Hill of Old Bond Street for your hair

128 *Sixteen curious garments worn by Royalty*

1 Five diamond necklaces
Worn all at the same time by Queen Mary to a party at
Buckingham Palace on 16 November, 1938.

2 Weighted kilts
Worn by the present Royal Family, specially designed to
withstand the wind.

**3 A black coat of pink spangles and shoes with high
scarlet heels**
A favourite costume of George IV

4 A large black spider
Worn by Queen Elizabeth I on the shawl that covered her bare
breast. Many people mistook it for a real one.

5 Suits with two pairs of trousers
Always ordered by King Edward VIII. His father, King George
V, considered trousers creased in the front to be vulgar, so
Edward used to order two pairs, one creased in the front, the
other at the sides.

6 A tartan dinner jacket
Worn by King George VI in 1950

7 A black suede dinner jacket
Worn by Prince Philip in the 1960s

**8 Tweed knickerbockers, long leather boots and a
brown velvet anorak**
Spotted being worn by Lord Snowdon in the Scottish village of
Ballater in 1965.

9 Roman togas
Worn by King George III's two youngest sons, Prince William
and Prince Edward, when they were aged four and two
respectively. The occasion was a special ceremony instituted by
the King in which the great of the land paid homage to the Royal

children. The two elder sons, aged seven and six, wore scarlet and gold and blue and gold, with medals.

10 A hunting green zip-up tunic with a belt of black corded silk

Worn without the obligatory sword by Lord Snowdon at the Investiture of Prince Charles. Less *avant-garde* in his tastes, The Duke of Norfolk said that Lord Snowdon looked like 'a bell hop at a hotel'.

11 Baby's pyjamas

Worn by Prince Albert every night, according to Queen Victoria, who wrote this description soon after his death: *'He slept in long white drawers, which enclosed his feet as well as his legs, like the sleeping suits worn by small babies.'*

12 A see-through dress

In the hope of preventing press photographers from pestering her further as she went about her duties at the Young England Kindergarten before her engagement, Princess Diana posed with two children in St George's Square. Unfortunately, the light shone through her dress, providing a good view of her legs.

13 An extremely gaudy parrot

On her visit to Paris in 1855, Queen Victoria hoped to charm the fashionable French. Her strange get-up caused quite a stir; she arrived carrying a very large handbag upon which her daughter had embroidered a gaudy parrot, and wore at a state dinner a dress from which substantial bunches of geraniums projected at irregular intervals, and rings on all her fingers, including thumbs.

14 A wedding veil

Queen Victoria was buried in white, with her wedding veil covering her face.

15 A bearskin

When King Edward VIII was the Prince of Wales, he used to enjoy wearing his Guards' Bearskin in leisure moments at weekends.

16 A short kilt

When King George IV visited Scotland in 1828, he wore a kilt for the first time. He soon expressed his embarrassment that the kilt was too short. *'As your Majesty stays so short a time in Scotland'*, replied Lady Jane Hamilton Dalrymple, *'the more we see of you the better!'*

129 *The heights of individual members of the Royal Family*

The Queen – *Five feet four inches*
The Queen Mother – *Five feet two inches*
Princess Margaret – *Five feet two inches*
Princess Anne – *Five feet six and a half inches*
Princess Diana – *Five feet ten inches*
Prince Philip – *Five feet eleven and a half inches*
Prince Charles – *Five feet nine and a half inches*
Prince Andrew – *Six feet*
Prince Edward – *Six feet*

130 *Four motifs on the Queen's evening dresses to honour the countries she visits*

1 Wattle
The national flower of Australia trimmed a yellow dress worn there by the Queen in 1954

2 Maple leaves
The theme of a dress worn on a visit to Canada in 1957

3 Bees
The Napoleonic emblem of industry swarmed all over a dress worn by the Queen on her State Visit to France in 1957.

4 Cherry blossoms
Worn on her State Visit to Japan in 1975

131 *Four peculiarities in Queen Victoria's use of the language*

1 Plurality
Queen Victoria always considered the word 'news' to be plural; a typical reaction was: 'The news from Khartoum are frightful.' She always did the same in a crisis, preferring 'crisises'.

2 Mimicry

She often spoke with a Scottish accent in the Highlands. Lady Lyttelton once heard the Queen ask her servant if he had any money to give a cottager. 'Aboot twelve shillings', he said. 'Ah, that won't do a-tall, I always give her five poond,' said the Queen.

3 Germanicisms

Her Hanoverian background affected Queen Victoria's spelling until the end of her life. Although she wrote her personal letters in French or German, her English notations on state papers had a Teutonic flavour: 'schocking' and 'bewhildering' were usual.

4 Malapropisms

Once, when annoyed with Gladstone, she suggested that it would be a good idea to 'take the sails out of that abominable old G. man.' Another time, the Queen pleaded with Lord Salisbury to 'do all you can to pour oil on the flames' when her grandson the Kaiser had made some particularly inflammatory statement.

Five lipread remarks of Royalty 132

1 'Up socks! Everything's going fine!'

Prince Philip, who was giving the bride away, to Princess Margaret before she walked up the aisle of Westminster Abbey.

2 'I think I've got indigestion!'

The Queen on the balcony of Buckingham Palace after Princess Anne's wedding.

3 'Put that out, Tony.'

The Queen at the Investiture of Prince Charles, catching sight of Lord Snowdon smoking one of his French cigarettes.

4 'Go on, give her a kiss.'
'I'm not going in for that caper – there are millions watching.'

Prince Andrew and Prince Charles on the balcony of Buckingham Palace after Prince Charles's wedding. After a little more persuasion, Prince Charles turned a blind eye to the millions and kissed his new wife.

5 'You look wonderful.'
'Wonderful for you.'

Prince Charles and Princess Diana as they met at the altar for their wedding.

and one member of the Royal Family who did her own lip-reading . . .

Princess Andrew of Greece

Increasingly deaf as the years went by, Prince Philip's mother was a near-perfect lip reader. She loved going to cinemas which showed silent films for the pleasure of lip-reading what was really being said. One of her favourite scenes was in von Stroheim's *Greed*. The hero is in the middle of a love scene and seems to be making passionate advances to the heroine. In fact, he is telling her that he is being evicted for non-payment of rent.

133 *Nine objects destroyed by Royalty*

1 New sheets
As a child, the Queen Mother once shredded her fresh sheets with a pair of scissors.

2 The New Palace at Kew
King George IV ordered the palace, which had been built by King George III in 1806 but never lived in, to be blown up in 1827.

3 A tea cup
On her first solo public engagement, at the Iver Secondary School, the sixteen-year-old Princess Alexandra dropped a tea cup. She insisted on picking up all the pieces herself.

4 Statuettes of John Brown
On the death of Queen Victoria, King Edward VII smashed a number of memorial statuettes of her presumptuous servant with his own hands.

5 The Great Seal
Before going into exile in 1689, King James II dropped the Great Seal into the Thames.

6 A table
While leaning over to sign the Visitor's Book after opening the Sue Ryder Foundation's museum in Cavendish in 1979, the Queen Mother was surprised when the table collapsed.

7 A billiards table
Playing billiards at Sandringham with his father, King Edward VIII miscued and destroyed the felt of the billiards table. King George V forbade him to play for a year.

8 All mastiffs
In a fit of temper and paranoia, King Henry VII ordered that all the mastiffs in the land should be destroyed, as they could attack a lion, the King of Beasts.

9 A house

A fireworks display specially laid on for Queen Elizabeth I on a visit to Warwick Castle in 1572 resulted in a nearby house being burnt to the ground. The inconvenienced husband and wife were given £25.00 compensation after a quick whip-round amongst the Queen's courtiers.

Eighteen dislikes of Queen Victoria 134

1 Babies
'An ugly baby is a very nasty object – and the prettiest is frightful.'
2 The music of Handel
'Tiresome'
3 Education for the working classes
'It is rendering the working classes unfitted for good servants and labourers.'
4 Gladstone
'The abominable G. Man'; 'That half-mad firebrand.'
5 Loud voices
6 Hot rooms
7 Bishops
'I do not like Bishops.'
8 Meeting people she knew when out for her afternoon drive
9 Men staying behind after dinner
'I think it is a *horrid* custom', she told Melbourne, allowing him to stay behind a maximum of five minutes.
10 Tobacco fumes
11 Cars
'I am told that they smell exceedingly nasty, and are very shaky and disagreeable conveyances altogether.'
12 The hairstyle of the 1880s
'The present fashion of fringe and frizzle in front is frightful.'
13 Votes for women
'She ought to get a good whipping,' she said after the daughter of Lord John Russell, her former Prime Minister, had spoken for female suffrage.
14 Getting her head wet when sea bathing
15 The telephone
Although she did allow two to be installed for use by guests to order their carriages.

16 The Danish Royal Family
17 Coal fires
If she allowed them at all, fires had to be wood fires; she very often ordered fires to be put out, declaring it 'quite warm enough'.
18 Death duties
She feared they would cause hardship 'to poor widows'.

135   *Six dislikes of the Queen Mother*

1 Hot, stuffy rooms
2 The Duchess of Windsor
3 Wearing trousers. (She never does except when she pulls her waders on over a skirt, when salmon fishing.)
4 *The Times* since the Murdoch takeover. (Describing it as 'common' she switched to the *Daily Telegraph*.)
5 Prince Charles' beard. ('I told him quite frankly that I didn't like it at all.')
6 Wearing uniforms. ('They do not like me.') She never wore a uniform during the war.

136   *Seventeen dislikes of the Queen*

1 Ivy
2 Any talk of King Edward VIII
3 Snails. '*How can you eat those beastly things?*' she once asked Prince Philip.
4 Tennis
5 Magenta
6 Milk pudding
7 The cold
8 Grouse
9 Charles Dickens
10 Dictating letters
11 Laying foundation stones
12 Cigar smoke
13 Sailing
14 Wimbledon

15 Listening to after–dinner speeches
16 Oysters. *'We've supplied the Royal Household since the time of William IV'*, complained the manager of Wilton's Restaurant in 1963, *'but since the Duke of Windsor left, they haven't eaten any at all.'*
17 Garlic

Four dislikes of King James I 137

1 Naked steel
2 Witches
3 Pigs
4 The sea

Five dislikes of King Edward VIII 138

1 Overdone beef
2 Wagner
3 Black people. (During his time in the Bahamas, he made them use the back door.)
4 Cats
5 Stiff shirts

Eight dislikes of Prince Charles 139

1 Red wine
2 The *Daily Express*
3 Tricia Nixon ('artificial and plastic')
4 Criticism of King George III
5 Golf
6 Braces
7 The smell of paint. ('I hate the smell of new paint. It sticks in my nose and makes me feel nauseous. Why do people paint everything when I am due somewhere?')
8 Being addressed simply as 'Prince' in America. ('You do get fed up with being referred to like an RAF police dog.')

140 *Six dislikes of Princess Anne*

1 Smoking
2 Alcohol
3 Long speeches
4 Exotic food
5 Netball
6 Oysters

141 *Fourteen miscellaneous dislikes of Royalty*

1 Riding
Princess Diana: *'I fell off a horse as a child and lost my nerve.'*
2 The smell of leather
Queen Elizabeth I.
3 Parsnips
Princess Alexandra
4 The dark
Princess Margaret
5 Being alone
King Edward VIII
6 The opera
King George VI once threw a book at an aide who suggested he should be seen at the opera more often.
7 Alexander's 'Ragtime Band'
Queen Mary: *'Very vulgar . . . not what I call music.'*
8 Peter Townsend
Prince Philip. King George VI had given Townsend the job of ascertaining Philip's suitability for his daughter. 'What infernal cheek for a man who was already heading for divorce to set himself up as a marriage counsellor.'
9 Champagne
Princess Margaret
10 Balzac
Queen Mary. She congratulated Madame Bricka upon burning Balzac's *'Petites Misères de la Vie Conjugale.'*
11 Motorcycles in the countryside
King George V

12 Moustaches on clergymen
King Edward VII. He insisted that the Archbishop of York
prevent them from being worn.
13 Sitting in rooms with open doors
Princess Margaret
14 Foreign travel and foreign ways
King George V

Seven Royal comments on education   142

1 'Ever since I can remember, it has been from people rather
  than from text books that I have got my education.' King
  Edward VIII.
2 'I'm one of those stupid bums who never went to university
  and it hasn't done me any harm.' Prince Philip.
3 'I think it's a very much over-rated pastime.' Princess Anne on
  Higher Education, 1971.
4 'I'm one of those stupid bums who went to university. Well, I
  think it's helped me.' Prince Charles.
5 'More history for children to learn in a hundred years' time.'
  The Queen, aged 14, on hearing of the outbreak of the Second
  World War.
6 'To make women learned and foxes tame has the same effect –
  to make them more cunning.' King James I, forbidding his
  daughter Elizabeth to learn Latin and Greek.
7 'My favourite programme is "Mrs Dale's Diary." I try never
  to miss it because it is the only way of knowing what goes on
  in a middle-class family.' The Queen Mother.

Ten areas of George V's conservatism   143

1 Dress
He expected his sons to wear morning coat whenever they visited
him, and white tie, tails and the Garter Star whenever they dined
with him, even if there were no other guests.
2 Food
He hated exotic food. Once when Edward VIII ordered him an

avocado as a treat he was disgusted. 'What in heaven's name is this?' he demanded.

3 Drink
He closed down all the pubs in the five parishes of Sandringham, replacing them with village clubs.

4 Sleep
He always went to bed at exactly 11.10 p.m.

5 Furniture
So furious was he when a housemaid slightly altered the position of some furniture in his sitting room that the housekeeper took a photograph of the correct position so that it would never happen again.

6 Legs
When Queen Mary was considering wearing a shorter, more fashionable skirt, a Lady-in-Waiting suggested that it would be safer if she wore one first, to test the King's reactions. King George was furious; Queen Mary abandoned the idea, sadly, since she considered her legs her 'best feature'.

7 Studs
He used the same collar stud all his life, having it filled with gold when it showed signs of failing, and he kept the same set of brushes, finally having them re-bristled.

8 Films
He hated mushy love scenes in films: '*Get on with it, man!*' he'd shout at the screen when particularly annoyed by kissing.

9 Foreigners
He utterly disapproved of foreign travel, foreign ways and cosmopolitan society, and never took holidays abroad.

10 Homosexuality
He muttered, upon hearing that an elderly personage of his acquaintance was a homosexual, '*I thought chaps like that shot themselves.*'

144 *Five Royal views of politicians*

1 '*He speaks to me as if I were a public meeting!*' Queen Victoria on Gladstone.
2 '*I could not have a better Prime Minister.*' King George VI on Churchill.
3 '*I would have as soon expected to see a pig in church.*' King George IV on seeing Peel at Ascot.

4 *'Why don't my Ministers talk to me as the President did tonight? I feel exactly as though a father were giving me his most careful and wise advice.'* King George VI on President Roosevelt.

5 *'I NEVER liked him.'* Queen Victoria on Palmerston.

Five Royal views on politics 145

1 *'We are all socialists nowadays.'* King Edward VII, 1895.

2 *'If only politicians had to sweat it out to get to the Olympics they may not be quite so keen to say to sportsmen, "Sorry, you're not going." '* Princess Anne, 1980.

3 *'There is no central machinery to provide a substitute for the good neighbour.'* King Edward VIII, 1935.

4 *'I tell you, Mr Wheatley, that if I had to live in conditions like that I would be a revolutionary myself.'* King George V, having heard the cruel life story of an old man.

5 *'I am not anti-socialist, but I regret to say that it was nationalism and socialism which produced Nazis and Fascists.'* Prince Philip.

Thirteen Royal reactions to the press 146

1 Disingenuousness
Prince Philip at the Rock of Gibraltar, faced with both apes and newspapermen, said 'Which are the monkeys?'

2 Aggression
Prince Edward to a photographer at Sandringham in January 1981. He emphasised his point by shooting at a bird behind the man and scattered a bit of shot in his vicinity.

3 Silence
When Capt. Mark Phillips was asked if he had anything good to say about the Press, he said nothing, and smiled.

4 Incivility
Prince Andrew refers to the Press as 'My Presstitutes'.

5 Condemnation
'A bloody awful newspaper', Prince Philip said of the *Daily Express*. 'It is full of lies, scandal and imagination. It is a vicious newspaper.'

6 Despair
'I've been misrepresented and misreported since the age of 17 and I long ago gave up reading about myself.' Princess Margaret.

7 Displeasure

'I wish you would go away!' shouted the Queen to photographers who hoped for a glimpse of Lady Diana Spencer at Sandringham in 1981.

8 Malediction

'May I take this opportunity to wish you all a Happy New Year – and your editors a particularly nasty one.' Prince Charles before his engagement was announced to a group of photographers, 1980.

9 Regret

'I don't fit into the slot they think I ought to.' Princess Anne.

10 Commiseration

'You have the mosquitoes, we have the Press.' Prince Philip to the people of Dominica.

11 Avoidance

'I am happiest when, like plain Mr Jones, I can go to a race meeting without it being chronicled in the papers the next day that his Royal Highness the Prince of Wales has taken to gambling very seriously, and yesterday lost more money than ever he can afford to pay.' King Edward VII.

12 Knowledge

'I simply treat the press as though they were children.' Princess Diana.

13 Indignation

On 24 December 1980, Princess Diana's mother, Mrs Shand Kydd, becoming increasingly distressed at press harassment of her daughter (this was over two months before the announcement of her engagement) wrote a letter to *The Times*: 'May I ask the editors of Fleet Street whether, in the execution of their jobs, they consider it necessary or fair to harass my daughter from dawn to dusk? Is it fair to ask any human being, regardless of circumstances, to be treated in this way?' She went on to add that she had written the letter solely on her own initiative.

The ten members of the Royal Family Jean Rook would like to interview and the questions she would put to them

1 The Queen

Are you ever as nervous of meeting anyone else as they are of you? What do you keep in that white (it isn't really plastic, is it?) handbag? What did you say, word for word, when Margaret told you she was breaking up with Lord Snowdon? Why haven't you changed your hair-do for 40 years, and is it dyed? Why do you wear horn-rimmed specs with the Crown? What are you thinking about when they play the National Anthem? If you hadn't been the Queen, what would you have been?

2 King Harold

Did you see it coming?

3 King Edward VIII

When you found 'no damned ink in the pot' to sign the Abdication did you, for a split second, still think of backing out, and were you sorry they lent you a fountain pen? Was Mrs Simpson worth it? Did you honestly love her to the last, or did you stick to her because you daren't cause another global fuss? Did you ever look at her in bed one morning and think, 'God, I gave up the Crown and Emperor of India for *that?*'

4 Queen Elizabeth I

Were you a virgin? And remember I'm taking a shorthand note.

5 Princess Margaret

Did you marry Tony on the rebound, and if they'd let you have Peter Townsend instead, would it have worked? Were you in love with Roddy Llewellyn and how did you feel on his wedding day? Is it true you're a harridan who throws plates?

6 Lord Snowdon

Was she a bitch? Which year did it start going wrong? Do you ever look up at Buck House's balcony on your way to a job, and think, 'I stood up there, with most of the world cheering'? What do you miss about her, and what are you thinking when you watch her on telly?

7 Queen Victoria

Do you know what John Brown wore under his kilt?

8 Anne Boleyn

That May morning you laid your 'very little neck' on the block, what was your last thought before the sword dropped? Did you look in the mirror before you went down to be executed? How did you look? Was Henry any good in bed?

9 Prince Charles

They say you mind that Andrew is better- and sexier-looking than you – true or false? Are you Action Man because you're still trying to live down those toddler pictures of the shy little bat-eared boy in the velvet collared coat? Did you fall head over heels with Diana, or were you pushed by your father to get your finger out and marry somebody? What Did Diana say to you at Cheltenham races, and were you privately having one hell of a row? Are you going bald?

10 Princess Diana

Do you accept what Charles just told me? Why don't you pull yourself together and look less sulky, at times, in public – face it, you knew what came with his job, and that you'd never stop him working himself into a lather over horses. Are you as sweet and shy as millions think, or, deep inside there, is there a very stubborn and occasionally quite nasty-tempered little girl?

Any regrets? Name them.

Jean Rook's outspoken comments and tough interviews in the *Daily Express* have so far barred her from putting these questions personally to the Royal Family.

148 *Eight rebukes to the Press by Princess Anne*

1 *'Don't you think I've got enough problems without you?'* To cameramen at a 1972 horse trial in Ayrshire.
2 *'You're getting on my goat. I've just got this horse settled and now you've upset him. How long are you going to keep this up?'* To the press at a horse trial shortly after the announcement of her engagement.
3 *'Everything I've seen written thus far is a copy of every falsification I've ever seen written about me. Even the pictures are not of me.'* To the press in Massachussetts in 1975.
4 *'I hope you've got your money's worth now.'* To the press in Kiev in 1973, after her horse *Goodwill* had thrown her.
5 *'Is this close enough?'* Sticking her head six inches from a press cameraman, shortly after the announcement of her British Leyland sponsorship.

6 *'Do you mind? It's their day, not yours.'* To TV cameramen at a riding school for the disabled in Swansea, 1976.
7 *'I am not your love. I am your Royal Highness.'* To an Australian photographer who had said, 'Look this way, love.'
8 *'Why don't you just naff off?'* to the press at the Badminton Horse Trials, 1982.

Six malicious remarks in the feud between 'Poor Fred' and his parents 149

The King and Queen had never liked their oldest son, whom they had left in Hanover. His grandfather's death, when the boy was twenty, made him Heir Apparent. They then summoned him to England and treated him to every insult they could devise. So great was their preference for his younger brother (who grew up to be 'The Butcher Cumberland') that they considered disinheriting Frederick in his favour. The King, popularly known as 'Old Gruff' for his parsimony and surliness, was further incensed at Frederick's increasing popularity and eventually banned the Court from having anything to do with him. At the height of their feud he actually had Frederick arrested.

1 *'His popularity makes me spew.'* Queen Caroline on her son.
2 *'The greatest ass, liar and beast in the world.'* King George II on his son.
3 *'A miserly martinet with an insatiable sexual appetite.'* Frederick on his father, the King.
4 *'False, lying, cowardly, nauseous puppy.'* King George II on his son.
5 *'I wish the ground would open this minute and sink the monster into the lowest hole in hell.'* Queen Caroline on her son.
6 *'I have lost my eldest son, but I was glad of it.'* King George II after Frederick had died after being hit by a cricket ball aged forty-four.

Twenty-six times Royalty has said No

1 No mirror
Towards the end of her life, Queen Elizabeth I refused to have a mirror in any of her rooms.

2 No invitation
Though General Idi Amin publicly asked to be invited to Princess Anne's wedding, his request was turned down.

3 No masonry
Prince Charles has broken with a long Royal tradition and has refused to become a Freemason.

4 No homosexuals
'I won't knight buggers', King George V.

5 No Kermit
At the Hyde Park Children's Party in 1979, Princess Anne refused to hold a Kermit the Frog toy for photographers. 'I'm not Mrs Thatcher', she informed them.

6 No undressing
On his wedding night, William of Orange went to bed wearing his woollen drawers. When King Charles II suggested that he might do better to take them off, William refused, saying that since he and his wife would have to live together for such a long time she would have to get used to his habits sooner or later.

7 No go
King George III became the first and only British monarch to go on strike when, made miserable by the treatment he was receiving to cure his mental conditions, he declared that 'no earthly consideration should induce him to sign his name to any paper or to do one act of government whatever' until he be reunited with his Queen. This industrial action paid off, and the King joined the Queen in Dutch House over the road.

8 No rude measurements
Prince Charles has always refused to give away the measurements of his inside leg.

9 No black stockings
On founding the Buckingham Palace Girl Guide Troop, King George VI refused to let the girls wear 'those hideous long black stockings' and insisted they wore knee length beige stockings instead. Soon, the whole Guide Movement followed the King's lead.

10 No pardon
King Edward IV twice refused Sir Thomas Malory a pardon from imprisonment.

11 No poet's burial
Irritated by the sneering tone of William Makepeace Thackeray's lectures on the Four Georges, Queen Victoria refused to let him be buried in Poet's Corner.

12 No twins
The day after the announcement of Princess Diana's pregnancy, Prince Charles refused to accept the gift of a pig's bladder from a Morris dancer in Chesterfield. The Morris dancer had assured the Prince that the pig's bladder would help produce twins. 'You can keep the bloody thing,' said the Prince.

13 No boots
Visiting a bootmakers Queen Mary asked the manager how much the cobblers were paid. On being told that they earned eight shillings a week, she turned on her heels saying, 'I will not buy boots made by sweated labour.'

14 No kiss
When her aunt, the Princess Royal, came to inspect the Queen's ATS unit during the war, the Queen refused to kiss her, preferring a formal salute.

15 No abbey
Prince Charles refused the advice of the Lord Chamberlain's office that he should marry Princess Diana in Westminster Abbey. When told that they wouldn't have enough soldiers to man the route properly he said, 'Well, stand them far apart.'

16 No present
Shortly after his Abdication, King Edward VIII refused to accept a Christmas present of a gold box from his brother the Duke of Kent. He returned it with a note saying, 'The only box I have come to expect from my brothers is a box on the ear.'

17 No invitations
Prince Philip's three sisters and their husbands were not invited to his wedding. All three had married Germans. His sister Sophie's husband was particularly unwelcome, as an intimate of Goering, and because of his war work as head of the Gestapo.

18 No country
In 1575, Queen Elizabeth refused the sovereignty of the Netherlands.

19 No shorts
As a child, Prince Andrew refused to wear tartan shorts under his kilt. 'Papa doesn't wear them' he remonstrated.

20 No hard cap
At a pageant at Benenden, Princess Anne refused to wear a protective cap beneath her Tudor bonnet. She said, 'I won't do it. I'll phone Mummy.'

21 No inadequate cipher

The Queen returned the Coronation gift of a gold cup wrongly inscribed to the Scots who had sent it, with the request that they add 'II' to the 'E.R.' – as they had engraved it to signify that they had never been ruled by Elizabeth I.

22 No spitting

When King Edward VII visited President Buchanan in the White House in 1859 he was surprised to see so many guests at a reception spitting. It was explained to him that the national pastime was killing flies with a squirt of tobacco juice. He declined an invitation to participate.

23 No more sea voyages

Queen Mary was a very bad sailor, and on one occasion was so seasick on the royal yacht that she went below to lie down. A little later on, the King, who had remained on deck, sent a sailor down to enquire after her. *'Well,'* said the King, when the sailor returned, *'and how is Her Majesty?'* The sailor replied: *'Her Majesty says never again, buggered if she will!'*

24 No mini skirt

In the late 1960s, Princess Anne suggested to her mother that she should wear a mini skirt. *'I'm not a film star'*, replied the Queen.

25 No obedience

Princess Diana was the first Royal bride to choose to omit the word 'obey' in her marriage vows.

26 No special treatment

On a visit to Jamaica in 1953 the Queen nervously walked around the white linen jacket schoolteacher Warren Kidd laid down in her path in imitation of Sir Walter Raleigh. Kidd was later arrested and sent for observation to a lunatic asylum.

151 *Seven favourite mottoes of Royalty*

1 *'Your work is the rent you pay for the room you occupy on Earth.'* The Queen Mother
2 *'Never relax, never relax, never relax.'* Prince Albert
3 *'A woman can never be too rich or too thin.'* The Duchess of Windsor
4 *'Look after the children and the country will look after itself.'* King George VI
5 *'I must not take the easy way out.'* The Queen as a child
6 *'I serve.'* Prince Charles has said, ' "I serve" is a marvellous

motto to have, and I think it is the basis of one's job.'
7 *'One must move with the times.'* Queen Mary

Five memorable Royal notices 152

1 'No smoking.'
Queen Victoria had 'No smoking' notices, glazed and framed, put up in strategic places around Windsor Castle. King Albert of Saxony had been a guest for two days before he remembered that he was a king himself. He then walked down the Grand Staircase puffing at a long cigar.

2 'Lavatory. Under Repair.'
Shortly after moving into Marlborough House, King Edward VII asked his mother, Queen Victoria, to come and look round. Their guided tour had only just begun when Edward remembered the smoking room and his mother's passionate hatred of smoking. He whispered the dilemma to Lord Charles Beresford who immediately rushed away. When mother and son arrived at the door to the smoking room they saw a notice saying 'Lavatory. Under Repair'. The Queen walked on.

3 'Cleanliness is next to godliness.'
This notice hung in King George VI's bathroom in Buckingham Palace.

4 'I am Caesar, the King's dog.'
This was attached to the collar of Caesar, King Edward VII's favourite dog.

5 'Maggie's playroom'
Prince Philip put this sign on the door of Princess Margaret's bedroom during his engagement to the Queen to highlight the age-gap between the two girls, so that Margaret would not insist upon joining in everything they did.

Four Royal reactions to Germany 153

1 Queen Mary
'I did not realise that I could really hate people as I do the Germans, tho' I never liked them.' (1941)

2 King Edward VIII
'Every drop of blood in my veins is German.' (Said in conversation with Diana Mosley.)

3 Princess Margaret

At the end of the war, aged fourteen, she threw all her German text books to the floor and said that she wasn't going to learn any more of Hitler's language.

4 King Edward VII

'You can tell when you have crossed the frontier into Germany because of the badness of the coffee.'

154 *Twenty-one Royal reprimands*

1 *'You dress like a cad. You act like a cad. You are a cad. Get out!!!'* King George V to his son, King Edward VIII, when Edward was well into his thirties.

2 *'My name's Diana.'* Princess Diana before her marriage to someone who had shouted 'Good old Di!' at Sandown Park.

3 *'We are not amused.'* Queen Victoria to Sir Alick York, after she had made him repeat a risqué joke which she had missed.

4 *'Actually, Captain, I think they've come to see me.'* The Queen from her state carriage to an escort commander who had allowed his horse to step in front of the rear wheel for a third time.

5 *'Damn you, what the devil are you doing here?'* King George V to King Edward VIII, who had rushed back to his father's bedside from Africa, having been informed by the Prime Minister that he was very ill.

6 *'Who's paying you to do this?'* Princess Anne to anti-blood sport campaigners who were blocking her way.

7 *'Hang him up then! Hang him up!'* King Henry VIII, on hearing that Henry Norris, his groom of the stole was reluctant to give evidence against Anne Boleyn and 'would rather die a thousand deaths than accuse the Queen of that which I believe her in my conscience innocent'.

8 *'You must not touch those toys. They are mine. And I may call you Jane but you must not call me Victoria.'* Queen Victoria aged 6 to Lady Jane Ellice, also aged 6.

9 *'Less of the wisecracks and stick to the commentary. You're turning the match into a barn dance.'* Prince Charles to Nassau polo commentator Tom Oxley.

10 *'I have never seen such good acting.'* Princess Margaret to friends after Lord Snowdon had been looking miserable on Australian television following their separation.

11 *'A very fine Prince, Sir James.'* Queen Victoria to Sir James Graham, after he had complimented her on giving birth to 'a very fine boy' in 1841.

12 *'Don't do it again. My advice to you is to leave this art to the Highlanders. They know what they're doing.'* King George V on first hearing his son King Edward VIII playing the bagpipes.

13 *'Come back, Philip, and do it properly!'* The Queen to Prince Philip, who was rushing through the final rehearsal for the Coronation.

14 *'If you don't come at once you won't be crowned Queen.'* King Edward VII to the tardy Queen Alexandra on the morning of their Coronation.

15 *'When I want you to wear something different from what I am wearing, I'll give you warning.'* King Edward VIII to his equerry, Fruity Metcalfe, who was wearing a dinner jacket with a shawl collar.

16 *'Does Mr Gladstone think that this is a public tent?'* Queen Victoria noting her Prime Minister entering her tent in the reception after King George V's wedding.

17 *'You can call me that once a day, and no more. I'm sick of it.'* King George VI, to a gardener who kept calling, him 'Your Royal Highness'.

18 *'I was not aware that my Palace is damp.'* King George V to a courtier who was wearing fashionable turn-ups on his trousers.

19 *'I don't mind you throwing stones at me, but what would the American tourists think?'* The Queen Mother, who had stopped her car in Windsor Great Park, to young hooligans who had been throwing stones at passing traffic. The youths immediately dispersed.

20 *'If a Princess of Great Britain and Ireland can eat biscuits out of a hair box, I presume the daughter of a Dresden dentist can!'* Queen Mary to her daughter's governess, Fraulein Gutman, who had refused to eat biscuits out of a hair box.

21 *'What a pompous remark, if I may say so.'* The Queen to the then editor of the *News of the World*, Barry Askew, at a Buckingham Palace meeting with editors to discuss press harassment of Princess Diana. Askew had suggested that Princess Diana would avoid cameramen if she sent a footman out to buy her winegums for her.

1 Votes for women
'A mad, wicked folly.' Queen Victoria

2 A sex film
In a rare moment of outspokenness, the Queen condemned a proposal that a Swedish film company be allowed in to make a film on the sex life of Jesus Christ in 1976, as 'quite obnoxious'.

3 Irish pigs (or jigs)
Shortly after the death of Lord Mountbatten, Princess Margaret was said to have referred to the Irish as 'pigs' at a private dinner party in Chicago attended by the Irish-American mayor, Jane Byrne. Later, the mayor issued a statement saying that Princess Margaret had merely been talking of 'Irish Jigs'.

4 Unemployment
Visiting the derelict steelworks at Dowlais in Wales in 1936, Edward VIII made his famous demand, 'Something must be done.'

5 A forty-acre field
'There is a limit to how interesting a forty-acre field can be, in my opinion.' Princess Anne in an interview, 1979.

6 Universal disarmament
'It is the great rubbish and nonsense I have ever heard of.' Edward VII, 1892

7 Smoking
'They were making a sooty kitchen of their inward parts,' wrote James I in 'A Counterblaste on the Use of Tobacco', a polemic in which he suggested that smoking originated with the Indians, who needed an antidote to syphilis.

8 St Kilda beach, Australia
'It's like swimming in sewage', Prince Charles, after surfing there in 1970

9 The Russians
'Oh! If the Queen were a man she would like to go and give these Russians, whose word one cannot believe, such a beating!' Queen Victoria to Disraeli

10 The Roman Catholic church
When Pope Paul VI refused a church wedding to Princess Michael of Kent, Prince Charles made a speech condemning Churches for 'the needless distress' that resulted from rigid doctrines.

Five things condemned by Prince Philip

1 The loo
'*This is the biggest waste of water in the country by far. You spend half a pint and flush two gallons.*' During an inspection of cisterns, May 1965.

2 The American moonshots
'*It seems to me that it's the best way of wasting money that I know of. I don't think investments on the moon pay a very high dividend.*' To a press conference in São Paulo, November 1968.

3 The red carpet
'*The man who invented the red carpet needed his head examining.*' On disembarking from the royal plane, 1968.

4 Government interference in the Olympics
'*The politicians have no right to tell us what to do.*' In a speech, 1980.

5 British cooking
'*You know, British women can't cook, They are very good at decorating food and making it attractive. But they have an inability to cook.*' Speaking at the Scottish Womens Institute Display, June 1966.

Four Monarchs and their religious views

1 '*I do not mind what religion a man professes, but I distrust him who has none.*' King Edward VII
2 '*There is only one Jesus Christ and all the rest is a dispute over trifles.*' Queen Elizabeth I
3 '*Presbytery is not a religion for gentlemen.*' King Charles I
4 '*We went to Church this morning. Nice church, but the sermon was "rot" . . . I don't know what the man was driving at. He impressed on us that Buddhism and the Brahmin religions were better than ours in many ways – I have long thought so, but it is scarcely for a Church of England clergyman to tell one so!*' Queen Mary

Four Monarchs who had views on the English weather

1 King Charles II
He once said, '*In England there is no day of the year when a man may not be outdoors in comfort.*'

2 Prince Albert
Tired of bad weather, Queen Victoria once consoled herself by writing in her diary, '*Dear Albert said we could not alter it, but must leave it as it was.*'

3 The Queen
When the Queen visited Eton during a downpour in 1973, a boy shouted, '*Vive La Reine!*' and the Queen replied, '*Yes, it is pelting, isn't it.*'

4 King George V
When someone complained about the English weather, King George V replied, '*I like my own country best, climate or no, and I'm staying in it.*'

Eleven royal sightseers

1 Prince Charles on Australia
'Whenever I come back to Australia I experience a curious and inexplicable sensation that I belong.'

2 Queen Mary on Norway
'Norway is certainly a grand country and the scenery is so beautiful, a mixture of Scotland and Switzerland.'

3 King Edward VII on Rome
'You look at two mouldering stones and are told it's the temple of something.'

4 The Queen on first sighting the Niagara Falls
'It looks very damp.'

5 Princess Alexandra on Mexico
'This country makes me gasp. And it isn't just the altitude.'

6 Queen Alexandra on Ireland
'Far more beautiful than Scotland.'

7 Queen Mary on Egypt
'The sphinx I thought most disappointing.'

8 Prince Charles on the Taj Mahal
When asked if he had been touched by it, he replied, 'Well, I did bang my head against the ceiling at one point.'

'Rather damp'

9 Queen Mary I
'When I am dead and opened, you shall find "Calais" lying in my heart.'

10 Queen Mary on India
'When I die India will be found written on my heart.'

11 Princess Margaret on her official visit to Morocco
'It was more like being kidnapped.'

Thirteen favourite Royal pastimes   160

1 Arguing
'Arguing is to my mind one of life's most fascinating occupations,' Angus Ogilvy.

2 The name game
The Queen and Prince Philip particularly like this for putting guests at their ease. Guests are told the lineage of a recent addition to the Royal stables and invited to think of a witty name for the new horse: (*Lost Marbles* out of *Amnesia* by *Lord Elgin*).

3 Making friends
Chosen by the Queen Mother as a child as her favourite pastime when writing in a friend's autograph album.

4 Sitting in bed eating chocolates and reading poems
Chosen by the Queen Mother in later life as her favourite pastime.
5 Running home movies backwards
A great favourite of King George VI, who particularly liked
watching swimmers leap from a pool onto a diving board.
6 Watching fires
As a young man, King Edward VII kept firemen's uniforms at
Chandos Street and at Watling Street. He would dress up in them
so that he could watch fires in anonymity. After watching a fire,
he would eat tripe at a restaurant in the Tottenham Court Road.
7 Listening to Gilbert and Sullivan
Queen Victoria regularly hired members of the D'Oyly Carte
Opera Company to perform songs from Gilbert and Sullivan
behind screens at her dinner parties.
8 Snowballing
King Edward VII and his family used to enjoy making their
guests stand as cockshies while they pelted them with snowballs.
9 Riding on buses
Princess Alice, Countess of Athlone, loved riding on buses up
until the time of her death in 1981 aged 97. Aged 86, she travelled
on a banana boat to Barbados.
10 Turning cartwheels
A favourite pastime of Princess Alexandra when she was a child.
11 Training corgis
As a child, Princess Anne spent a long time teaching her corgi,
Sherry, to jump through a hoop.
12 Tap-dancing
Princess Diana is a keen tap-dancer.
13 Button making
King George III was particularly keen on making buttons with his
own hands on quiet evenings.

And the Favourite Pastime of One Royal Servant . . .
Connecting the Queen to the Queen Mother
A senior telephone operator at Buckingham Palace has admitted
that her favourite pastime is connecting the Queen and the Queen
Mother each morning with the words: 'Your Majesty? Her
Majesty, Your Majesty.'

Six of the Queen Mother's favourite games

1 Racing Demon
2 Bringing in the Sentence
3 Murder in the Dark
4 Parade – everyone marches past her and the King while she pretends to review them
5 Charades
6 Canasta

Seven likes of King Edward VIII

1 Gardening
2 Burgundy
3 Dancing
4 Very crisp bacon
5 Sleight of hand
6 Eating the heads of game birds
7 Old snuff boxes

Twelve things the Queen particularly likes

1 Horse-racing. (*Were it not for my Archbishop of Canterbury, I should be off in my plane to Longchamps every Sunday.*')
2 Warm weather
3 Scottish country dancing
4 Jig-saw puzzles
5 Long-stemmed deep pink carnations
6 Champagne
7 Deerstalking
8 Quiet evenings at home, watching television with her supper on a tray
9 Crossword puzzles
10 Bright red dresses
11 The Beatles film *Yellow Submarine*. She has seen it four times
12 Sandringham. (*At Sandringham I feel a great deal more remote from London than at Balmoral.*')

Four unexpected talents of the Queen Mother

1 She is an expert fly-fisher. She will land at least one 20lb salmon each summer at Balmoral.
2 She can play the bongo drums. She was taught by Ian Hall, the founder of the Bloomsbury Society, in 1974.
3 She is a gifted big-game hunter. On holiday in Kenya in 1925 she shot a rhinoceros with a .275 rifle.
4 She is an expert billiards player, as she demonstrated impressively at the Press Club in London.

The Queen Mother plans her next pot

Six unexpected talents of the Queen

1 She can strip and service an engine. She was taught at Aldershot during the war. 'We had sparking plugs last night all the way through dinner,' remarked the Queen Mother to a friend.

2 She can drive a railway engine. In 1950 she drove the engine named after her from its shed to the platform on a visit to Swindon, and she has also driven engines in South Africa and Canada.

3 She is an expert at crosswords, usually completing the *Daily Telegraph*'s and one other every day.

4 She is a superb mimic, specialising in the politicians whom she has had to receive over the last thirty years.

5 She can operate lock machinery. In November 1953 she helped a banana boat through a lock on the Panama Canal.

6 She is a skilled dancer, excelling at tap dancing and the Twist.

Sixteen things designed or invented by Royalty   166

1 **The handkerchief** Invented by King Richard II
2 **The Aviary at London Zoo** Designed by Lord Snowdon
3 **The Rose Garden at Windsor** Designed by Prince Philip
4 **Pigsties** Designed by Prince Albert
5 **The George Cross** Based on a design by King George VI
6 **A John Brown Memorial Brooch** Designed by Queen Victoria to commemorate her forthright servant. Made in gold, it had Brown's head on one side and the Royal monogram on the other.
7 **A swivel for the kettle at Buckingham Palace** Designed by Prince Philip.
8 **A chairmobile for the disabled** Invented by Lord Snowdon.
9 **The Balmoral Tartan** Designed by Prince Albert.
10 **The Sirloin of Beef** A title invented by James I, when he knighted a loin of beef at Hoghton Tower in Chorley.
11 **Princess Margaret's engagement ring** Designed by Lord Snowdon.
12 **The Windsor uniform** Designed by George III and revived by Queen Victoria, it consists of a dark blue tail-coat with red collar and cuffs, to be worn by family and entourage.
13 **Quick-release polo breeches** Designed by Prince Philip.
14 **The Yard** Invented by King Henry I, who decreed it to be the distance between the end of his thumb and his nose.
15 **Bubble-top car** When bad weather threatened to prevent her subjects seeing the Queen on her Canadian tour in 1951, Prince Philip proposed that a plexiglas bubble be constructed to cover the open car, an idea subsequently used by other heads of

state. 'How do I look?' the Queen asked her husband's
Equerry. 'Like an orchid wrapped in cellophane' was his reply.

16 **An extraordinary centrepiece** The Royal Plate includes a
silver gilt table decoration designed by Prince Albert. It is 30
inches high, and displays Queen Victoria's favourite dogs in
active pursuit of rats. There is one dead rat and one live rat in
a trap guarded by the Queen's terrier Islay and her dachshund
Waldmass.

Ten Royal comments on Art

1 On Victor Pasmore's *Relief Construction*
Seeing this sculpture in the San Francisco Art Museum Prince
Philip said, 'That looks to me like something to hang a towel on.'

2 On *The Adoration* by Rubens
Visiting King's College Chapel, Cambridge for the first time
Prince Edward said he found Rubens's painting, *The Adoration*,
'out of keeping with the rest of the chapel'.

3 On John Piper's Windsor Castle paintings
During the Second World War King George VI commissioned
John Piper, who was well known for his brooding, stormy
pictures, to paint a series of Windsor Castle. For a long time after
delivering the paintings, the artist heard nothing. Then he was
presented to the King at a garden party. 'Ah, yes . . . Piper' said
the King. 'Pity you had such awful weather.'

4 On the Arts in general
King George II would often say in his thick German accent, 'No
more bainting, blays or boetry!'

5 On Caton Woodville's painting of herself
'We are *redder* than that', said Queen Victoria of her Jubilee
portrait, before exiting from the room.

6 On Cézanne
Upon looking over a Cézanne at an art exhibition, King George
V hailed the Queen: 'Come over here, May, there's something
that will make you laugh!'

7 On Dutch Old Master paintings
'A very *low* style', said Queen Victoria, who preferred the Italian
painters through Albert's influence.

8 On an acquisition of King George IV
'Ay – it seems pretty – I dare say it is. My brother was very fond
of this Knicknackery. Damned expensive taste, though.' King
William IV upon being shown a picture from the splendid
collection amassed by his brother King George IV.

9 On Lely's portrait of himself
'Odds fish, I am an ugly fellow' said King Charles II on first seeing this painting.

10 On Henry Moore
Prince Philip once referred to a Henry Moore sculpture as a 'monkey's gallstone'.

'A Monkey's Gallstone' – Henry Moore looks at his own sculpture with more appreciative eyes than Prince Philip

Twelve of the Queen Mother's favourite painters

1 John Piper
2 Rex Whistler
3 Paul Nash
4 Cecil Beaton
5 Sidney Nolan
6 Duncan Grant
7 Augustus John

8 L S Lowry
9 Edward Seago
10 John Bratby
11 George Stubbs
12 Noel Coward

169 *Three Royal comments on Shakespeare*

1 *'I hear a great deal about Shakespeare, but I cannot read him, he is such a bombast fellow.'* King George II
2 *'Was there ever such stuff as the great part of Shakespeare? Only it's Shakespeare and nobody dare abuse him.'* King George III
3 *'He's a great man. I quote him occasionally. He comes in very useful.'* Prince Andrew

170 *Eleven favourite writers of Royalty*

1 *Mary Stewart* A favourite of Princess Diana.
2 *John Bunyan* King George VI's favourite book was *Pilgrim's Progress*.
3 *Alexander Solzhenitzyn* A favourite of Prince Charles.
4 *Tolstoy* Queen Mary first read the works of Tolstoy and Dostoevsky when she was over 80. She then declared them her two favourite writers.
5 *Marie Corelli* A favourite of Queen Victoria. Others included Lewis Carroll, Charles Dickens, Harriett Beecher Stowe, Charlotte Bronte and George Eliot.
6 *P G Wodehouse* A favourite of the Queen Mother. She offered to fly personally to America to knight him when she heard he was too weak to travel to England to accept a knighthood.
7 *John Buchan* A favourite of King George V.
8 *E F Schumacher* A favourite of Prince Charles, who particularly admires *Small Is Beautiful*.
9 *Jane Austen* A long time favourite of the Royal Family. King George IV had a set of her novels in each of his houses. In response to his request, Jane Austen dedicated *Emma* to him. The Queen Mother and the Queen are both keen readers of her.
10 *Arthur Koestler* A favourite of the Queen Mother. During the war she tried to persuade Churchill that *Darkness at Noon* should be made required reading for his whole cabinet.
11 *Daphne du Maurier* A favourite of Princess Diana.

Nine favourite books of the Queen and Princess Margaret when they were very young

1 *Peter Pan*
2 *Dr Doolittle*
3 *Black Beauty*
4 *The Rose and the Ring*
5 Lamb's *Tales from Shakespeare*
6 All the books of Beatrix Potter
7 *When We Were Very Young* (especially 'Changing the Guard at Buckingham Palace')
8 *At the Back of the North Wind*
9 *Alice in Wonderland*

Sixteen Books written by Royalty

1 *The Old Man of Lochnagar* by Princes Charles. A children's book originally written for his brothers.
2 *A Guide to the Chatting Up of Girls* by Prince Charles. An adult manual written for the men of the Royal Regiment of Wales and never published.
3 *Our Life in the Highlands* by Queen Victoria.
4 *More Leaves from a Journal of a Life in the Highlands* by Queen Victoria
5 *A Biography of John Brown* by Queen Victoria. Her friends dissuaded her from publishing this life of her forward manservant. Instead, she had it privately circulated.
6 *A Tract Against the Pope* by Edward VI, aged twelve.
7 *A Counterblaste on the Use of Tobacco* by James I, who also wrote books on the Bible and demonology.
8 *Necessary Doctrine and Evolution for any Christian Man* by Henry VIII, greatly assisted by Cranmer, emphasising the Royal Supremacy.
9 *Family Album*
10 *The King's Story* an autobiography by Edward VIII.
11 *The Heart Has Its Reasons* an autobiography by the Duchess of Windsor.
12 *For My Grandchildren* an autobiography by Princess Alice.
13 *The Coronation, 12 May 1937* by the Queen aged eleven,

written in a penny exercise book, inscribed 'To Mummy and Pa
in memory of their Coronation, from Lilibet, By Herself.'
14 *Private View* by Lord Snowdon.
15 *Wildlife Crisis* by Prince Philip.
16 *A Question of Balance* by Prince Philip

173 *Seven favourite television and radio programmes of members of the Royal Family*

1 King George VI: *Lift up Your Hearts, ITMA*
2 The Queen Mother: *Dad's Army, Crossroads, Mrs Dale's Diary*
3 The Queen: *Kojak, Dad's Army, Brideshead Revisited, The Good Life,* anything with Dudley Moore
4 Prince Charles: *The Goons, Monty Python's Flying Circus, Horizon, Edward and Mrs Simpson, Life on Earth, World About Us*
5 Princess Diana: *Crossroads, The Muppet Show, Not the Nine O'Clock News*
6 Princess Anne: *Pebble Mill at One*
7 Prince Andrew: *Fawlty Towers*

174 *Six famous people who have taught Royalty*

1 Mendelssohn
Taught Queen Victoria to sing
2 Landseer
Taught Queen Victoria to paint in watercolours
3 Lloyd George
Taught Edward VIII enough Welsh for his Investiture as Prince of Wales
4 Dan Maskell
Gave Princess Anne and Princess Alexandra tennis lessons
5 Graham Hill
Helped teach Prince Andrew to drive
6 Edward Seago
Gave painting lessons to Prince Philip and Prince Charles

1 *Passion, Poison and Putrefaction*
Prince Andrew acted the part of Adolphus Bastable in a Lakefield College production of Shaw's play.

2 *Aladdin and His Wonderful Lamp*
In a 1943 Buckingham Palace production, the Queen played Aladdin and Princess Margaret played Princess Roxanna. Prince Philip was in the audience.

3 *The Boy With a Cart*
While at Benenden, Princess Anne played Alfred, son of Mrs Fipps, in Christopher Fry's play.

4 *A Midsummer Night's Dream*
Queen Mary played the part of 'Wall'.

5 *Macbeth*
Prince Philip played the attendant Lord, Donalbain, in a Gordonstoun production. His son, Prince Charles, played Macbeth himself.

6 *Black Comedy*
Prince Edward played the male lead in Peter Shaffer's play at Gordonstoun.

7 *Oliver*
Prince Andrew played the part of Mr Brownlow in a Lakefield College Production.

8 *The Christmas Child*
The Queen played a King and Princess Margaret played Jesus in a 1940 Windsor Castle production. Princess Margaret sang a solo of 'Gentle Jesus Meek and Mild'.

9 *Fedora*
For one night only, King Edward VII played the part of the dead prince, opposite Sarah Bernhardt, in an 1882 Paris production of Sardou's play.

10 *Cinderella*
Princess Anne played the title role in a Girl Guides Pantomime at Buckingham Palace. Princess Margaret played the title role in a Windsor Castle production in 1941. The Queen played Prince Charming.

11 *HMS Pinafore*
Late in her life, Queen Victoria sang the role of Buttercup accompanied by Princess Louise on piano.

12 **And on film. . . .**
Princess Margaret played Queen Victoria in a film produced by Peter Sellers. Britt Ekland and Lord Snowdon had supporting roles. Properly edited and with full soundtrack at a total cost of

£6000 the film was presented to the Queen on her thirty-ninth birthday in 1965.

176 *Eight roles acted by Prince Charles*

1 Reg Sprott, the singing dustman
2 The Duke of Wellington
3 Lord Butler
4 Macbeth
5 The Duke of Gloucester (in *Richard III*)
6 The Pirate King (in *The Pirates of Penzance*)
7 The Duke of Exeter (in *Henry V*)
8 A Guardsman (in *Patience*)

177 *Four memorable impersonations by Royalty*

1 Miss Piggy
Princess Diana likes to impersonate her to friends
2 Arthur Negus
Impersonated by Prince Charles in a Cambridge revue
3 King George III
Often impersonated as a madman by his son, later King George IV.
4 Sophie Tucker (the last of the Red-Hot Mamas)
Impersonated in full dress by Princess Margaret at her forty-eighth birthday party in Scotland.

178 *Five favourite hymns sung at Royal weddings*

1 'Lead us heavenly father'
Sung at the wedding of King George VI and the Queen Mother
2 'O perfect love'
Sung at the wedding of the Duke and Duchess of Windsor

3 'Jesu Joy of man's desiring'
Sung at the wedding of Prince Philip and the Queen
4 'Glorious things of Thee are spoken'
Sung at the wedding of Mark Phillips and Princess Anne
5 'I vow to thee my country'
Sung at the wedding of Prince Charles and Princess Diana

Six modern songs associated with Royalty 179

1 'Yes, we have no bananas'
Queen Mary specially learnt the words to it
2 'The Merry Widow Waltz'
Princess Margaret could hum it aged 11 months
3 'Daisy' (A bicycle built for two)
Chosen by King George V to be played at his wedding
4 'Yankee doodle dandy'
Sung by General Tom Thumb to Queen Victoria
5 'The red flag'
Sung at Oxford by the Duke of Windsor to his own banjo
accompaniment.
6 'The Camptown races'
Sung by Mr Gladstone, the Prime Minister, accompanying
himself on the banjo, at the insistence of King Edward VII and his
guests at Sandringham. The act received a number of encores.

Four odd locations for the National Anthem 180

1 In the sea
When King George III went swimming in his blue serge costume,
he would be accompanied by a contraption filled with fiddlers
playing, 'God Save the King', and young ladies draped with
sashes and bonnets bearing the same message.

2 In Paris
On Queen Victoria's visit to the Hotel de Ville in Paris in 1855,
the officials ordered the band to play 'God Save the Queen' as a
polka.

3 On the smallest record player in the world

The gramophone in the children's nursery of Queen Mary's dolls' house plays the National Anthem.

4 On the English Channel

When Charlotte of Mecklenburg-Strelitz made her trip across the English Channel to marry King George III in 1761, she got into the swing of things by playing 'God Save the King' on her harpsichord over and over again. Dull of ear and weak of stomach, her English attendants spent the voyage being seasick.

181   *Three older members of the Royal Family and their favourite music*

1 The Queen

Oklahoma (particularly 'People will say we're in love', which she used to request from bands when Prince Philip was courting her).

Handel's *Water Music*.

Military Marches (she has a tape of them in her Rolls Royce).

2 Prince Philip

Louis Armstrong

Ella Fitzgerald

'Rule Britannia'

3 The Queen Mother

The Sound of Music

Bach Chamber Music

Gracie Fields

182   *Six of Princess Diana's favourite musicians and composers*

1 Abba
2 Dr Feelgood
3 Tchaikovsky
4 Grieg
5 Neil Diamond
6 The Police

Prince Charles's favourite music   183

1 Beethoven
2 Bach
3 The Beatles
4 Mozart
5 Berlioz
6 The Seekers
7 The Three Degrees
8 Verdi

Prince Andrew's favourite music   184

1 Genesis
2 Pink Floyd
3 The Eagles
4 Olivia Newton-John

Princess Margaret's eight 'Desert Island Discs'   185

1 '16 Tons' by Tenessee Ernie Ford
2 'The Waltz' in Act Two of Tchaikovsky's *Swan Lake*
3 Brahms's 2nd Symphony, 1st movement
4 'Rock, Rock, Rock' by Carol Ravezza and Sid Phillips and his Band
5 'Scotland the Brave' by The Royal Highland Fusiliers
6 'Rule Britannia' from the last night of the Proms
7 'King Cotton' a march by Sousa
8 'Cwm Rhondda' by the Pendyrus Male Choir (Her luxury for her Desert Island was a piano, her book *War and Peace* and her single favourite piece of music the Waltz from *Swan Lake*.)

186   *Lord Snowdon's eight 'Desert Island Discs'*

1 'The Green Cockatoo' by Roberto Inglez and his Orchestra
2 'London Pride' by Noel Coward
3 'Night and Day' by Cole Porter
4 'The Boys in the Back Room' by Marlene Dietrich
5 The Prologue from *West Side Story*
6 The Waltz in Act One of Tchaikovsky's *Swan Lake*
7 Beethoven's 'Ninth Symphony in D Minor', 4th Movement
8 'Land of My Fathers' by the Treorchy Male Voice Choir. (His luxury for his Desert Island was a canvas, oil paints and brushes, his book *A History of Architecture on the Comparative Method* by Sir Bannister Fletcher. His single favourite piece of music was the Waltz from *Swan Lake*.)

187   *Six Royal poems*

1 Henry VIII (to Anne Boleyn):
Now unto my lady
Promise to her I make
From all others only
To her I me betake.

2 George III (who was in love with Sarah Lennox – since her father was only a Duke, they were unable to marry):
I'd crowns resign
to call thee mine. . . .

3 Elizabeth I:
Christ was the Word that spake it,
He took the bread and brake it,
And what the Word doth make it,
I do believe and take it.

4 Henry VI (written in the Tower of London):
Kingdoms are but cares,
State is devoid of stay,
Riches are ready snares
And hasten to decay.

5 Henry VIII:
The hardest stones are pierced through with tools,
The wisest are with princes made but fools.

6 Prince Charles:
Insistent, persistent, the press never end,
One day they will drive me right round the bend;
Recording, re-phrasing every word that I say:
It's got to be news at the end of the day.

Disgraceful, most dangerous, to share the same plane,
Denies me the chance to scratch and complain;
Oh where, may I ask you, is the monarchy going
When Princes and pressmen are in the same Boeing?

1975

Six Royal reactions to the National Anthem 188

1 Impatience
When the conductor Sir Landon Ronald was conducting, 'God Save the King' he suddenly heard King Edward VIII command him to 'Hurry it up!'

2 Favour
As a child, Queen Victoria charmed her uncle, King William IV when he asked her her favourite tune by replying, 'God Save the King'. A century later, our own Queen made exactly the same reply, with exactly the same effect, to her grandfather, King George V.

3 Spirituality
After a concert at the Albert Hall which had ended with the National Anthem, King George V said, 'I do wish you musicians would not play God Save the King so quickly. You hurry through it as if you wanted to get it over. You see it means a great deal to me. I look upon it almost as a hymn.'

4 Upset
Returning to England for the first time since his Abdication, the Duke of Windsor was saddened to realise that the band had played the shortened version of the National Anthem. 'The Monarch always gets the full treatment', he later explained dejectedly 'and the others only get the first six bars.'

159

5 Distaste

Once when the Queen Mother was watching television with friends, the National Anthem was played. 'Switch it off,' she said. 'Unless one is there it's embarrassing – like hearing the Lord's Prayer while playing Canasta.'

6 Possessiveness

George V considered it 'his' song. When, after his long illness, the king was serenaded by a military band he said: 'I used to hear that good old thing almost every day, but I have not heard it now for 5 months. It is rather moving to hear it once again.'

189 *Seven books to which Prince Charles has written the Introduction*

1 *King George III* (1972)
2 *Captains and Kings* (1972)
3 *The Living World of Animals* (1970)
4 *The Puffin Annual No. 1* (1974)
5 *More Goon Show Scripts* (1973)
6 *The World Underwater Book* (1973)
7 *The Country Life Book of The Queen Mother* (1978)

190 *Six musical members of the Royal Family*

1 Princess Margaret

She sings satirical songs and accompanies herself on the piano.

2 Prince Charles

He can play the banjo and the cello. He knows 'The Ying Tong Song' by heart.

3 Queen Victoria

She had a beautiful singing voice. Fanny Kemble remarked 'The Queen's voice is exquisite.' Ellen Terry compared it to 'a silver stream flowing over golden stones'.

4 King Edward VIII

He could play the banjo, the ukelele and the bagpipes. He once composed a tune on the bagpipes. He named it 'Majorca'.

5 Queen Elizabeth I
She could play the virginals.
6 The Duchess of Kent
She sings very well. She has performed with the Bach Choir at
The Albert Hall.

Fourteen Monarchs portrayed by actors 191

1 *Henry VIII*
   Charles Laughton, Anthony Quayle, Keith Michell, Robert Shaw
2 *Elizabeth I*
   Flora Robson, Anna Robens, Bette Davis, Glenda Jackson
3 *Charles I*
   Alec Guinness
4 *Henrietta Maria*
   Dorothy Tutin
5 *Charles II*
   James Villiers
6 *George IV*
   Peter Ustinov
7 *Queen Victoria*
   Pamela Stanley, Prunella Scales, Anna Neagle, Dorothy Tutin, Annette Crosbie
8 *Prince Albert*
   Robert Hardy
9 *Edward VII*
   Timothy West, Thorley Walters
10 *Edward VIII*
   Peter Barkworth, Edward Fox, Charles Laughton (he based his portrayal of Emperor Claudius in *I Claudius* on King Edward VIII's Abdication speech).
11 *Queen Mary*
   Wendy Hiller, Peggy Ashcroft, Greer Garson
12 *Queen Elizabeth II*
   Pamela Stephenson, Jeanette Charles, Elaine May
13 *Princes Charles*
   Mike Yarwood, Russell Davies, Marc Sinden
14 *Princess Diana*
   Eve Lohman, Pamela Stephenson, Suzanne Danielle

Five things censored for Royalty

1 The Prime of Miss Jean Brodie

A ten-second sequence of two girls giggling over a drawing of a naked man was cut from the Royal Film Performance of *The Prime of Miss Jean Brodie* lest it should embarrass the Queen Mother.

2 Shakespeare's plays

Because Queen Mary II had taken her father's throne, she censored all reference in Shakespeare and other writers to unfilial behaviour, resulting in a total ban on *King Lear* and the cutting of an entire act in *Richard III*.

3 A tenant's book

When Mrs Cresswell, a tenant of King Edward VII at Sandringham, published a book called *Eighteen Years on the Sandringham Estate* which detailed her grievances at the King's game eating all her crops, the King instructed his Norfolk agent, Edward Beck, to buy up the entire edition and burn it.

4 An interview with Prince Philip

When he was asked by an interviewer on Tyne Tees television in 1968 what his reaction would be to one of his children marrying a coloured person, Prince Philip hummed and hawed, saying it was a difficult question to answer. Immediately after the recording, the master copy of the interview was locked in a safe, and both the question and the answer were cut from the transmitted version.

5 A painting of Queen Victoria

In 1855, Sant painted a picture of Queen Victoria and her children listening to Lord Cardigan relating the story of the Charge of the Light Brigade. Some time later, when, mainly due to the flamboyance of his wife, Cardigan became ostracised by society, Queen Victoria had herself painted out.

Ten 'Most Glorious Royal Brides': a list by Barbara Cartland

'1 Eleanor of Castile

Eleanor of Castile married Edward I in 1254. Beautiful and adored by the King, when she went with him on a Crusade, she sucked the poison from his wound. After her death the King erected "Eleanor Crosses" at the twelve places the coffin rested.

2 HM Queen Victoria

Victoria married Albert of Saxe Coburg and Gotha in 1840. She was madly in love with him and wrote: "He is perfection in every way – in beauty, in everything. . . . Oh, how I adore and love him. . . ."

3 HM Princess May of Teck (Queen Mary)

HM Princess May of Teck married George, Duke of York in 1893. She was called Mary after she married, and became one of our most admired, dignified and impressive Queens.

4 Lady Elizabeth Bowes Lyon

Lady Elizabeth Bowes Lyon married the Duke of York in 1923. Her charm, her sweetness and the love and admiration she has created wherever she goes have made her the Queen of every English heart.

5 HRH Princess Marina of Greece

Prince George, Duke of Kent, fell head over heels in love with the exquisite Princess Marina. After eight ecstatically happy years he was killed flying in the RAF.

Miss Barbara Cartland

6 HRH Princess Elizabeth

Princess Elizabeth, very sweet and lovely, married in 1947 the handsome, dashing Philip of Greece. Her brilliant intelligence and her sense of humour have made her an outstanding Queen, helped and sustained by her husband's love and understanding.

7 HRH Princess Margaret

No one who saw the marriage of Princess Margaret in 1960 to Anthony Armstrong-Jones will forget her beauty and a radiance which seemed to light the Abbey. To the crowds watching, it was a fairy story come true.

8 Miss Katharine Worsley

After a courtship of two years, Katharine Worsley married Edward, Duke of Kent in 1961. Her train was fifteen feet long and 2,000 guests were entertained before the happy couple left in a Heron of the Queen's Flight for their honeymoon.

9 HRH Princess Alexandra of Kent

Lovely, captivating and sensitive Princess Alexandra brought sunshine into Westminster Abbey in a gown of gold sequins when she married dark, handsome, clever Angus Ogilvy in 1962. They are very happy.

10 Lady Diana Spencer

Just like a Barbara Cartland novel, dashing and adored, the Prince of Wales fell in love with the sweet, gentle, shy little girl who loved children. They were married in 1981 and the whole world prayed that they would live happily ever afterwards.'

194 *Ways in which the Royal Family are related other than by marriage*

1 The Queen and Prince Philip

(a) Third cousins: through their descent from Queen Victoria.
(b) Second cousins once removed: through King Christian IX of Denmark.
(c) Fourth cousins once removed: through collateral descendents of King George III.

2 Princess Anne and Mark Phillips

(a) Thirteenth cousins once removed: through Edward I.
(b) Thirteenth cousins three times removed: through Sir William Griffin.

3 Prince Charles and Princess Diana

(a) Seventh cousins once removed: through William Cavendish, 3rd Duke of Devonshire.

(b) Tenth cousins twice removed: through King James I in three different ways.

(c) Eleventh cousins: through Elizabeth, Queen of Bohemia.

(d) Eleventh cousins once removed: through another line of descent from King James I.

(e) Fifteenth cousins once removed: through King Henry VII in at least four different ways.

Six first meetings of Royal husbands and wives   195

1 King George IV meets Caroline of Brunswick Wolfenbuttel

On first seeing his arranged wife, King George IV turned to an aide and gasped, 'Harris, I am not well, pray get me a glass of brandy.'

2 The Duke of Windsor meets Mrs Simpson

Late in his life, the Duke of Windsor recalled his first meeting with his future wife. At a houseparty, he asked her if she missed American central heating. 'I'm sorry, Sir, but you disappoint me', she replied. 'In what way?' 'Every American woman who comes to your country is always asked the same question. I had hoped for something more original from the Prince of Wales.'

3 King Henry VII checks out the Queen of Naples

Before meeting his intended bride, the widowed Queen of Naples, King Henry VII sent envoys with very strict instructions: they were to find out whether she was tall simply because of high heels; to discover how much her complexion owed to cosmetics; to 'mark her breasts and paps whether they be big or small; to mark whether there appear any hair about her lips or not'; to discover how much she ate and drank, and, one final instruction, 'that they endeavour them to speak with the said young queen fasting . . . and to approach as near to her mouth as they honestly may, to the intent that they may feel the condition of her breath, whether it be sweet or not.'

4 Prince Charles meets Lady Diana Spencer

Princes Charles first met his future wife in a ploughed field in 1977:

Prince Charles: 'I remember thinking what a very jolly and amusing and attractive sixteen-year-old she was. I mean, great fun – bouncy and full of life and everything. I don't know what you thought of me, but – '
Princess Diana: 'Pretty amazing.'

5 King George I checks out Princess Caroline for his son

On meeting her future father-in-law, King George I, Princess Caroline was given a thorough examination: 'As soon as I entered the room he took a wax light and examined me from head to foot'.

6 King Henry VIII meets Anne of Cleves

So unlike her portraits was the king's new wife that Henry VIII was moved to ask his courtiers if they had brought him the Flanders Mare.

196 Six Royal messages of love

1 *'. . . As a woman in love I was prepared to go through rivers of woe, seas of despair, and oceans of agony for him.'* The Duchess of Windsor writing about King Edward VIII in her memoirs.

2 *'Although I have often told it you before, I repeat it once more, that I love you darling child, with my whole heart and soul and thank God every day that I have such a wife as you, who is such a great help and support to me and I believe loves me too.'* King George V in a letter to Queen Mary.

3 *'I was so proud of you and thrilled at having you so close to me on our long walk in Westminster Abbey, but when I handed your hand to the Archbishop I felt that I had lost something very precious.'* King George VI in a letter to the Queen after her wedding.

4 *'I have read the most sweet letters of your Highness lately given to me, from which I have easily perceived your most entire love for me.'* Arthur, Prince of Wales, in a letter to Princess Catalina of Aragon in 1499. He was aged thirteen and she was aged twelve. They had yet to meet.

5 *'Wishing Myself (especially of an evening) in my sweetheart's arms, whose pretty dukkys I trust shortly to kiss.'* King Henry VIII in a letter to Anne Boleyn.

6 The Duke of Windsor: *'What would you have if you were granted one wish?'* The Duchess of Windsor: *'You.'* (In conversation at a dinner party in Paris in the 1960s.)

Eight things Prince Charles and Princess Diana have said they have in common

1 Music
2 Dancing
3 The outdoors
4 Skiing
5 The same sense of humour
6 Opera
7 Walking
8 Fishing

Six things Earl Spencer has said about his daughter Diana and her marriage

1 *'She was a delightful child, and as a baby she could have won any beauty competition.'*
2 *'She loved her soft toys nearly as much as she loved babies. She always loved babies.'*
3 *'The average family wouldn't know what had hit them if their daughter married the future king . . . but my family go back to the Saxons – so that sort of thing's not a bit new to me.'*
4 *'Diana had to marry somebody, and I've known and worked for the Queen since Diana was a baby.'*
5 *'The press made Diana's life difficult but she behaved very well. It has proved to be a test, though it wasn't meant to be, and she came through with flying colours. I wouldn't have done it myself at 19. I would have collapsed.'*
6 *'I'm afraid I'll never see my daughter again, you know. I expect I won't see her any more. They fix his schedule two years in advance, you know.'*

Seven Royal reflections on marriage

1 *'It is like taking a poor lamb to be sacrificed.'* Queen Victoria on the marriage of her eldest daughter Victoria to Frederick, the future Emperor of Prussia.

2 *'I shouldn't wonder if their children are four-legged.'* The Queen on the marriage of Princess Anne to Mark Phillips.

3 *'One marriage leads to another.'* Prince Andrew soon after Prince Charles's wedding.

4 *'I can see that you are sublimely happy with Philip which is right but don't forget us is the wish of Your ever loving and devoted Papa.'* King George VI in a letter to the Queen after her wedding to Prince Philip.

5 *'You can get used to anyone's face in a week.'* King Charles II.

6 *'If he was a cowboy I should love him just the same and would marry no-one else.'* Queen Alexandra in a letter to one of her future sisters-in-law.

7 *'It's the last decision on which I would want my head to be ruled by my heart.'* Prince Charles.

Six Kings who were much older than their Queens

1 Henry I
36 years older than his second wife, Adeliza of Louvain
2 Edward I
40 years older than his second wife, Margaret of France
3 Richard II
23 years older than his second wife, Isabelle of France
4 Henry VIII
25 years older than his fourth wife, Anne of Cleves
30 years older than his fifth wife, Catherine Howard
21 years older than his sixth and last wife, Catherine Parr
5 James II
25 years older than his second wife, Mary of Modena
6 William IV
27 years older than Queen Adelaide

1 King Henry II (born 1133) eleven years younger than Eleanor of Aquitaine.
2 King Philip of Spain (born 1527) eleven years younger than Queen Mary I.
3 King Henry VIII (born 1491) six years younger than Catherine of Aragon.
4 King Edward IV (born 1442) five years younger than Elizabeth Woodville.
5 King Edward III (born 1312) a year younger than Philippa of Hainault.
6 King Richard II (born 1367) a year younger than Anne of Bohemia.
7 King George II (born 1683) six months younger than Queen Caroline.

Eight things which have gone wrong 202
at Royal Weddings

1 A bouquet mislaid
Before the Queen set out for her wedding, there was a frantic search for her bouquet. Eventually it was located in a refrigerator, where it had been placed by a well-meaning footman.

2 A premature orchestra
At the wedding of King Edward VII, the orchestra became so bored by the Archbishop's lengthy sermon that they began tuning up.

3 A train snagged
Both on her way to the altar and on her way from it, the Queen got her train caught on the altar steps. Her father and the best man managed to free it both times.

4 A name misplaced
Princess Diana called her husband 'Philip Charles . . .' when she made her wedding vows.

5 A meaning reversed
Soon after Princess Diana's mistake, Prince Charles, instead of saying 'All my worldly goods with thee I share', said, 'All thy goods with thee I share.'

6 A necklace forgotten
Before the Queen's wedding, the bride suddenly remembered that

she had left her pearl necklace – a present from her parents – in St James's Palace, where it was on display to the public along with other wedding presents. The Queen's Private Secretary, Sir John Colville fought his way through the crowds and, after some difficulty in convincing the police of his identity, retrieved the necklace.

7 A dress stained
At the wedding of Augusta of Saxe-Gotha to Frederick, Prince of Wales in 1736, the bride was sick.

8 A handbag swung
At the wedding banquet of Prince Philip's parents, Olga, Duchess of Wurttemberg, who had secured her tiara with elastic, had her spectacles knocked off. In a myopic fury she swung her handbag, hitting the wrong suspect.

203 *Four members of the Royal Family and their Circle whose wedding nights were exceptional*

1 King William III
Tucked up in bed with his wife on their wedding night, Prince William of Orange was surprised by King Charles II drawing back the curtains of the bed and yelling, 'Now, nephew, to your work! Hey! St George for England!'

2 King George IV
Queen Caroline once complained that amongst other misdemeanours committed by her husband King George IV on their wedding night, he had forced her to smoke a pipe.

3 Philip Herbert
The morning after the wedding of his favourite, Philip Herbert, King James I appeared in the bedchamber in his nightgown, leapt into the bed and romped around with bride and groom.

4 Prince Michael of Kent
Prince Michael of Kent spent his wedding night all alone because Princess Michael of Kent wished to remain pure enough to receive Roman Catholic communion for the last time on the following day.

Six marriages of King Henry VIII and their durations

1 *Catherine of Aragon:* 23 years and 11 months (divorced 1533).
2 *Anne Boleyn:* 3 years and 4 months (beheaded 1536).
3 *Jane Seymour:* 1 year and 5 months (died after childbirth 1537).
4 *Anne of Cleves:* 6 months (divorced 1541).
5 *Catherine Howard:* 1 year and 6 months (beheaded 1542).
6 *Catherine Parr:* 3 years and 6 months (widowed in 1547, she married Lord Seymour the same year).

Five Royal reactions to pregnancy

1 *'It really is* too dreadful *to have the first year of one's married life and happiness spoilt by discomfort and misery . . . I was furious at being in that position.'* Queen Victoria to her eldest daughter.
2 *'It's what we're made for.'* The Queen, to a friend who asked if she was nervous.
3 *'Of course it is a great bore for me and requires a great deal of patience to bear it, but this is alas the penalty for being a woman.'* Queen Mary to King George V.
4 *'Being pregnant is an occupational hazard of being a wife.'* Princess Anne in an interview, 1981.
5 *'Some days I feel terrible. Nobody told me about morning sickness.'* Princess Diana to Mrs Janet Lukic on a walkabout in Chesterfield, November 1981.

Four stages of procreation by Prince Philip

1 *'People want the first child very much when they marry.'*
2 *'They want the second child almost as much.'*
3 *'If a third comes along they accept it as natural − but they haven't gone out of their way to try to get it.'*
4 *'When the fourth child comes along, in most cases it's unintentional.'*

Days of the week on which Kings and Queens (and their consorts) were born

Monday
Edward VIII, Henry V, Richard III, Anne of Cleves, Mary Tudor, James II, William III, George I, Queen Adelaide, Queen Victoria.
Tuesday
Edward II, Richard II, Queen Caroline (George II), Queen Caroline, (George IV), Edward VII.
Wednesday
James I, Charles I, Mary II, William IV, Elizabeth II.
Thursday
Henry VII, Henry VIII, George IV, Prince Albert (consort of Queen Victoria).
Friday
Edward I, Catherine of Aragon, Edward VI, the Duchess of Windsor, Prince Philip.
Saturday
Henry IV, Edward IV, Charles II, Queen Mary of Modena (wife of James II), Queen Charlotte, George V, Edward VIII, George VI, The Queen Mother.
Sunday
Edward V, Charles I, Queen Catherine of Braganza (wife of Charles II), Queen Anne, George III, Queen Alexandra, Queen Mary.

Days of the week on which members of the Royal Family were born

Monday's child is fair of face,
Tuesday's child is full of grace,
Wednesday's child is full of woe,
Thursdays's child has far to go,
Friday's child is loving and giving,
Saturday's child works hard for his living,
And the child that is born on the Sabbath Day
Is bonny and blithe, and good and gay.

Monday
Princess Michael of Kent (15 January 1945)
Tuesday
Princess Anne (15 August 1950)
Prince Edward (10 March 1964)
Peter Phillips (15 November 1977)
Earl of St Andrews (son of the Duke of Kent, 26 June 1962)
Lady Helen Windsor (his sister, 28 April 1964)
Wednesday
The Queen (21 April 1926)
Mark Phillips (22 September 1948)
Princess Alice, Duchess of Gloucester (25 December 1901)
The Duchess of Kent (22 February 1933)
Thursday
Princess Margaret (21 August 1930)
The Duchess of Gloucester (20 June 1946)
Earl of Ulster (son of the Duke of Gloucester, 24 October 1974)
Lady Gabriella Windsor (daughter of Prince Michael of Kent, 23 April 1981)
Friday
Prince Philip (10 June 1921)
Prince Andrew (19 February 1960)
Zara Phillips (15 May 1981)
Lord Snowdon (7 March 1930)
Lord Linley (3 November 1960)
Lady Sarah Armstrong-Jones (1 May 1964)
Lord Frederick Windsor (6 April 1979)
Princess Alexandra (25 December 1936)
Hon. Angus Ogilvy (14 September 1928)
Saturday
The Queen Mother (4 August 1900)
The Princess of Wales (1 July 1961)
The Duke of Gloucester (26 August 1944)
Lady Davina Windsor (daughter of the Duke of Gloucester, 19 March 1977)
Lady Rose Windsor (her sister, 1 March 1980)
The Duke of Kent (9 October 1935)
Lord Nicholas Windsor (his son, 25 July 1970)
Prince Michael of Kent (15 January 1942)
James Ogilvy (29 February 1964)
Sunday
The Prince of Wales (14 November 1948)
Marina Ogilvy (31 July 1966)

209 *Five Royal children and their weights at birth*

Prince Charles: 7 pounds 6 ounces
Princess Anne: 6 pounds
Prince Andrew: 7 pounds 3 ounces
Prince Edward: 5 pounds 7 ounces
Princess Diana: 7 pounds 12 ounces

210 *Four second sons who succeeded to the Throne*

1 Henry VIII

The second son of King Henry VII, he succeeded to the Throne after his elder brother Arthur, Prince of Wales died in 1502 following his marriage to Catherine of Aragon (who Henry then married).

The first photograph to be taken of King George VI after his Accession in 1936

2 Charles I

The second son of James I, whom he succeeded after the death of his elder brother Henry Frederick, Prince of Wales.

3 George V

The second son of Edward VII. His elder brother Albert Victor, Duke of Clarence, having died shortly after his engagement to Princess May of Teck. Like Henry VIII, King George V married the wife intended for his elder brother.

4 George VI

The second son of George V. His elder brother, Edward VIII abdicated after less than a year on the Throne.

Ten Queens who bore children late in life

1 Queen Eleanor of Aquitaine

The wife of Henry II, she was 40 when her first child was born (a girl) and it was not until she was 45 that she gave birth to the future King John.

2 Queen Eleanor of Provence

The wife of Henry III was over 40 when her last child, Prince Henry was born.

3 Queen Eleanor of Castile

Presented King Edward I with an heir (the future King Edward II) when she was in her forty-first year. She was 46 when her fifteenth and last child, Princess Blanche, was born.

4 Queen Philippa of Hainault

The wife of Edward III, she gave birth to her twelfth child when she was 43.

5 Elizabeth Woodville

Queen consort of Edward IV was 43 when her last child, Princess Bridget was born.

6 Queen Caroline

She was 41 when she gave birth to the ninth child of George II.

7 Queen Charlotte

The wife of King George III gave birth to her fifteenth and last child when she was 38. The King said 'My quiver is full.'

8 Queen Victoria

Was aged nearly 38 when she gave birth to her ninth and last child, Princess Beatrice, in 1857.

9 Queen Mary
Had her sixth and last child, Prince John, when she was 38.
10 The Queen
Queen Elizabeth II was aged nearly 38 when Prince Edward, her fourth child was born in 1964.

212 Five Royal conversations with children

1 The Queen Mother meets a little girl
Once when the Queen Mother was on a Royal walkabout, a little girl asked her, 'Is it true that your daughter's the Queen?' To which the Queen Mother replied, 'Yes. Isn't it exciting?'
2 Princess Alexandra meets a little boy
When Princess Alexandra was still a teenager, she was greeted by a little boy with the expression, 'Wotcher!' 'Wotcher!' replied the Princess.
3 The Queen meets a little girl
Touring Poole General Hospital in 1968, the Queen stopped by the bed of a little four-year-old girl. 'Do you know who this is?' the nurse asked the little girl. 'Yes,' came the reply. 'It's Granny.'
4 The Queen meets a little boy
When she was visiting families at an RAF station in 1949, the Queen was asked by a little boy, 'Where's your pussy cat?' The Queen quickly realised that he was referring to the nursery rhyme, "Pussy cat, pussy cat, where have you been?" "I've been to London to look at the Queen", and apologised for not bringing him.
5 Queen Victoria meets Queen Wilhelmina of the Netherlands
When the elderly Queen Victoria met Queen Wilhelmina, who was then only ten years old, she made her feel at home by saying, 'As we're Queens together, we can say what we like.'

Five pieces of Royal advice on how to deal with children

1 Prince Charles's advice
'If your children want to alter society, listen to their reasons and the idealism behind them. Don't crush them with some clever remark straight away.'

2 King Edward III's advice
'Let the boy win his spurs' (said of his son, the Black Prince, at the Battle of Crécy, 1345).

3 Prince Philip's advice
'It's no use saying do this, do that, don't do that . . . it's very easy when children want something to say *No* immediately. I think it's quite important not to give an unequivocal answer at once. Much better to think it over. Then, if you eventually say *No*, I think they really accept it.'

4 Queen Victoria's advice
'Make him sit upright, keep his hands out of his pockets, refrain from dandyism, slang, banter, mimicry and practical jokes.' (Orders given to the three equerries of the adolescent Prince of Wales who became King Edward VII.)

5 King George V's advice
'My father was frightened of his mother, I was frightened of my father, and I am damned well going to see to it that my children are frightened of me.'

Four favourite childhood toys of Prince Charles

1 A blue Austin Car
2 A Train Set
3 'Jumbo' – a fluffy elephant on wheels
4 A Beatle wig

Nine favourite childhood games of the Queen and Princess Margaret

1 *Happy Families*.
2 *Horses*. The then Archbishop of Canterbury, Cosmo Lang, once saw the Queen as a child playing horses with her grandfather, King George V, leading him by the beard as he shuffled along the floor on his hands and knees.
3 *Old Maid*.
4 *Playing with Pinkle Ponkle*. When she was little girl, Princess Margaret played with a fantasy friend called Pinkle Ponkle who lived in the air and ate caterpillar sandwiches and green jam.
5 *Bears*. When the Queen was a little girl, she enjoyed playing a game of bears on hands and knees with her parents. When Princess Margaret was born, one of the Queen's first reactions was, 'Now there will be four bears instead of three.'
6 *Demon Pounce*.
7 *Waving*. The Queen and her grandfather, King George V, used to greet each other every morning by looking through binoculars and waving from the Queen's home, 145 Piccadilly, to the King's, Buckingham Palace.
8 *Delivering Groceries*. The Queen enjoyed riding around on her reined nanny delivering groceries to imaginary customers.
9 *Animal Grab*.

Eighteen Royal views on the younger generation

1 *'He is intelligent, has a good sense of humour and thinks about things the right way.'* King George VI on Prince Philip.
2 *'The better I know and the more I see of your dear little wife, the more charming I think she is and everyone fell in love with her here.'* King George V to King George VI on the Queen Mother.
3 *'I always hated the rascal, but now I hate him yet worse than ever.'* King George II on Frederick, Prince of Wales.
4 *'They are such miserable, puny children (each weaker than the preceding one).'* Queen Victoria on King Edward VII's children.
5 *'I think the Prince will marry an English girl, but if he does marry an American let's just hope it's not a divorced one.'* The Duchess of

'More Royal than the rest of us' – the Queen

Windsor on Prince Charles in an interview, 1974.

6 'Elizabeth would always know her own mind. There's something very steadfast and determined about her.' Queen Mary on the Queen before her marriage to Prince Philip.

7 'What a curious child he is.' Queen Alexandra on her grandson, King Edward VIII.

8 'Anne's much more positive than I was, so I think she'll be all right.' Princess Margaret on Princess Anne before her wedding announcement.

9 'I pray to God that my eldest son will never marry and have children, and that nothing will come between Bertie and Lilibet and the Throne.' King George V on his eldest son, King Edward VIII, his second son, King George VI and his grandaughter, the Queen.

10 'Oh, she's more Royal than the rest of us.' The Queen on Princess Michael of Kent.

11 'Wild as hawks. They are such ill-bred, ill-trained children that I

cannot fancy them at all.' Queen Victoria on King George V and the Duke of Clarence, aged 7 and 8.

12 *'The only nice thing to have happened this year.'* Queen Mary on the birth of Princess Alexandra in the year of the Abdication.

13 *'If my children are a guide, there is nothing they like better than a little blood.'* Prince Philip, on being asked if the whaling shots in the film of *Around the World in Eighty Days* were too gory.

14 *'Your sweet little daughter . . . has four teeth now, which is quite good at 11 months old, she is very happy and drives in a carriage every afternoon, which amuses her.'* King George V to King George VI on the Queen.

15 *'A very common-looking child, very plain in the face.'* Queen Victoria on Prince Leopold, her fourth son.

16 *'She's highly strung and somewhat emotional. It's all that foreign blood in her.'* Queen Mary on Princess Alexandra as a baby.

17 *'He is too sweet stumping around the room and we shall love having him at Sandringham. He is the fifth generation to live there and I hope he will get to love the place.'* King George VI to the Queen on Prince Charles.

18 *'I fear the seventh granddaughter and fourteenth grandchild becomes a very uninteresting thing – for it seems to me to go on like the rabbits in Windsor Park.'* Queen Victoria.

217 *Ten Royal views on the older generation*

1 *'A man who by the simple qualities of loyalty, resolution and service won for himself such a place in the affection of all of us that when he died millions mourned for him as for a true and trusted friend.'* The Queen on her father, King George VI, at the unveiling of his memorial in the Mall in 1955.

2 *'Motherdear is the most selfish person I have ever known.'* King George V on Queen Alexandra.

3 *'I don't mind praying to the eternal father, but I must be the only man in the country afflicted with an eternal mother.'* King Edward VII on Queen Victoria after her Diamond Jubilee Service.

4 *'I'm very lucky, because I have very wise and incredibly sensible parents who have created a marvellous, secure, happy home.'* Prince Charles.

5 *'Grandpa has gone to heaven and I'm sure God is finding him very*

useful.' Princess Margaret on King George V after his death.

6 *'I know that Old Man kind. That's you, grandpapa . . . you are old, and you are very, very kind.'* The Queen as a child to King George V, after she had heard carol singers with 'joy to you and all mankind'.

7 *'The vulgar view of King George III is quite simply that he was mad, and to make matters worse, that he also succeeded in losing the American colonies. The fact that he had wide and civilised interests, was a great patron of the arts and sciences and devoted a vast quantity of time to affairs of State has been conveniently neglected.'* Prince Charles on King George III.

8 *'How horribly* boneless *it felt!'* King Edward VIII on having to hold the hand of his great-grandmother, Queen Victoria.

9 *'Too disgusting, because his face was covered with grease paint.'* Queen Victoria on having to sit on the knee of her uncle, King George IV and kiss him.

10 *'A strange busload to be travelling through eternity together.'* King George V on his ancestors buried in St George's Chapel, Windsor. He used to call them 'a mixed grill'.

Thirteen famous Britons who are related to Princess Diana

1 Oliver Cromwell
   (first cousin eleven times removed)
2 Lady Antonia Fraser
   (fifth cousin four times removed)
3 George Orwell
   (eleventh cousin three times removed)
4 Virginia Woolf
   (twelfth cousin three times removed)
5 Oliva de Havilland
   (fifth cousin three times removed)
6 Graham Greene
   (thirteenth cousin once removed)
7 Sir Alec Douglas-Home
   (third cousin once removed in two different ways)
8 Bertrand Russell
   (half second cousin three times removed)
9 Jane Austen
   (seventh cousin six times removed)

Wilhelm Duke of Schleswig-Holstein-Sonderburg-Glücksburg (1785–1831) Princess Louise of Hesse-Cassel (1789–1867)

Landgrave Wilhelm of Hesse-Cassel (1787–1867) Princess Charlotte of Denmark (1789–1864)

Nicholas I, Emperor of Russia (1796–1855) Princess Charlotte of Prussia (1798–1860)

Joseph, Duke of Saxe-Altenburg (1789–1868) Duchess Amalie of Württemberg (1799–1848)

Ludwig II, Grand Duke of Hesse (1777–1848) Princess Wilhelmine of Baden (1788–1836)

Moritz, Count von Hauke (1775–1830) Sophie de la Fontaine (1790–1831)

Prince Karl of Hesse (1809–1877) Princess Elisabeth of Prussia (1815–1885)

Prince Albert of Saxe-Coburg and Gotha (1819–1861) Victoria, Queen of Great Britain (1819–1901)

Christian IX, King of Denmark (1818–1906)

Princess Louise of Hesse-Cassel (1817–1898)

Grand Duke Constantine of Russia (1827–1892)

Princess Alexandra of Saxe-Altenburg (1830–1911)

Prince Alexander of Hesse (1823–1888)

Julie, Princess of Battenberg (1825–1895)

Ludwig IV, Grand Duke of Hesse (1837–1892)

Princess Alice of Great Britain (1843–1878)

George I, King of The Hellenes (1845–1913)

Grand Duchess Olga of Russia (1851–1926)

Louis Mountbatten, 1st Marquess of Milford Haven (1854–1921)

Princess Victoria of Hesse (1863–1950)

Prince Andrew of Greece (1882–1944)

Princess Alice of Battenberg (1885–1969)

Prince Philip, Duke of Edinburgh (1921–   )

Charles,

Prince Albert of Saxe-Coburg and Gotha
(1819–1861)
Victoria, Queen of Great Britain
(1819–1901)

Christian IX, King of Denmark
(1818–1906)
Princess Louise of Hesse-Cassel
(1817–1898)

Duke Alexander of Württemberg
(1804–1885)
Countess Claudine Rhédey de Kis-Rhéde
(1812–1841)

Adolphus, Duke of Cambridge
(1774–1850)
Princess Augusta of Hesse-Cassel
(1797–1889)

Thomas Bowes-Lyon, Lord Glamis
(1801–1834)
Charlotte Grimstead
(1797–1881)

Oswald Smith
(1794–1863)
Henrietta Mildred Hodgson
(1805–1891)

Lord William Cavendish-Bentinck
(1780–1826)
Anne Wellesley
(1788–1875)

Edwyn Burnaby
(1799–1867)
Anne Caroline Salisbury
(1806–1881)

Edward VII, King of Great Britain
(1841–1910)

Princess Alexandra of Denmark (1844–1925)

Francis, Duke of Teck
(1837–1900)

Princess Mary Adelaide of Great Britain
(1833–1897)

Claude Bowes-Lyon, 13th Earl of Strathmore (1824–1904)

Frances Dora Smith (1832–1922)

Rev Charles Cavendish-Bentinck (1817–1865)

Caroline Louisa Burnaby
(1832–1918)

George V, King of Great Britain
(1865–1936)

Princess Mary of Teck
(1867–1953)

Claude George Bowes-Lyon, 14th Earl of Strathmore
(1855–1944)

Nina Cecilia Cavendish-Bentinck
(1862–1938)

George VI, King of Great Britain
(1895–1952)

Lady Elizabeth Bowes-Lyon
(1900–   )

Elizabeth II, Queen of Great Britain
(1926–   )

Prince of Wales
948–   )

183

Ancestral chart of
the Princess of Wales

George John Spencer, 2nd Earl Spencer (1758–1834)
Lady Lavinia Bingham (1762–1831)

Sir Horace Beauchamp Seymour (1791–1851)
Elizabeth Malet Palk (–1827)

Henry Baring (1777–1848)
Cecilia Anne Windham (1803–1874)

John Crocker Bulteel (1792/3–1843)
Lady Elizabeth Grey (1798–1880)

James Hamilton, 1st Duke of Abercorn (1811–1885)
Lady Louisa Jane Russell (1812–1905)

Richard William Penn Curzon-Howe, 1st Earl Howe (1796–1870)
Hon Anne Frances Gore (1817–1877)

George Charles Bingham, 3rd Earl of Lucan (1800–1888)
Lady Anne Brudenell (1809–1877)

Charles Gordon-Lennox, 5th Duke of Richmond and Lennox (1791–1860)
Lady Caroline Paget (1796–1874)

Edward Roche (1771–1855)
Margaret Honoria Curtain (1786–1862)

Frederick Spencer, 4th Earl Spencer (1798–1857)

Adelaide Horatia Elizabeth Seymour (1825–1877)

Edward Charles Baring, 1st Baron Revelstoke (1828–1897)

Louisa Emily Charlotte Bulteel (1839–1892)

James Hamilton, 2nd Duke of Abercorn (1838–1913)

Lady Mary Anna Curzon-Howe (1848–1929)

George Bingham, 4th Earl of Lucan (1830–1914)

Lady Cecilia Catherine Gordon-Lennox (1838–1910)

Edmund Burke Roche, 1st Baron Fermoy (1815–1874)

Charles Robert Spencer, 6th Earl Spencer (1857–1922)

Hon Margaret Baring (1868–1906)

James Albert Edward Hamilton, 3rd Duke of Abercorn (1869–1953)

Lady Rosalind Cecilia Bingham (1869–1958)

Albert Edward John Spencer, 7th Earl Spencer (1892–1975)

Lady Cynthia Elinor Beatrix Hamilton (1897–1972)

Edward John Spencer, 8th Earl Spencer (1924–   )

James Brownell Boothby (1791–1850)
Charlotte Cunningham
(1799–1893)

John Work
(1781–1823)
Sarah Boude
(1790–1860)

John Wood
(1786–1848)
Ellen Strong
(ca 1802–1863)

David Gill
(1797–1868)
Sarah Ogston
(1797–1872)

William Smith Marr
(1810–1898)
Helen Bean
(1814/5–1852)

William Littlejohn
(1803–1888)
Janet Bentley
(1811–1848)

James Crombie
(1810–1878)
Katherine Scott Forbes
(1812–1893)

Eliza Caroline Boothby (1821–1897)

Frank Work
(1819–1911)

Ellen Wood
(1831–1877)

Alexander Ogston Gill
(1833–1908)

Barbara Smith Marr
(1843–18   )

David Littlejohn
(1841–1924)

Jane Crombie
(1843–1917)

James Boothby
Burke Roche, 3rd
Baron Fermoy
(1851–1920)

Francis Ellen
Work
(1857–1947)

William Smith Gill
(1865–1957)

Ruth Littlejohn
(1879–1964)

Edmund Maurice Burke Roche,
4th Baron Fermoy
(1885–1955)

Ruth Sylvia Gill
(1908–   )

Hon Frances Ruth Burke Roche
(1936–   )

Lady Diana Frances Spencer
(1961–   )

185

10 T E Lawrence (Lawrence of Arabia)
    (fourth cousin three times removed)
11 Samuel Pepys
    (second cousin ten times removed)
12 Winston Churchill
    (sixth cousin once removed and fourth cousin twice removed)
13 Lord Lucan
    (second cousin once removed)

221 *Fifteen famous Americans who are related to Princess Diana*

1 Humphrey Bogart – actor
   (seventh cousin twice removed)
2 George Washington – First American President
   (eighth cousin seven times removed)
3 Calvin Coolidge – 30th President of the United States
   (tenth cousin)
4 F D Roosevelt – 32nd President of the United States
   (seventh cousin three times removed in six different ways)
5 Lillian Gish – silent screen star
   (double seventh cousin three times removed)
6 Orson Welles – actor and director
   (eighth cousin twice removed)
7 Harriet Beecher Stowe – author and anti-slavery campaigner
   (sixth cousin four times removed)
8 Ben Bradlee – editor-in-chief of the *Washington Post* newspaper
   (tenth cousin once removed)
9 Ralph Waldo Emerson – essayist
   (fifth cousin five times removed)
10 Erle Stanley Gardner – crime writer
   (double eighth cousin thrice removed)
11 Lee Remick – actress
   (tenth cousin)
12 Gloria Vanderbilt – heiress and designer of blue jeans
   (eighth cousin thrice removed)
13 Nelson Bunker Hunt – tycoon
   (ninth cousin once removed)
14 John Singer Sargent – portrait painter
   (fifth cousin twice removed)
15 Louisa M Alcott – author of *Little Women*
   (seventh cousin four times removed)

Nine famous foreigners who are related to Princess Diana

1 The Marquis de Sade
   (double fourth cousin seven times removed)
2 Georges Sand
   (sixth cousin four times removed)
3 Giscard D'Estaing
   (quintuple ninth cousin once removed)
4 Goethe
   (tenth cousin five times removed)
5 The Aga Khan
   (seventh cousin)
6 Herman Göering
   (tenth cousin three times removed)
7 Bismarck
   (eighth cousin five times removed)
8 King Juan Carlos
   (half ninth cousin)
9 Catherine the Great
   (fourth cousin six times removed)

Adam Plattenberg-Witten zu Meitengen's favourite foreign monarchs

'1 Bernabo Visconti

Joint Ruler of Lombardy in the fourteenth century. This man was subject to uncontrollable rages. Once when he found that one of his 500 hunting dogs was out of condition he had all the keepers hung. He was perpetually at odds with the Pope, and was eventually excommunicated; his furious reaction was to force the Papal Legate to eat the Bill of Excommunication – including the ribbons and lead seals. He then, to demonstrate his spite for the Church publicly, roasted 4 nuns and an Augustan friar. His final act of vengeance came in 1350 when he captured Bologna and forced one of the city's priests to pronounce an Anathema on the Pope from a high tower.

2 Vlad the Impaler

Some believe he was the model for Count Dracula. Offended that some Ottoman emissaries had not removed their turbans, he was informed that no insult was intended, but that they had to wear them for religious reasons. Announcing that he was a great respecter of religion, Vlad ordered that the turbans be nailed onto the unfortunate diplomats' heads. His favourite method of punishment was to impale his victims upon huge wooden stakes. One lucky man, a foreign merchant, escaped this fate through honesty. His cache of gold had been stolen, and Vlad ordered it to be replaced. When the merchant found that his saddlebags contained twice the original amount of gold, he returned and informed Vlad of this discovery. The despot assured him that if he had failed to mention it he would have been impaled.

3 King Boris of Bulgaria (1918–1943)

This king was a keen mechanic and railway enthusiast. King Edward VIII, on a visit to the king in the 1930s recalled that the official farewell was curtailed by an argument between Boris and his brother over who was going to drive the train back.

4 King George I of the Hellenes (1845–1913)

Prince William of Glucksburg's first intimation that he had been elected King of Greece in 1863 was from the greasy newspaper which wrapped a sardine sandwich he had taken in his lunch-packet to the Danish Military Academy. When he took up the post, he found the vast ballroom of his palace at Athens a perfect place for roller skating and would weave in and out of the pillars, followed by his whole family in order of seniority.

5 King Basil II Bulgaroctones (Slayer of the Bulgars) (958–1025)

He blinded 15,000 Bulgarian prisoners "as an example", which proved very satisfying to his subjects. The Bulgar king is said to have died of shock at hearing of the deed.

6 Dom Pedro II, Emperor of Brazil (1831–1889)

Due to his quick intervention, the judges of the Brazilian Centennial Exhibition arranged to let Alexander Graham Bell exhibit his new invention – the telephone – for the first time.

7 King Zog of Albania (d. 1961)

Aubrey Herbert describes this king as a reader of Shakespeare and a "fine fighting man". He fled Albania after the Italian invasion in 1938 and came to London. Having settled in, he tried to buy *The Times*, but was obliged to settle for the less-influential *Kensington and Chelsea Post*.'

Adam Plattenberg-Witten zu Meitengen is a lifetime student of history and a distant relation of the Hohenzollerns.

Eleven well-known nursery rhymes which are really about monarchs

1 *Ride a cock horse to Banbury Cross,*
  To see a fine lady upon a white horse,
  Rings on her fingers and bells on her toes,
  And she shall have music wherever she goes.
  The fine lady is Queen Elizabeth I

2 *Wee Willie Winkie runs through the town,*
  Upstairs and downstairs in his nightgown,
  Rapping at the window, crying through the lock,
  Are the children all in bed, for it's now eight o'clock?
  Wee Willie Winkie was the Jacobite name for William III

3 *There was an old woman who lived in a shoe*
  She had so many children she didn't know what to do
  She gave them some broth without any bread
  She whipped them all soundly and put them to bed.
  The old woman is Queen Caroline, wife of King George II, who had eight children

4 *Sing a song of sixpence,*
  A pocket full of rye,
  Four and twenty blackbirds
  Baked in a pie.
  The four and twenty blackbirds are the twenty-four manorial deeds King Henry VIII had confiscated; the rye is tribute in kind. Later in the rhyme, the King is King Henry VIII, the Queen is Catherine of Aragon and the maid is Anne Boleyn.

5 *Charlie over the water, Charlie over the sea,*
  Charlies caught a pretty bird, can't catch me.
  Charlie is Bonny Prince Charlie, the Young Pretender

6 *Little Jack Horner*
  Sat in the corner
  Eating a Christmas pie
  He put in his thumb
  And pulled out a plum,
  And said, What a good boy am I!

Jack Horner was a messenger sent by the Abbot of Glastonbury with a pie containing twelve memorial title deeds to King Henry VIII, in an attempt to soften him against destroying the monastery. Jack Horner opened up the pie on the way to London and took for himself the deeds for the manor of Mells. The Horner family live in Mells to this day.

7 *Here comes the candle to light you to bed,*
Here comes a chopper to chop off your head,
Chip! Chop! Chip! Chop!
  (From 'Oranges and Lemons.')
  The rhyme is about the many marriages of King Henry VIII and his decisive action in concluding them.

8 *Rowley Powley, pudding and pie,*
Kissed the girls and made them cry,
When the boys came out to play,
Rowley Powley ran away.
  Rowley Powley is King Charles II. Georgie Porgie can be substituted: Georgie is King George I.

9 *Mary, Mary, quite contrary,*
How does your Garden grow?
With silver bells and cockleshells
And pretty maids all in a row.
  Mary is Mary, Queen of Scots. The cockleshells were the decorations on a dress she was given by the Dauphin, the pretty maids were her ladies-in-waiting.

10 *Rock-a-bye baby in the treetop,*
When the wind blows, the cradle will rock,
When the bough breaks, the cradle will fall,
And down will come cradle, baby and all.
  The baby is James Stuart, the child of King James II. The wind is bringing William of Orange.

11 *Hark, Hark, the dogs do bark*
The beggars are coming to town
Some in rags,
And some in jags,
And one in a velvet gown.
  The beggars are the Dutchmen in the train of William III, and the one in the velvet gown is William himself.

Five London streets named after monarchs

1 Birdcage Walk
It was here that King Charles II kept his aviary in St James's Park.
2 Hanover Square
In honour of George I
3 Kingsway
Named as a compliment to King Edward VII
4 Regent Street and Regents Park
For the Prince Regent, later King George IV
5 The King's Road
The King is Charles II, who converted a country lane into the main road between St James Palace and Hampton Court Palace. The King's Road remained the monarch's private road until the reign of King George III.

Five euphemisms in Queen Victoria's Court Circular

(Started by King George III, the Court Circular relates the major royal events of each day. It reached its zenith of prolixity in the reign of Queen Victoria, who liked to record every fact, no matter how minor, in suitable language, no matter how pompous. Even the fact that the Queen had *not* caught a cold merited inclusion: 'Her Majesty has not suffered from the inclemency of the weather during the last week.')

1 A Promenade: *a walk*.
2 Equestrian exercise: *riding*.
3 Graciously invited to partake of a collation: *stayed for a meal*.
4 An auspicious return of her natal day: *the Queen's birthday*.
5 The efforts elicited the approbation of the Royal circle: *there was applause*.

Twelve Royal catchphrases

1 *'Keep your hair on.'*
King George VI

2 *'That's quite another thing.'*
King George III

3 *'That's not really so.'*
Mark Phillips. (Peter Tidman, the public relations expert hired in 1981 to improve Mark Phillips's television manner, later commented, 'Ask him if it's true that when you ring Buckingham Palace, Roddy Llewellyn answers the telephone and he only says, "That's not really so".')

4 *'Delicious.'*
The Queen's favourite adjective.

5 *'Unhelpful.'*
A favourite adjective of the Queen Mother. For instance, reference to the Duchess of Windsor will be regarded as 'unhelpful'.

6 *'Poor little man.'*
Queen Alexandra's expression for almost anyone who wasn't Royal.

7 *'Okey-Dokey.'*
One of King Edward VIII's recurrent Americanisms. Others included, 'prezzies', 'makin' whoopee' and 'hot-diggerty-dog'.

8 *'So to speak.'*
One of the phrases Princess Anne frequently inserts in her sentences. Others include 'as it were' and 'if you like'.

9 *'Such Fun.'*
The Queen Mother

10 *'Hey!'*
George III used this expression so often that it became a national joke. Another favourite of his was 'What! What!'

11 *'Don't you think so?'*
The Queen Mother often ends sentences with this phrase, or 'isn't it?', to invite a sense of shared experience.

12 *'Exactly so, ma'am.'*
Snoozing through conversations, King William IV tended to wake up with a start and say 'Exactly so, Ma'am' before lapsing back into sleep.

Eight things named after Royal houses

1 A lipstick
The lipstick the Queen wore at her Coronation was specially concocted to go with her crimson and purple robes. It is red with blue undertones, and it is now known as the Balmoral lipstick.

2 A cathedral
On returning to Los Angeles after marrying the Duke and Duchess of Windsor, the imaginative Reverend R A Jardine named a church 'Windsor Cathedral'. But congregations dwindled, and the church was closed down.

3 The time
Many of the letters of King George V are headed by the time, and then the letters 'S T'; this stands for 'Sandringham Time'. King George, a stickler for punctuality, always kept the Sandringham clocks half an hour early, much to the displeasure of King Edward VIII.

4 A snack
'The Balmoral Buttie', much loved by the Royal Family, and Prince Edward in particular, is a roll filled with barbecued meat or fish.

5 A soup
'Brown Windsor Soup' is a particularly glutinous soup beloved by Queen Victoria.

6 A knot
The Windsor Knot, one of the distinguishing marks of the Duke of Windsor when he was Prince of Wales, particularly irritated his father, and put his tailor to a lot of trouble. The ties had to be specially reinforced with extra material to produce the desired bulky knot.

7 A suiting
'The Prince of Wales check' was favoured by the future Edward VIII. It is a complicated black-and-white check which has grown more discreet with time.

8 A hat
The Balmoral Cap is a flat Scottish cap.

Five American states named after Royalty

1 Virginia
Named for The Virgin Queen, Elizabeth I
2 Georgia
Named in honour of George II
3 New York
After the Duke of York, brother of Charles II, to whom the King gave proprietary rights in 1665.
4 North and South Carolina
Called successively in honour of Charles I and Charles II.
5 Maryland
Given as a compliment to Queen Henrietta Maria, wife of Charles I.

Six pub names with Royal associations

1 The Rising Sun:
The Arms of King Edward III
2 The Swan and Antelope:
The Arms of King Henry IV
3 The Royal Oak:
The oak tree in which King Charles II hid from Cromwell's men.
4 The White Hart:
The Arms of King Richard II
5 The Golden Lion:
The Arms of King Henry I
6 The Blue Boar:
'The Boar' was the nickname of King Richard III, and was a popular pub name in his day. After the Battle of Bosworth, publicans switched their allegiance and retitled their pubs 'The Blue Boar'.

1 Norman and Ruby Gordon
Used by Princess Margaret and Lord Snowdon during their courtship for booking theatre tickets.

2 Miss Buckingham
The name under which Princess Diana appeared in the appointment book of Bellville Sassoon, her dressmaker, during her pre-wedding days.

3 Ralph Robinson
Nom de plume of King George III when he contributed an article to *Annals of Agriculture* in 1787.

4 Mr James and Janet
Code names agreed between King Edward VIII and Mrs Simpson for speaking to each other on public telephones.

5 Edward Bishop
In 1977 Prince Edward went by this name on a school trip to the Italian Alps.

6 Nurse Kent
The name by which Princess Alexandra was known during her time as a nursing student at the Great Ormond Street Children's Hospital.

7 Mrs Morley and Mrs Freeman
Queen Anne and Sarah, Duchess of Marlborough, used these names in their *billets doux*: the Queen (Mrs Morley) feeling that to be addressed as 'Your Highness' would impede their passionate friendship.

8 Charlie Chester
Prince Charles, who numbers among his titles Earl of Chester, used this soubriquet signing himself into a club where he saw 'A Night at the Opera'.

9 Miss Kirby
Assumed by Princess Alexandra for a private visit to Ireland in 1960.

10 Mr and Mrs Brown
Princess Margaret and Roddy Llewellyn's travelling disguise on a trip to Mustique in 1980.

11 Mr Johnson
King George V's name aboard the battleship *Collingwood*.

12 Countess of Balmoral
During a holiday in France, Queen Victoria used this name in the belief that her presence would go unnoticed, and it succeeded up to a point.

13 Mr and Mrs Butler and Mr and Mrs Kent
Both names used on business trips to Spain and Portugal by
Princess Alexandra and Angus Ogilvy.
14 Charles Renfrew
Lady Diana Spencer told friends she was out with 'Charles
Renfrew' those evenings she spent with the Prince of Wales before
their engagement was announced. An earlier Prince of Wales also
used this subsidiary title. Edward VII travelled unofficially to the
United States using this name.
15 Lady Killarney
Queen Mary used this as her travelling name from Victoria
Station to St Moritz before her marriage to George V.
16 Andrew Cambridge
Prince Andrew's effort to fly to Canada without being noticed on
his way to a term at Lakefield College.
17 William Guelph
The name by which William IV as a midshipman was known to
the other boys on his ships.
18 Mr and Mrs Hardy
The Prince and Princess of Wales flew to the Bahamas for a short
holiday in 1981 using this name but their presence did not escape
notice.
19 Countess of Lancaster
Another of Queen Victoria's travelling names.
20 The Duke of Lancaster
Chosen by King Edward VIII to emphasise the private nature of
his Mediterranean holiday with Mrs Simpson in 1936.
21 Lord and Lady Churchill
Prince Albert and Queen Victoria adopted these names as a joke
on their first high-spirited journey through the Highlands.
22 Florizel
The whimsical name by which the young George IV signed all his
letters to an actress, Perdita Robinson, with whom he thought he
was in love.
23 Mr and Mrs Harris
Lord Brownlow and Mrs Simpson, hoping to elude the chaos of
the Abdication's press coverage, pretended to be married for their
journey from Newhaven to Dieppe.
24 Victoria
Nom de guerre adopted by Queen Victoria's grandson, the Duke of
Clarence, for his visits to the notorious Hundred Guineas Club,
which required guests to assume female names.
25 Earl of Baldwin
When a woman tourist asked Prince Philip, who was then a

student at Gordonstoun, to sign her autograph book, he wrote this name and then disappeared up the mast of the boat he was working on before she could call him back.

Three Kings with the most baptismal names

232

1 Edward VIII (1936): *1 Edward, 2 Albert, 3 Christian, 4 George, 5 Andrew, 6 Patrick, 7 David*
2 George V (1910–1936): *1 George, 2 Frederick, 3 Ernest, 4 Albert*
3 George VI (1936–1952): *1 Albert, 2 Frederick, 3 Arthur, 4 George*

Three Queens with the most baptismal names

1 Mary, wife of King George V: *1 Victoria, 2 Mary, 3 Augusta, 4 Louisa, 5 Olga, 6 Pauline, 7 Claudine, 8 Agnes*
2 Alexandra, wife of King Edward VII: *1 Alexandra, 2 Caroline, 3 Mary, 4 Charlotte, 5 Louisa, 6 Julia*
3 Adelaide, wife of King William IV: *1 Adelaide, 2 Louisa, 3 Theresa, 4 Caroline, 5 Amelia*
> NB Prince Albert, the husband of Queen Victoria, had five baptismal names: Francis Albert Augustus Charles Emmanuel.

Ten Royal words and their translations

233

1 Hoosh-Mi
Princess Margaret's childhood word for chopped-up food.
2 The bore hunts
The Duke and Duchess of Windsor's expression for dull parties.
3 My props
The Queen Mother's expression for her clothes.

4 Boy

King Edward VII's word for champagne. He started using it at a picnic in Homburg, where the champagne was being served by a young boy. Anyone waiting more would shout 'Boy!'. The King noticed a girl had nothing in her glass and asked her what she would like to drink. 'I'll have some Boy like everyone else,' she replied. 'And I'll have some Boy too', said the King. The expression caught on, and for some time enjoyed a vogue in smart circles.

5 Fundungus

Prince Philip's word for all the artificial trappings of monarchy.

6 The aunt heap

Prince Charles's expression for Kensington Palace. King Edward VIII invented the term.

7 Granny's chips

The Royal Family's term for Queen Mary's brooches, ring and necklace made from the vast Cullinan diamond. The brooch alone has one 92 carat diamond and another 62 carat diamond.

8 Up the road

The Queen Mother talks of going 'up the road' when she leaves for Buckingham Palace.

9 Windy water

Princess Margaret's childhood expression for Soda Water.

10 My house in Pimlico

King George V's expression for Buckingham Palace.

234 *Eight titles by which members of the Royal Family are known*

1 Deputy Sheriff of Harris County, Texas

Prince Philip was given this promotion in the 1960s.

2 Lord of Man

This is how the Queen should be toasted in the Isle of Man.

3 Soya Hun

This was the name bestowed on Prince Andrew by the Algonquin Indians. It means 'Heir of the Earth'.

4 Duke of Lancaster

Under this masculine title, the Queen owns the Chapel Royal of the Savoy. In this chapel alone, the words of the National Anthem are traditionally altered to: 'God Save our Gracious Queen, Long

Live Our Royal Duke, God Save the Queen.' In Lancashire the loyal toast is 'the Queen, Duke of Lancaster.'

5 His Royal Highness Prince Red Chow
This was the title bestowed on Prince Charles by the Kainai tribes of Alberta when they made him a Red Indian Chieftain.

6 Miss Diana
This was the name by which the children of the Young England kindergarten in Pimlico knew the future Princess of Wales.

7 Number-one-fellah-belong-missus-Queen
The natives of Papua New Guinea who speak Pidgin-English use this mouthful to indicate Prince Philip.

8 The Duke of Rothesay
In Scotland, the heir to the throne is known as The Duke of Rothesay.

Six names of the Duchess of Windsor   235

1 Bessiewallis Warfield
2 Wallis Warfield (she dropped the Bessie, saying it reminded her of cows)
3 Mrs Earl Spencer
4 Mrs Ernest Simpson
5 Mrs Wallis Warfield
6 The Duchess of Windsor

Seven different names of the Duke   236
of Windsor

1 Prince Edward of York
2 Prince Edward of Cornwall and York
3 Duke of Cornwall
4 Edward, Prince of Wales
5 King Edward VIII
6 Prince Edward
7 Duke of Windsor

Nine recurring names associated with Royalty

1 Sharp
(a) Detective Inspector Derek Sharp, assigned to protect Prince Charles
(b) 'Sharp' – Queen Victoria's favourite collie

2 Earl Spencer
(a) The father of Princess Diana
(b) Lieutenant Earl Spencer – the first husband of the Duchess of Windsor

3 William Hamilton
(a) The Scottish MP who is the current Royal Family's most vociferous critic.
(b) The man who, in 1849, was sentenced to seven years' transportation for attempting to assassinate Queen Victoria.

4 Davy Crockett
(a) the young Prince Charles's pet South American love bird
(b) King Edward VIII's favourite pug

5 Peter Townsend
(a) The man Princess Margaret once wished to marry
(b) A pug which once belonged to the Duke and Duchess of Windsor. ('But', the Duchess once told James Pope-Hennessy, 'we gave the Group-Captain away.')

6 Lady Diana Spencer
(a) The Princess of Wales
(b) The young lady who, in 1734, Frederick, Prince of Wales considered marrying but decided against.

7 Caesar
(a) King Edward VII's favourite dog
(b) The Queen's childhood rocking-horse

8 Keppel
(a) William III's catamite
(b) King Edward VII's mistress
(c) Prince Edward's governess

9 Marion Crawford
(a) The Queen and Princess Margaret's governess, writer of *The Little Princesses*
(b) The writer of *'Corleone'*, one of Queen Victoria's favourite romantic novels

1 Fishface
Princess Diana's nickname for Prince Charles
2 Duck
Kaiser Wilhelm II's nickname for his grandmother, Queen Victoria
3 Fog
Prince Charles's nickname for Mark Phillips ('Thick and wet')
4 That She-devil
King George IV's nickname for his wife, Queen Caroline
5 Lilibet
The Royal Family's nickname for the Queen
6 The Firm
King George VI's nickname for his family
7 Grandpapa England
The Queen's nickname for her grandfather, King George V
8 The Flanders Mare
King Henry VIII's nickname for his fourth wife, Anne of Cleves. He also knew her as 'The Dutch Cow'.
9 Charley's Aunt
The nickname Princess Margaret gave herself after the birth of Prince Charles.
10 The Monster of Glamis
King Edward VIII's nickname for the Queen Mother. He also called her 'The Dowdy Duchess' and 'That Fat Scotch Cook'.
11 Toots, Gawks and Snipey
Nicknames given to themselves by King Edward VII's daughters Princesses Louise, Victoria and Maud.
12 Uncle Pineapple
The Queen and Princess Margaret's nickname for the late Duke of Gloucester; Queen Victoria's name for William IV.
13 Dickie
The Royal Family's nickname for Lord Mountbatten
14 Pussy
Her family's nickname for Queen Victoria's eldest daughter, the Princess Royal.
15 The Bicycle Kings
The British Royal Family's nickname for the Scandinavian Royal Families
16 Gan-Gan
The Queen's nickname for her grandmother, Queen Mary. Also

King Edward VIII's name for *his* grandmother, Queen Victoria.

17 Drina

Her family's nickname for Queen Victoria as a child: a diminutive of her first Christian name, Alexandrina.

18 Collars and Cuffs

His family's nickname for King George V's older brother, the Duke of Clarence. His peculiarly long neck obliged him to wear a very high starched collar, and he always wore his cuffs too long.

19 Our Val

The Royal Family's nickname for Princess Michael of Kent

20 The Foreman

The Royal Family's nickname for King George VI

21 The Fiend

George IV's nickname for his wife, Queen Caroline

22 Uncle King

Queen Victoria's nickname as a child, for George IV

23 Philip In His Glory

His European relations' nickname for Prince Philip

24 Piggyface

The Royal Family's nickname for the Queen when she is in a bad mood.

'The Foreman'

Eight names applied to members of the Royal Family by their schoolmates

1 Flop
Prince Philip at Cheam
2 Bat Lugs
King George VI at Dartmouth (like his grandson, he had large ears).
3 Pragger-Wagger
King Edward VIII at Magdalene College, Cambridge
4 Pommy Bastard
Prince Charles at Timbertops, Australia
5 Sardine
King Edward VIII at Dartmouth
6 The Sniggerer
Prince Andrew at Gordonstoun
7 Jaws
Prince Edward at Gordonstoun (he wore braces on his teeth)
8 Earl
Another name for Prince Edward at Gordonstoun (from the initials of his Christian names Edward Antony Richard Louis).

Fifteen nicknames for Royal servants

1 Crawfie
Marion Crawford, the Governess to the Queen and Princess Margaret
2 Mispy
Catherine Peebles, the Governess to Prince Charles
3 Bambi
Catherine Peebles, when she was Governess to the Kent children
4 Mambo
Mabel Anderson, the Nanny to the Royal Family
5 Golly
The Queen and Princess Margaret's name, when young, for their cook, Mrs MacDonald
6 Water
Queen Elizabeth I's name for Sir Walter Raleigh

7 The Fuehrer

The Queen Mother's name for her horse trainer, the late Peter Cazalet

8 Alla

Clara Cooper Knight, the Queen's nurse

9 Mider

Mr Hansell, tutor to King George VI and King Edward VIII

10 Fruity

Major David Metcalfe, equerry to King Edward VIII

11 Oddjob

Cambridge students' name for Prince Charles's detective at Cambridge

12 Goosey

Mabel Lander, the music teacher to the Queen and Princess Margaret

13 Bobo

Margaret Macdonald, the Queen's Dresser

14 Cousin Halifax

The imaginary relation Princess Margaret used to blame for all her wrongdoings

15 Gruffenough

The Queen and Princess Margaret's name, when young, for Marion Crawford, when cross.

241 Eighteen commoners' nicknames for members of the Royal Family

1 Peter Pan

Ernest Simpson's name for King Edward VIII

2 Andy Pandy

The Royal Household's name for Prince Andrew when he was young

3 Randy Andy

The popular press's nickname for Prince Andrew now he is older.

4 The Faery

Disraeli's name for Queen Victoria

5 Old Rowley

His Court's name for King Charles II (after a remarkably procreative Royal stallion)

6 Carlo

Welsh demonstrators' nickname for Prince Charles at the time of his Investiture. 'Carlo' is Welsh for 'dog'.

7 Farmer George

The popular name for King George III

8 King Edward the Eighth and Mrs Simpson the Seven-Eighths

The Court's nickname for them before the Abdication

9 Mrs Brown

The radical press's name for Queen Victoria. It referred to her intimacy with her brawny servant, John Brown.

10 Tum-Tum

His friends' nickname for King Edward VII

11 Fum the Fourth

Lord Byron's nickname for King George IV in 'Don Juan'

12 The She-Wolf of France

The popular name for Queen Isabella, wife of Edward II. She later had him murdered.

13 The Baker

The nickname given to King Edward VIII by the household staff of his mistress, Mrs Freda Dudley Ward. Like the baker, the King called every morning.

14 Guelpho the Gay

The Court's name for King Edward VII as a young man

15 Charles the Third

Nell Gwynne's nickname for King Charles II. Her previous lovers had been Charles, Lord Buckhurst and Charles Hart.

16 Acid Drops

Royal servants' codename for the Queen and Prince Philip when they have quarrelled or are in dangerously bad moods.

17 Sprat and Herring

King George V and his brother the Duke of Clarence were known to their fellows on the Britannia as boys by these names.

18 Mrs Fagin

The Maharajah of Punjab's name for Queen Victoria. He resented her possession of the Koh-i-Noor diamond.

Nine things with Royal names 242

1 A breed of dog

The King Charles Spaniel

2 A rude gesture

If you put your thumb to your nose with your fingers spread out you are making a Queen Anne's Fan.

3 A strip show

After Prince Andrew had visited a strip act in Trader Jon's, Florida, in 1980, the stripper who had entertained him, a Vietnamese lady called Linda Lynn, renamed her act, 'The Randy Andy Eye Popper'.

4 Rebellious youths

The Teddy Boys of the 1950s were so named for aping the Edwardian style of dress. The Edwardian Age was itself named after King Edward VII. It is doubtful whether the King would have countenanced the antics of his namesakes.

5 A bodice

The Spencer bodice had its origins in 'The Spencer' an early type of waistcoat pioneered by George, 2nd Earl Spencer in the eighteenth century.

6 A cow

Queen Victoria was so horrified at the sight of her daughter suckling her own child that she had a cow in the Royal dairies named 'Princess Alice'.

7 A watch chain

An 'Albert' in Victorian times was a watch-chain which stretched across the waistcoat from one pocket to the other: it was named after the Prince Consort, who popularized the style in the 1850s.

8 A cake

The Battenberg cake when sliced is seen to be composed of sponge in quarters of different colours.

9 Two puddings

Apple Charlotte and Charlotte Russe are named after the wife of King George III, Queen Charlotte. They are puddings, enclosed in sponge flavoured with apple and coffee respectively.

243 *Eight unexpected middle names of the Royal Family*

1 Olga, Christabel:
   Princess Alexandra
2 Louise:
   Princess Anne
3 Angela:
   The Queen Mother
4 Christian:
   Prince Andrew

5 Antony, Louis:
Prince Edward
6 Ophelia:
Lady Gabriella Windsor
7 Franklin:
Prince Michael of Kent (after President Roosevelt, his godfather)
8 Pauline, Claudine, Agnes:
Queen Mary

Private Eye's *nicknames for the* Royal Family

1 Brenda: The Queen
2 Yvonne: Princess Margaret
3 Brian: Prince of Wales
4 Keith: Prince Philip
5 Erica: Princess Diana

Five names of Prince Philip

1 Philippos
The name in which his father registered his birth.
2 Prince Philip of Greece
Listed in the *Almanach de Gotha* as sixth in line to the Greek throne.
3 Lieutenant Philip Mountbatten, RN
The name he took upon naturalization as a British subject in 1947.
4 Baron Greenwich, Earl of Merioneth and Duke of Edinburgh
Created by King George VI the day before his wedding to the Queen.
5 Prince Philip
The Queen created her husband a Prince after 10 years of marriage on 22 February 1957 in recognition of his work in the previous decade.

1 **1, 2, 3** The numbers adopted by King George VI, the Queen and Princess Margaret during practice sessions of their own firefighting unit during the war.

2 **230873** The Queen's ATS number at Aldershot during the war.

3 **102 and 89** Prince Charles's school numbers at Hill House and at Cheam.

4 **1** Prince Philip's passport number. (He lists his profession as 'Prince of the Royal Household'.)

5 **10, 2 and double 3** The numbers scored by Princess Diana with three darts at her first public throwing of darts in The John Boste Youth Club, Newcastle, March 1982.

6 **7¼** The size of Princess Diana's head, revealed when she visited James Lock and Co for a fitting for a riding hat soon after her honeymoon. 'It may be large, but there's not much in it', she joked.

247   *Seven decorations worn with the Queen's full uniform at her Birthday Parade*

1 The Imperial Order of the Crown of India
2 Defence Medal
3 War Medal 1939–45
4 Jubilee Medal of King George V
5 Coronation Medal of King George VI
6 The Canadian Forces Decoration (Silver)
7 The Riband and Star of the Order of the Garter

248   *Seven official appointments to the Court of King George III*

1 The Keeper of the Fire Buckets
2 The Keeper of the Orchard Gate
3 The Keeper of the Ice House
4 The Distiller of Milk Water

5 The Carrier of His Majesty's Despatches Between His Court
or Residence and the Post Office
6 The Keeper of the Lions, Lionesses and Leopards in the Tower
7 The Embellisher of Letters to the Eastern Princes

Eight old-fashioned posts that exist   *249*
in the Queen's Household

1 Hereditary Grand Falconer
2 Grand Almoner
3 Royal Bargemaster
4 Master of the Queen's Music
5 The Queen's Raven Master
6 The Clerk of the Closet
7 Keeper of the Queen's Swans
8 The Queen's Racing Pigeon Manager

Mr Len Rush, The Queen's Racing Pigeon Manager

250 *Five lucky holders of warrants from King Edward VIII*

1 An Optician in Calcutta
2 A Photographer in Southsea
3 A Chemist in Sunningdale
4 A Cartage Contractor in Portsmouth
5 A Cigarette Maker in Malta

251 *Five school prizes awarded to Princess Diana*

1 The Legatt Cup for Helpfulness
2 The Palmer Cup for Pets' Corner
  (won with the aid of her guinea-pig, Peanuts)
3 The Parker Cup for Swimming
4 The West Heath Dancing Cup
5 The Miss Clark Lawrence Award for Service to the School
  ('We don't give this every year. It's presented only to
  outstanding people', commented her Headmistress, Miss
  Rudge.)

252 *Forty-two firms holding warrants of appointment to the Queen*

1 James Allan & Son, Ltd: *Boot and Shoemakers*
2 Hardy Amies, London: *Dressmakers*
3 William Anderson & Sons, Edinburgh: *Tailors and Kiltmakers*
4 Ashton & Mitchell, London: *Theatre Ticket Agents*
5 Barrow Hepburn, London: *Manufacturers of Royal Maundy Purses*
6 Calman Links, London: *Furriers*
7 Cartier, London: *Jewellers and Goldsmiths*
8 J & J Cash, Coventry: *Manufacturers of Woven Name Tapes*
9 William C. Cassie, Aberdeen: *Piano Tuner*
10 Frederick J Chandler, Marlborough: *Saddlers*
11 Harold Cox, Windsor: *Jeweller*

12 Cyclax, London: *Suppliers of Beauty Preparations*
13 Deimel Fabric Co., London: *Manufacturers of Dr Deimel Garments*
14 Emile et Cie, London: *Hairdressers*
15 Gallyon & Sons, King's Lynn: *Cartridge Makers*
16 General Trading Company, London: *Suppliers of Fancy Goods*
17 D. Gilbert & Son, Newmarket: *Suppliers of Racing Colours*
18 Hamley Brothers, London: *Toymakers*
19 Harrison & Wilson, King's Lynn: *Saddlers*
20 Hatchard's, London: *Booksellers*
21 Norman Hartnell, London: *Dressmakers*
22 Henderson's, Ballater: *Outfitters*
23 M L Ironside, Ballater: *Chemist*
24 Herbert Johnson, London: *Hatters*
25 S Launer & Co., London: *Suppliers of Handbags*
26 R G Lawrie, Glasgow: *Bagpipe Makers*
27 Lilliman & Cox, London: *Dry Cleaners*
28 Lillywhites, London: *Outfitters*
29 S Lock, London: *Embroiderers*
30 Simone Mirman, London: *Milliner*
31 C Patman, Cambridge: *Clock Repairer*
32 C J Reid, Eton: *Chemists*
33 Rigby & Peller, London: *Corsetiéres*
34 Simpson (Piccadilly), London: *Outfitters*
35 Frank Smythson, London: *Stationers*
36 Spratt's Patent Ltd, Barking: *Suppliers of Dog Foods*
37 A B Stevens, Waltham Cross: *Rose and Carnation Suppliers*
38 Studio Lisa, London and Welwyn: *Photographers*
39 Aage Thaarup, London: *Milliners*
40 R Tyson, Dublin: *Makers of Racing colours*
41 Wartski Jewellers, London: *Jewellers*
42 Bernard Weatherill, London: *Riding Clothes Outfitters*

Four people who have refused Honours from the Queen   253

1 Evelyn Waugh
Offered a CBE, Evelyn Waugh wrote back saying that he would prefer to wait until he won his spurs.
2 Graham Greene
On receiving a letter offering him a knighthood, Graham Greene

passed it to his secretary, asking her to 'refuse in the normal way'. He later became the Companion of Honour as it is personally bestowed by the Queen.

3 Winston Churchill

At dinner in 1955, the Queen turned to Sir Winston Churchill and asked, 'Would you like a Dukedom or anything like that?' He refused.

4 Harold Macmillan

Harold Macmillan turned down an Earldom and the Order of the Garter.

254 *Twenty-two awards and distinctions earned by members of the Royal Family*

1 The under-twelves high jump medal

Won by Prince Philip at Cheam with his effort of 3 feet 10 inches.

2 Farmyard race rosette

At a gymkhana in Barbados when he was 17, George VI won the race in which mounted competitors had to imitate a farmyard animal on completing the course. He won the prize with a donkey imitation.

3 The King's dirk

Won by Prince Philip as the best all-round cadet in his term at Dartmouth.

4 Child making the most effort citation

Given to Prince Edward at his day school for his level best at a school concert.

5 Half-Blue at Cambridge

Prince Charles won his 'Half-Blue' for Polo at Cambridge in 1969.

6 The Howard-Eardley Crochett Prize for best cadet

A book token worth £2 which Prince Philip won at Dartmouth. He spent it on Liddell-Hart's *The Defence of Britain*.

7 Captain of the hockey team

A distinction earned by Princess Diana at West Heath school

8 Small ponies private turn-out rosette

Princess Alexandra won with her white pony 'Tony' when she was eight.

9 School Guardian
Gordonstoun's way of saying 'Head Boy'. Prince Charles had this distinction in his last year at school, as had his father before him.
10 *Country Life* crossword competition
The 3 guinea prize has been won several times by Princess Margaret
11 A hole-in-one
Made in Brazil by King Edward VIII in 1921
12 A biscuit-eating competition
Won in Paris by Prince Philip when he was seven
13 A tennis trophy
King George VI won the RAF Doubles at Wimbledon in 1926 partnered by Cmdr Louis Grieg.
14 The Newmarket Plate
Won by Charles II on his own horse, in 1671 and 1674
15 Life-saving certificate
Earned by both the Queen and Princess Margaret when they were young
16 Heavy Goods Vehicle licence
Gained by Princess Anne
17 First prize for the best pig
King Edward VII bred many prize-winning pigs at Sandringham

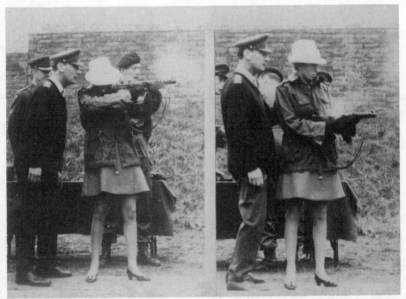

Princess Anne fires a Sterling sub-machine gun with considerable accuracy

18 Eleven bullseyes

Scored by Princess Anne, firing 20 rounds of ammunition from a submachine gun at her hip when visiting an army base

19 A picnic set of plastic forks and spoons

Won by Princess Diana in a tombola at the Dick Sheppard Comprehensive School at Tulse Hill in January 1982 on three 25p tickets. Prince Charles won nothing. In a subsequent raffle, Princess Diana failed to win a suede coat.

20 First prize in the Fur and Feather Show

Awarded to Princess Diana's guinea-pig 'Peanuts' at Sandringham in 1967

21 Three Derby wins and the Grand National

Won by King Edward VII. The first Derby triumph was with the King's famous horse, *Persimmon*, in 1896. He won the Derby with Minoru in 1909. But 1900 was his best racing year – his horse Diamond Jubilee won five classic races – he took the Two Thousand Guineas, the Newmarket Stakes, the Eclipse Stakes, the Derby and the St Leger. This series of wins was unprecedented in racing history.

22 The European Horse Trials

Won by Princess Anne at Burleigh in 1971

255   *Twenty-three holders of the Order of Merit*

Founded by King Edward VII in 1902, The Order of Merit is one of the most cherished medals as it is in the Monarch's own gift.

1 Sir Frank Macfarlane Burnet
2 Henry Moore
3 Dorothy Hodgkin
4 Sir William Walton
5 Ben Nicholson
6 Lord Zuckerman
7 Lord Penney
8 Dame Veronica Wedgwood
9 Sir Isaiah Berlin

10 Sir George Edwards
11 Sir Alan Hodgkin
12 Paul Dirac
13 Harold Macmillan
14 Lord Hinton
15 Lord Clark
16 Sir Ronald Syme
17 Lord Todd
18 Lord Franks
19 Sir Frederick Ashton
20 J B Priestley
21 Lord Olivier
22 Sir Peter Medawar
23 Group Captain Leonard Cheshire

Five superlatives bestowed on Royalty

1 'Hooligan of the Year'
Awarded to Prince Charles in 1978 by the RSPCA after he had hunted boar in Liechtenstein.

2 'Male personality who did most to promote hairstyles in 1973'
Awarded to Mark Phillips by the Birmingham Branch of the National Hairdressers Federation. He beat Jeremy Thorpe and Terry Wogan.

3 'Best Dictator for Britain'
Awarded to Prince Philip, topping a *Daily Telegraph* public opinion poll in 1969. He beat Enoch Powell, Harold Wilson and David Frost.

4 'Chosen by God'
Awarded to the Queen, after a public opinion poll discovered that 30 per cent of Britons believed her to be chosen by God to reign.

5 'Best Dressed Man of the Year'
Awarded to Prince Charles in March 1954, when he was five years old, by the *Tailor and Cutter*.

Nine disastrous poems about Royalty: the worst passages

1 *They love her for her wisdom and her pride*
  Her friendship and her quiet majesty.
  And soon the streets of Britain will be thronged
  With crowds rejoicing in her Jubilee.
    Mary Wilson, 'The Opening of Parliament', 1977

2 *Along the wire the electric message came:*
  He is no better, he is just the same.
    Alfred Austin on King Edward VII's spell of typhoid,
    1871

3 *In cities, multitudinous voices swell*
  We have a King who loves His subjects well,
  We have a Queen, and never was more fair;
  Long may they reign and ever grow more dear!'
    Sir Osbert Sitwell, 'Ode for the Coronation of Their
    Majesties, 12 May 1937'

4 *'To such a Crown all broken spirits turn:*
  And we, who see this young face passing by,
  See her as symbol of a Power Etern,
  And pray that Heaven will bless her till she die.'
    John Masefield, 'On the Wedding of Princess Elizabeth
    and Philip'

5 *'Bride of the heir of the kings of the sea –*
  O joy to the people and joy to the throne,
  Come to us, love us and make us your own:
  For Saxon or Dane or Norman we,
  Teuton or Celt, or whatever we be,
  We are each all Dane in our welcome of thee, Alexandra!
    Alfred, Lord Tennyson, 'A Welcome to Alexandra',
    1863

6 *. . . You, sir, inherit*
  A weight of history in a changing world,
  Its treasured wisdom and its true
  Aspirings the best birthday gift for you.
    C Day-Lewis 'For the Investiture', 1969

7 *O'er the vast deep, great Monarch, dart thine eyes,*
  A watery prospect bounded by the skies
    John Tickell, 'On the Arrival of King George I'

8 *Wherever you are*
Wherever you be
Please take your hand
Off the Princess's knee
> Recited by Spike Milligan in a Soho Jazz Club, 1965, to Peter Sellers, who was escorting Princess Margaret at the time

9 *Thy choicest gifts in store*
On her be pleased to pour,
Long may she reign.
May she defend our laws
And ever give us cause
To sing with heart and voice
God Save Our Queen.
> The third verse of 'God Save the Queen' anonymously composed in 1743

Three terrible passages from the Royal poems of William McGonagall 258

1 *Most August! Empress of India, and of Great Britain the Queen,*
I most humbly beg your pardon, hoping you will not think it mean,
That a poor poet that lives in Dundee
Would be so presumptuous to write unto thee.
> From 'A Requisition to the Queen', 1877

2 *And as this is her first Jubilee Year*
And will be her last, I rather fear
> From 'An Ode to the Queen on her Jubilee year'

3 *The Queen, from first to last, was the crowning glory of the ceremony*
Her beauty, her grace, her exquisite dress was lovely to see,
And her train of crimson and gold was borne by eight gentlemen
Which certainly was a grand honour conferred upon them.
> From his Coronation poem, 1902 (the last he ever wrote)

217

Three 'D's' of the Queen Mother

In a speech to a school, the Queen Mother recommended three qualities worthy of cultivation:

1. Discernment: The power to judge what needs doing
2. Decision: to act
3. Designing: a plan of action

'One of those extraordinarily rare people . . .'

260 Four words of advice: how to be Royal

1 Prince Albert's advice (issued to all those attendant to Edward VII)

'A prince should never say a harsh or a rude word to anybody, nor indulge in satirical or bantering expressions. . . . These remarks apply, of course, in a still stronger degree to anything approaching to a practical joke, which should never be permitted.'

2 George V's advice (to Edward VIII)

'Never refuse an invitation to take the weight off your feet, and seize every opportunity you can to relieve yourself'.

218

3 The Queen's advice (to Princess Margaret, when they were both children)

'If you see someone with a funny hat you must not point at it and laugh, and you must not be in too much of a hurry to get through the crowds to the tea table. That's not polite either.'

4 Prince Charles's advice

'I've learnt the way a monkey learnt, by watching its parents.'

Five comments of Prince Charles on members of his Family 261

1 His mother

'She is just a marvellous person and a wonderful mother.'

2 His grandmother, the Queen Mother

'One of those extraordinarily rare people whose touch can turn everything to gold.'

3 His 'Honorary Grandfather', Lord Mountbatten

'I admire him, I think almost more than anybody else. He's a very great man.' 'I adored him – and miss him so dreadfully now.'

4 His brother, Prince Andrew

'Ah, the one with the Robert Redford looks.'

5 His father, Prince Philip

'He lets one get on with what you want to do. He gives one the opportunity to do these things. He says, "We think it might be an idea; what do you think?" In that sense, he's been an influence – but a moderating influence and an influence of great wisdom.'

Ten Royal responses to their public images 262

1 Bafflement

'We suit each other admirably and I thank God every day that he should have brought us together . . . and people said I only married you out of sympathy and pity. That shows how little the world knows what it is talking about.' Letter from King George V to Queen Mary.

2 Acceptance

The Duchess of Windsor once asked a friend in common of hers and the Royal Family: 'Why do the King and Queen treat us as they do?' The friend replied, 'The public would not allow them to behave in any other way.' The Duchess said, 'Yes, I quite understand.' Later, the friend mentioned the incident and her explanation to the King. George VI said, 'Yes, that's right.'

3 Defensiveness

'The art world thinks of me as an uncultured polo-playing clot.' Prince Philip.

4 Satisfaction

'I'm so blonde and tall I walk into a room like an ostrich and no one can miss me.' Princess Michael of Kent.

5 Indifference

'I daresay that I could improve my image in some circles by growing my hair to a more fashionable length, being seen at the Playboy Club at frequent intervals, and squeezing into tight clothes.' Prince Charles.

6 Confusion

On his own image in 1963, Prince Philip said: 'I know I'm rude, but it's fun.' He later confessed: 'There's an awful lot of things, that if I were to re-read them now, I'd say to myself: "Good God, I wish I hadn't said that".'

7 Adaptation

In response to strong anti-German feeling, King George V in July 1917 ordered his family to relinquish all their German names and titles and to adopt British surnames. A great many Highnesses and Serene Highnesses were no more; Tecks became Cambridges, Battenbergs were turned into Mountbattens, and the Royal Family were simplified to Windsor instead of Saxe-Coburg-Gotha.

8 Exhibitionism

When James I, who hated being surrounded by the public, was told that they only wanted to see him he replied, 'God's wounds! I will pull down my breeches and they shall also see my arse!'

9 Gratification

After his Silver Jubilee parade in 1935, King George V, surprised by the welcome he had been given, said, 'I had no idea they felt like that about me. I'm beginning to think they must really like me for myself.'

10 Encouragement

'Sometimes I drive with the children in the park', wrote Queen Mary, 'and I am really quite touched at the nice reception we get from all classes, they all look so pleased to see one and crowd round the carriage. It is a great encouragement when I think of all that lies before us.'

Four aspects of life on which Royalty has been ignorant

1 Welsh history

During the weeks of clamour that preceded his Investiture in 1969, Prince Charles approached a Welsh Nationalist demonstrator, pointed to his banner, and asked, 'Who is Llewelyn?' The demonstrator pointed out to the Prince that Llewelyn was the last Welsh Prince of Wales.

2 Agriculture

When Queen Mary first went to Badminton in the war years, she looked at a field of hay in amazement and asked what it was. 'Oh, *that's* what hay looks like!' she gasped. She was then aged seventy-two.

3 Golf

Though King Edward VII was very fond of golf, his wife, Queen Alexandra, often mistook it for hockey. She thought that you had to prevent your opponent from putting his ball into the hole, and that the first into the hole was the winner. This meant that she would run between shots and then, when her opponent's ball was approaching the hole, she would try to hit it off course.

4 Sapphism

When an anti-homosexuality Bill was brought for her to sign, Queen Victoria refused to believe in the existence of such a thing as lesbianism. She struck out all references to sex between women in the Bill, and to this day female homosexuality cannot be prosecuted.

Five Pieces of advice to Royalty

1 Katherine Roger's advice to the Duchess of Windsor

'All you need to know is one French phrase – 'Je n'entends pas' – 'I don't understand.'

2 The Shah of Persia's advice to King Edward VII

'You'll have to have his head off when you come to the Throne.' (The Shah had considered the Duke of Sutherland, to whom he had been introduced, to be 'too grand for a subject'. His advice was not taken.)

3 A policeman's advice to Princess Diana

'Please lock up in future or your vehicle may be stolen.' (In a note left on the windscreen of her red Mini Metro, January 1981.)

4 Princess Margaret's advice to the Queen

'You look after your Empire and I'll look after my life.' (After the Queen had said, 'Behave yourself' when Princess Margaret motioned towards a group of good-looking sailors in Africa, 1947.)

5 The Government of Ghana's advice to the Queen

Before the birth of Prince Andrew, the newspaper of the Ghana Government, the *Ghana Times*, advised the Queen to christen her child 'Amma Ghana' if it was a girl and 'Kwame Ghana' if it was a boy.

265 Six reactions of sovereigns on hearing of their Accession to the Throne

1 *'This is the Lord's doing and it is marvellous in our eyes'*
   Queen Elizabeth I, 1558
2 *'The Crown is not my right, and pleaseth me not. The Lady Mary is the rightful heir.'*
   Lady Jane Grey, bursting into tears, 1554
3 *'It is a fine day'*
   Queen Anne in 1702, looking out of the window
4 *'Dat is vun beeg lie!'*
   King George II, 1727
5 *'I shall go back to bed. I have never slept with a Queen before'*
   King William IV, 1830
6 *'I will be good'*
   Queen Victoria, 1837

266 Thirteen Kings and Queens who were not crowned

1 **Matilda**, daughter of King Henry I, was proclaimed 'Lady of the English' on 7 April 1141, but never crowned.
2 **Margaret of France**, second wife of King Edward I, to whom she was married on 8 or 10 September 1299.

222

3 **King Edward V**, reigned from April to June 1483 and was deposed on 25 June 1483.

4 **Jane Seymour**, 3rd wife of King Henry VIII. (Her coronation was postponed because of the plague and she died in childbirth before it could take place.)

5 **Anne of Cleves**, 4th wife of King Henry VIII (No arrangement was ever made for the coronation of this Queen.)

6 **Catherine Howard**, 5th wife of King Henry VIII. (No arrangement was ever made for the coronation of this Queen.)

7 **Catherine Parr**, 6th wife of King Henry VIII. (No arrangement was ever made for the coronation of this Queen.)

8 **Lady Jane Dudley** (*née* Grey) was proclaimed Queen on 10 July 1553 and deposed on 19 July of same year.

9 **Henrietta Maria of France**, wife of King Charles I, was never crowned because of the religious difficulties involved.

10 **Catherine of Braganza**, wife of King Charles II, was never crowned for the same reason.

11 **Sophia Dorothea**, wife of King George I, was never acknowledged as Queen and had in fact been divorced from him in Germany before his accession to the throne.

12 **Caroline of Brunswick**, wife of King George IV, was forcibly excluded from her husband's coronation and denied the right to be crowned separately.

13 **King Edward VIII** abdicated in December 1936, his coronation having been arranged to take place the following May.

The five longest Reigns

1 Queen Victoria *63 years 7 months from 1837 to 1901*
2 King George III *59 years 3 months from 1760 to 1820*
3 King Henry III *56 years 1 month from 1216 to 1272*
4 King Edward III *49 years 9 months from 1327 to 1377*
5 Queen Elizabeth I *44 years 4 months from 1558 to 1603*

The five shortest Reigns

1 Lady Jane Grey *9 days in 1553*
2 King Edward V *77 days in 1483*
3 King Edward VIII *326 days in 1936*
4 King Richard III *2 years, 2 months from 1483–5*
5 King James II *3 years, 10 months from 1685–8*

Ten Institutions founded by Royalty

1 The Christian Sisterhood of Martha and Mary

Founded by Prince Philip's mother, Princess Andrew, in 1949. She became its life President, and dressed in its grey habit until her death in Buckingham Palace in 1969 at the age of 84.

2 Newmarket racecourse

Founded in 1634 by King Charles I

3 Ascot racecourse

Founded in 1711 by Queen Anne

4 The Royal Society

Founded for the pursuit of science by King Charles I in 1660

5 The Royal Mail

Founded by King Charles I in 1635. In those days, the person who received the letter had to pay for it.

6 The Marlborough Club

When an Extraordinary General Meeting of White's club threw out a motion proposed by King Edward VII that smoking, which was prohibited in certain places, should in future be allowed, the King exclaimed, 'Very well, I will found a club of my own in which I can smoke when and where it pleases me.' He then founded the Marlborough Club.

7 Eton College

Founded by King Henry VI in 1440

8 Greenwich Observatory

Founded by King Charles II in 1675

9 The Theatre Royal, Drury Lane

Founded by King Charles II in 1663

10 Trinity College, Cambridge

Founded by King Henry VIII in 1546

Seven annual ceremonies which still continue

1 The Trial of the Pyx
Since Saxon times, each year the Queen's Remembrancer and Senior Master of the Supreme Court presides over a jury of goldsmiths in Goldsmiths Hall to make certain that the coins issued by the Royal Mint are of the correct size and weight.

2 The search of Westminster
Since the Gunpowder Plot, the cellars, corridors and galleries of Westminster are searched before the Opening of Parliament with lanterns by the Yeomen of the Guard (recently assisted by the police, with torches and sniffing dogs).

3 Swan upping
Each year, the Dyers and Vintners companies place marks on swans, so that the Queen, who traditionally owns all mute swans that are unmarked, cannot lay claim to them.

4 Royal Maundy
Dating from the time of King Edward I, every Maundy Thursday the Queen distributes specially minted silver coins to twice as many elderly people as the number of her age. This tradition was abandoned by King James II but revived by King George V in 1932.

5 The presentation of leeks
On St David's Day, March 1, a member of the Royal Family presents leeks to the Welsh Guards

6 The offering at Epiphany
Each year, on the Feast of the Epiphany, January 6, two of the Queen's Gentlemen Ushers make an offering of gold, frankincense and myrrh on the Queen's behalf at a communion service in the Chapel Royal at St James' Palace. Afterwards, £30 is deposited in the Alms dish for the poor of the parish. The last monarch to attend this ceremony in person was King George III.

7 Stopping at Temple Bar
Whenever the Queen makes a ceremonial visit to the City, she stops at Temple Bar to seek permission of the Lord Mayor to enter the environs.

Date	Person Crowned	Place of Coronation	Officiant
25 Dec. 1066	William I the Conqueror	Westminster Abbey	Aldred, Archbishop of York
11 May 1068	Matilda of Flanders (wife of William I)	Westminster Abbey	
26 Sept. 1087	William II Rufus	Winchester Cathedral	Lanfranc, Archbishop of Canterbury
6 Aug. 1100	Henry I	Westminster Abbey	Maurice, Bishop of London
11 Nov. 1100 (also wedding day)	Matilda of Scotland (1st wife of Henry I)	Westminster Abbey	Anselm, Archbishop of Canterbury
3 Feb. 1121	Adeliza of Louvain (2nd wife of Henry I)	Westminster Abbey	Ralph d'Escures, Archbishop of Canterbury
26 Dec. 1135	Stephen	Westminster Abbey	William de Corbeil, Archbishop of Canterbury
22 March 1136	Matilda of Boulogne (wife of Stephen)	Westminster Abbey	William de Corbeil, Archbishop of Canterbury
25 Dec. 1141	Stephen is said to have been re-crowned)		
19 Dec. 1154	Henry II and Eleanor of Aquitaine	Westminster Abbey	Theobald, Archbishop of Canterbury
14 June 1170	Henry 'the Young King' (son and heir of Henry II)	Westminster Abbey	Roger of Pont l'Eveque, Archbishop of Canterbury
27 Aug. 1172	Henry 'the Young King' (again) and Margaret of France (his wife)	Winchester Cathedral	Rotrou, Archbishop of Rouen
3 Sept. 1189	Richard I	Westminster Abbey	Baldwin, Archbishop of Canterbury
12 May 1191 (also wedding day)	Berengaria of Navarre (wife of Richard I)	Chapel of St George, Lemesos, Cyprus	John FitzLuke, Bishop of Evreux
27 May 1199	John	Westminster Abbey	Hubert Walter, Archbishop of Canterbury
8 Oct. 1200	Isabella of Angoulême (wife of John)	Westminster Abbey	Hubert Walter, Archbishop of Canterbury
28 Oct. 1216	Henry III	Gloucester Cathedral	Peter des Roches, Bishop of

17 May 1220	Henry III (again)	Westminster Abbey	Stephen Langton, Archbishop of Canterbury
20 Jan. 1236	Eleanor of Provence (wife of Henry III)	Westminster Abbey	Edmund Rich, Archbishop of Canterbury
19 Aug. 1274	Edward I and Eleanor of Castile	Westminster Abbey	Edward Kilwardby, Archbishop of Canterbury
24 Feb. 1308	Edward II and Isabelle of France	Westminster Abbey	Henry Merewell (alias Woodlock), Bishop of Winchester
2 Feb. 1327	Edward III	Westminster Abbey	Walter Reynolds, Archbishop of Canterbury
20 Feb. 1328	Philippa of Hainault (wife of Edward III)	Westminster Abbey	Simon Meopham, Archbishop of Canterbury
16 July 1377	Richard II	Westminster Abbey	Simon Sudbury, Archbishop of Canterbury
22 Jan. 1382	Anne of Bohemia (1st wife of Richard II)	Westminster Abbey	William Courtenay, Archbishop of Canterbury
8 Jan. 1397	Isabelle of France (2nd wife of Richard II)	Westminster Abbey	Thomas Arundel, Archbishop of Canterbury
13 Oct. 1399	Henry IV	Westminster Abbey	Thomas Arundel, Archbishop of Canterbury
26 Feb. 1403	Joan of Navarre (2nd wife of Henry IV)	Westminster Abbey	Thomas Arundel, Archbishop of Canterbury
9 April 1413	Henry V	Westminster Abbey	Thomas Arundel, Archbishop of Canterbury
24 Feb. 1421	Catherine of France (wife of Henry V)	Westminster Abbey	Henry Chichele, Archbishop of Canterbury
6 Nov. 1429	Henry VI	Westminster Abbey	Henry Chichele, Archbishop of Canterbury
(17 Dec. 1431	Henry VI (as King of France)	Nôtre Dame, Paris	Cardinal Beaufort
30 May 1445	Margaret of Anjou (wife of Henry VI)	Westminster Abbey	John Stafford, Archbishop of Canterbury
29 June 1461	Edward IV	Westminster Abbey	Cardinal Bourchier, Archbishop of Canterbury

Date	Person Crowned	Place of Coronation	Officiant
26 May 1465	Elizabeth Woodville (wife of Edward IV)	Westminster Abbey	Cardinal Bourchier, Archbishop of Canterbury
6 July 1483	Richard III and Anne Neville	Westminster Abbey	Cardinal Bourchier, Archbishop of Canterbury
30 Oct. 1485	Henry VII	Westminster Abbey	Cardinal Bourchier, Archbishop of Canterbury
25 Nov. 1487	Elizabeth of York (wife of Henry VII)	Westminster Abbey	John Morton, Archbishop of Canterbury
24 June 1509	Henry VIII and Catherine of Aragon	Westminster Abbey	William Warham, Archbishop of Canterbury
1 June 1533	Anne Boleyn (2nd wife of Henry VIII)	Westminster Abbey	Thomas Cranmer, Archbishop of Canterbury
20 Feb. 1547	Edward VI	Westminster Abbey	Thomas Cranmer, Archbishop of Canterbury
1 Oct. 1553	Mary I	Westminster Abbey	Stephen Gardiner, Bishop of Winchester
15 Jan. 1559	Elizabeth I	Westminster Abbey	Owen Oglethorpe, Bishop of Carlisle
25 July 1603	James I and Anne of Denmark	Westminster Abbey	John Whitgift, Archbishop of Canterbury
2 Feb. 1626	Charles I	Westminster Abbey	George Abbot, Archbishop of Canterbury
(18 June 1633	Charles I (as King of Scots)	Edinburgh	John Spottiswood, Archbishop of St Andrews)
(1 Jan. 1651	Charles II (as King of Scots)	Scone	
23 April 1661	Charles II	Westminster Abbey	William Juxon, Archbishop of Canterbury
23 April 1685	James II and Mary of Modena	Westminster Abbey	William Sancroft, Archbishop of Canterbury
11 April 1689	William III and Mary II	Westminster Abbey	Henry Compton, Bishop of London

228

23 April 1702	Anne	Westminster Abbey	Thomas Tenison, Archbishop of Canterbury
20 Oct. 1714	George I	Westminster Abbey	Thomas Tenison, Archbishop of Canterbury
11 Oct. 1727	George II and Caroline of Brandenburg-Ansbach	Westminster Abbey	William Wake, Archbishop of Canterbury
22 Sept. 1761	George III and Charlotte of Mecklenburg-Strelitz	Westminster Abbey	Thomas Secker, Archbishop of Canterbury
19 July 1821	George IV	Westminster Abbey	Charles Manners Sutton, Archbishop of Canterbury
8 Sept 1831	William IV and Adelaide of Saxe-Meiningen	Westminster Abbey	William Howley, Archbishop of Canterbury
28 June 1838	Victoria	Westminster Abbey	William Howley, Archbishop of Canterbury
9 Aug. 1902	Edward VII and Alexandra of Denmark	Westminster Abbey	Frederick Temple, Archbishop of Canterbury William Dalrymple Maclagan, Archbishop of York
22 June 1911	George V and Mary of Teck	Westminster Abbey	Randall Thomas Davidson, Archbishop of Canterbury
12 May 1937	George VI and Elizabeth Bowes-Lyon	Westminster Abbey	Cosmo Gordon Lang, Archbishop of Canterbury
2 June 1953	Elizabeth II	Westminster Abbey	Geoffrey Francis Fisher, Archbishop of Canterbury

Eleven traditions abandoned by Royalty

1 The triplet bounty

Initiated by Queen Victoria in 1849, the tradition of sending £3 to each set of triplets born was ended in 1957. £4,428 was distributed to babies during the reign of King George VI. A congratulatory telegram is now sent instead.

2 Beefeaters' beards

Beards were compulsory wear for Beefeaters until King Edward VIII made them optional. This and the establishment of the King's Flight he regarded as the only practical reforms he made during his short reign. He had, however, also abolished the tradition of the Prime Minister writing daily to the Sovereign with news of the happenings in Parliament.

3 The Maundy washing

King George II abandoned the tradition of the sovereign washing the feet of the old on Maundy Thursday. The tradition dated back to King Edward I, though some of the burden had already been removed from the ceremony, as courtiers would wash and rewash the feet several times before the Sovereign made his dab. Queen Elizabeth I's enthusiasm for kissing the big toes of the old died with her.

4 Hair powdering

Prince Philip stopped footmen powdering their hair, condemning it as 'unmanly'.

5 The witnessing of the birth

Since the time of Queen Anne, all Royal births had been witnessed by the Secretary of State until King George VI discontinued the tradition. Princess Margaret's birth in 1930 was the last time this happened.

6 The Royal curtsey

When the Queen Mother came to the throne she abolished the tradition of the royal children curtseying to their parents, though Princess Elizabeth and Princess Margaret continued to curtsey to their grandmother, Queen Mary.

7 The finger bowl

King George I banished finger-bowls from Court as rather too many Jacobites used them to toast 'The King Over the Water'. Not until King Edward VII's reign did the finger-bowls return. The toast to 'The King Over the Water' was revived following the Duke of Windsor's exile.

8 The buckling of spurs

The buckling on of spurs to the Sovereign's ankles was an important part of the Coronation ceremony until the time of Queen Anne, whose ankles were too fat to hold them.

9 Touching for the King's Evil

Discontinued by King George I. This attempted 'cure' for scrofula was last tried by Queen Anne, who is said to have touched 100,000 for the affliction, including Samuel Johnson, who remembered his encounter with an 'old lady in a black cloak and diamonds'.

10 The presentation of debutantes at Court

After 250 years, this annual ceremony was abandoned by the Queen on 3 July 1958. The last debutante to be presented to the Queen was Miss Fiona Macrae of Edinburgh.

11 Night-time funerals

Until Queen Victoria's funeral in 1901 it had been customary for centuries for royal funerals to take place at night. They were private and not occasions for pomp. Queen Victoria left detailed instructions for a day-time funeral and lying-in-state and the same procedures have been followed ever since.

Fifteen Royal traditions which are still in force 273

1 Coal giving

Every Christmas, the Queen presents a hundredweight of coals to the 800–900 needy people over 65 years old in Windsor. She also gives all the members of her staff a plum pudding each.

2 Telegrams

The Queen sends a telegram to everyone on their hundredth birthday. The telegram reads, 'The Queen is much interested to hear that you are celebrating your one-hundredth birthday and sends you warm congratulations and good wishes.' Those who go on to reach 105 get another telegram, and others for every year afterwards.

3 Baptism

All Royal babies are baptised in Jordan water.

4 Mourning

British barristers dress as they do because they are still in mourning for Queen Mary, who died in 1694. Etonians are still in mourning for George III. Senior staff of the Royal Households still wear black livery in mourning for Prince Albert, who died in 1861.

5 St George's Day

Since 1342, the villages of the Manor of Fordington have sent the Prince of Wales a leg of a sheep roasted on the green as rent for their annual fair.

6 The Horse Guards

To this day, the Horse Guards do not have the post of Sergeant because Queen Victoria once – mistakenly – proclaimed 'Sergeant means servant, and there will be no servants in my Household Cavalry.'

7 The Waterloo Dinner

On June 18 each year, a dinner is held in the Waterloo Chamber at Windsor Castle to commemorate the British victory over the French in 1815. The present Duke of Wellington is the guest of honour, and the tables are decorated with flowers in his family colours, blue and yellow.

8 Perfuming the corridors

Before guests arrive to stay in any of the Royal houses, a footman walks along the corridors swinging a censer full of smouldering lavender.

9 Breakfasting to bagpipes

For fifteen minutes of the Queen's breakfast every morning, a Pipe Major from the Argyll and Sutherland Highlanders marches outside the Queen's dining room playing the bagpipes. This maintains a tradition started by Queen Victoria in 1843.

10 The extra equerry

Group-Captain Peter Townsend is still listed as an extra equerry to the Queen.

11 Pricking the sheriff

Following a tradition begun by Queen Elizabeth I, the Queen still announces the next Sheriff of each county by pricking his name on a vellum roll with a bodkin. Queen Elizabeth I had been sewing in her garden and used a bodkin in the absence of a pen.

12 The great Seal

Early in each new reign, the incoming Monarch damages the Seal of his predecessor with a hammer.

13 Vivat Rex

At every Coronation, the scholars of Westminster School still cry 'Vivat Rex' or 'Regina'. This privilege was originally bestowed on them by King James II, to reward them for publicly kneeling to pray for King Charles I on the day of his execution.

14 Christmas presents
Since the time of Prince Albert, the Royal Family have exchanged
presents on Christmas Eve rather than on Christmas Day. Each
member of the family and guest has his own table stacked with
presents.
15 Changing for dinner
The Queen Mother still changes every evening into formal
evening dress for dinner even if she is dining alone.

The four crowns of King William IV — 274

1 William I of Hanover
2 William II of Ireland
3 William III of Scotland
4 William IV of England

Eleven irregular aspects of Coronations — 275

1 King Henry IV's Coronation
One of the King's shoes dropped off in the procession, shortly
followed by a spur from the other leg; at the Coronation banquet
a gust of wind carried the crown from his head, which combined
to inspire in supporters a sense of insecurity.
2 King George III's Coronation
It was delayed for two days when the workmen went on strike.
On the morning of the Coronation it was discovered that the
canopy, the Chair of State and the Sword of State had been lost.
During the service the Bishop of Salisbury became so muddled
that he referred in his sermon to the extraordinary number of
years the King had already sat on the Throne. His concentration
cannot have been helped by what one witness described as 'the
general clattering of knives, forks, plates and glasses' that the
congregation required for sustenance during the six-hour service.
At the Coronation banquet the King's Hereditary Champion rode
in gorgeously attired to throw down the gauntlet, but his steed,

which had been hired for the occasion from Astley's Circus, presented its rump to the King. King George III was the last monarch to style himself King of France; but so fantastic was the conceit by that time that no one remarked upon the oddity of two actors being hired for the occasion to impersonate the Dukes of Normandy and Aquitaine come to give fealty. The Lord High Steward made matters worse by saying: 'I have taken care that the next Coronation shall be regulated in the best manner possible.'

3 James II and Mary's Coronation

To satisfy their religious scruples, James II and Mary had a secret Catholic Coronation at which they received communion before proceeding with their official Coronation.

4 George IV's Coronation

The King took the unusual step of choosing prize fighters as his pages, though the wisdom of his selection became obvious when his indiscreet estranged wife, Caroline, attempted to force herself into the ceremony by banging her fists on the doors of the Abbey and signalling her frustration by a high-pitched wailing.

5 King Charles II's Coronation

It had to be postponed because Oliver Cromwell had sold all the necessary regalia.

6 Queen Mary I's Coronation

Queen Mary, a fierce Catholic, refused to sit in the Coronation Chair because it had previously been sat in by her predecessor, King Edward VI, whom she considered a heretic. She also turned up her nose at the consecrating oil, saying that, as it had been used on him, it was 'no longer holy'.

7 Queen Anne's Coronation

Queen Anne was so extremely fat and gout-ridden that she had to be carried throughout the ceremony in a chair.

8 Queen Victoria's Coronation

Queen Victoria had ordered that a smaller Coronation ring be made to fit her tiny little finger. On the day, the Archbishop ceremonially put it on the wrong finger, where it got quite stuck and the Queen had to go to bed with her Coronation ring still on. The Bishop of Bath and Wells complicated matters by turning over two pages at the end of the service. When the Queen discovered this had happened, she ordered that they return to the right place and do it again.

9 Edward VII's Coronation

After one postponement when the King had to have his appendix removed, the ceremony went smoothly until Archbishop Temple asked his special protection for 'widowers' rather than 'widows'. The Archbishop would have placed the Crown on the wrong way round had the King not interfered. Rising from his knees, the Archbishop fell, and had to be caught by three bishops kneeling nearby. The Holy Oil was dripped down Queen Alexandra's nose. The Marchioness of Londonderry lost her tiara in the lavatory for Peeresses. It was fetched out by a doctor with a pair of forceps, which resulted in speculation.

10 George VI's Coronation
The Archbishop's thumb covered the words of the Oath; the Lord Chamberlain's hands were shaking so much that the King had to fix the belt of the Sword of State himself; the place in the Bible was lost; a chaplain fainted; the Crown was put on the wrong way round on the King's head; and for a short time the King was pinned to his position by a bishop who was standing on his robe.

11 The Queen's Coronation
Nothing seemed to go amiss until after the ceremony when the congregation had left. The Peers' vacated seats were found to be the final resting-place for an impressive number of empty half-bottles of spirits. The exact quantity has never been disclosed. Seven coaches, which had been sold from the Royal Mews to Sir Alexander Korda, had to be borrowed from his film studios to complete the impression of splendour.

How the Queen, Prince Philip and Prince Charles take their coffee   276

1 The Queen *White with sugar*
2 Prince Philip *Black with sugar*
3 Prince Charles *None at all – he doesn't like it*

Seven ingredients for a cocktail invented by King Edward VII   277

1 Rye whisky
2 Crushed ice
3 A square of pineapple
4 A piece of lemon peel
5 A dash of maraschino
6 Champagne
7 Powdered sugar

235

278 *Ingredients of a shooting lunch at Balmoral*

1 A stuffed roll
2 A slice of plum pudding
3 An apple
4 Diluted whisky

279 *Three human dishes served to Royalty*

1 A Jeffrey Hudson sandwich
One of King Charles I's favourite jests was to pretend to eat his 18-inch dwarf, Jeffrey Hudson, between two halves of a loaf of bread.

2 A Jeffrey Hudson pie
The versatile Jeffrey Hudson was also served up in a cold pie by the Duke of Buckingham in the middle of a banquet he was giving for Queen Henrietta. The Queen was delighted. For all his contributions to Royal mirth, Jeffrey Hudson was knighted.

3 Cora Pearl *au naturel*
In 1875, a voluptuous Englishwoman named Cora Pearl was served on a silver dish, naked save for a few sprigs of parsley and a string of pearls, to a beaming King Edward VII when he dined at the Café des Anglais in Paris.

280 *Eight dishes to set before the Queen*

1 Chicken salad
2 Dover sole
3 French beans
4 Peas
5 Saddle of lamb
6 Fresh fruit
7 Bendicks Bittermints
8 Coffee sugar – *she enjoys chewing it after dinner*

Three favourite dishes of Prince Charles 281

1 Scrambled eggs and smoked salmon
2 Bread and butter pudding
3 Peach melba

Edward VII's ideal menu 282

Eggs in Aspic
Plovers Eggs
Oysters

Trout

Well-cooked Roast Beef

Strawberries

Wine: Champagne, preferably Duminy extra sec, 1883. For bedside consumption: A cold fowl and a bottle of wine.

Queen Victoria's ideal menu 283

Brown Windsor Soup

Haggis

Boiled Chicken

Chocolate Cake
Cranberry Tart
Trifle

For chewing after dinner: caraway seeds. Wine: Claret 'strengthened' with whisky.

284 *Seven favourite snacks of Princess Diana*

1 Borsch
2 Chocolate Cake with Butter Icing
3 Ginger Biscuits
4 Lemon Souffle
5 Twiglets
6 Ham Salad
7 Cheese

285 *Six favourite sweets of Princess Diana*

1 Star Bars
2 Kit-Kat
3 Smarties
4 Wine Gums
5 Bubblegum
6 Lindt chocolate
7 Fruit Gums

286 *Six effects of Royal drinking*

1 Falling asleep on the wedding night
King George IV was so drunk on the night that he married Queen Caroline that he prompted this report from her. 'Judge what it was to have a drunken husband on one's wedding day and one who passed the greatest part of his bridal night under the grate, where he fell and where I left him.'

2 A hangover
'Please excuse me if I sound somewhat different today,' said Princess Anne in a speech to the Portland naval base after Prince Charles's wedding, 'but I am suffering from a hangover after a very enjoyable wedding.'

3 Notoriety
Queen Anne was a heavy drinker and very fond of brandy. On

her statue in St Paul's Churchyard (which faced a gin palace) a wag once wrote:
Brandy Nan, left in the lurch,
Her face to the gin-shop, her back to the church.

4 Death
In 1478, The Duke of Clarence, the brother of King Richard III, was drowned in a butt of Malmsey.

5 Near death
In Florida in 1980, Prince Charles was overcome with heat after playing polo on a very muggy April day. The effect of drinking ice cold champagne to revive himself precipitated his collapse. At first no one knew how ill he was. Eventually he was rushed to hospital. 'Don't leave me, Oliver,' he said to his equerry, Oliver Everett, 'I think I am dying.' At one stage his pulse rate was recorded at zero.

6 Bare cellars
Badminton House, where Queen Mary stayed throughout the war, sent an urgent demand to their wine merchants for more hock in 1942. The dowager Queen drank half a bottle every night and stocks were low.

Favourite drinks of eight members of the Royal Family 287

1 The Queen
Light sweet white wines like Moselle, or Sauternes. At the end of a particularly busy day she will have a gin and tonic, and she likes champagne. But her favourite drink of all, which is kept ready in quantity, is barley water.

2 The Queen Mother
Green and yellow Chartreuse (but only when one of her horses wins a race). Otherwise, she likes whisky and soda.

3 Prince Charles
French dry white wines, Martini Bianco, and champagne, especially Bollinger '75.

4 Prince Philip
He drinks beer with lunch and will have a pink gin in the evening.

5 Princess Diana
Drinks gin and tonic with lots of tonic.

6 Princess Anne
Coca-Cola.
7 Princess Margaret
Drinks whisky with her dinner, as did her grandfather, George V; this is possibly because she does not like white wine or champagne.
8 Prince Andrew
Ginger ale and shandy

The Royal Barley Water Recipe
    1 teacup pearl barley
    4 pints boiling water
    2 lemons
    6 oranges
    Demerara sugar to taste

Put barley in a large saucepan, add the boiling water and simmer over a low heat with the lid on for 1 hour. Strain the water from the barley into a basin, adding the rind of one lemon and three oranges. Add sugar. Allow to stand until cold. Strain off the rinds and add the orange and lemon juice. Keep in refrigerator.

Prince Philip enjoys a pint of Best Bitter

Causes of death of British monarchs

William the Conqueror:
Of burst bowels, aged 59, when jumping a trench on horseback, his stomach was forced onto the pommel.

William II:
Possibly murdered while hunting; died at 40 with an arrow through his heart.

Henry I:
A surfeit of lampreys (none too fresh) caused his death of ptomaine poisoning at 67.

Stephen:
A ruptured appendix, aged 57.

Henry II:
Cerebral haemorrhage at 55.

Richard I:
Gangrene resulting from an arrow wound in his shoulder in battle, 49.

John:
Of dysentery following a surfeit of peaches and cider when he was 49.

Edward I:
Dysentery and bowel haemorrhage, 68.

Edward II:
Murdered cruelly by his wife's confederates who thrust a red hot spit into his bowels through a horn forced into his rectum when he was 43.

Edward III:
Gonorrhoea contracted from his mistress at 65.

Richard II:
Anorexia nervosa from depression at 36 (Shakespeare has him murdered by a pole-axe by Sir Piers Exton, but his skull shows no sign of fracture).

Henry IV:
Acute chronic eczema and chronic intestinal toxaemia; died at 46.

Henry V:
Of 'a bloody flux' or dysentery, 35.

Henry VI:
Murdered by Gloucester in the Tower of London, 49.

Edward IV:
Pneumonia, aged 42.

Edward V:
Possibly smothered, aged 12, in the Tower.

Richard III:
Skull fracture from an axe at Bosworth Field, 36.
Henry VII:
Of gout and consumption at 52.
Henry VIII:
Syphilis, aged 58.
Edward VI:
Consumption and congenital syphilis, aged 15.
Lady Jane Grey:
Beheaded at the age of 16.
Mary I:
An influenza epidemic when she was 42.
Elizabeth I:
Infected tonsils, 69.
James I:
Chronic intestinal toxaemia aged 59.
Charles I:
Beheaded, 48.
Charles II:
Uremia caused by gouty kidneys, aged 54.
James II:
Died of a brain haemorrhage, aged 67.
Mary II:
Of smallpox at the age of 32.
William III:
Pneumonia caused by a lung infection after he had broken his shoulder when his horse stumbled over a mole hill, aged 51.
Anne:
Cerebral haemorrhage when she was 49.
George I:
Of apoplexy in his coach after eating a surfeit of melons at the age of 67.
George II:
When a large blood vessel in his heart burst, aged 77, when he was sitting in the loo.
George III:
Senile decay at 81.
George IV:
Rupture of the major blood vessel in the stomach, and cirrhosis of the liver, 67.
William IV:
Pneumonia and cirrhosis of the liver, 71.
Victoria:
Cerebral haemorrhage, aged 81.

Edward VII:
Heart failure, 69.
George V:
Bronchial infection, 71.
Edward VIII:
Cancer of the throat, aged 77.
George VI:
Lung cancer, when he was 57.

Seven members of the Royal Family 289
who have been cremated

1 *HRH The Duchess of Connaught* (Louise Margaret of Prussia, wife of Arthur, 1st Duke of Connaught, 3rd son of Queen Victoria) died 14 March 1917, was cremated at Golders Green Crematorium, and had her ashes buried in the Royal Burial Ground at Frogmore.

2 *HRH Princess Louise*, Duchess of Argyll (4th daughter of Queen Victoria) died 3 December 1939, was cremated at Golders Green Crematorium, and had her ashes buried in the Royal Burial Ground at Frogmore.

3 *Alastair Arthur*, 2nd Duke of Connaught (grandson of no. 1 above) died at Ottawa, Canada 26 April 1943, was cremated there, and had his ashes deposited in the Chapel at Mar Lodge, Braemar, Aberdeenshire.

4 *The Marchioness of Carisbrooke* (granddaughter-in-law of Queen Victoria) died 16 July 1956, was cremated at Golders Green Crematorium, and had her ashes deposited in the Battenberg Chapel at Whippingham Church, Isle of Wight.

5 *HRH Princess Arthur of Connaught* (granddaughter of King Edward VII, daughter-in-law of no. 1 above and mother of no. 3 above) died 26 February 1959, was cremated at Golders Green Crematorium, and had her ashes deposited in the Chapel at Mar Lodge, Braemar, Aberdeenshire.

6 *The Marquess of Carisbrooke* (grandson of Queen Victoria and husband of no. 4 above) died 23 February 1960, was cremated at Golders Green Crematorium, and had his ashes deposited in the Battenberg Chapel at Whippingham Church, Isle of Wight.

7 *David, 3rd Marquess of Milford Haven* (great-great-grandson of Queen Victoria) died 14 April 1970, was cremated at Golders Green Crematorium, and had his ashes deposited in the Battenberg Chapel at Whippingham Church, Isle of Wight.

243

Eight relics in the collection of St George's Chapel at Windsor at the end of the fifteenth century

1 A thorn of Christ's crown
2 Some of Christ's mother's milk
3 The shirt and some of the blood of St Thomas of Canterbury
4 The armbones of St William of York, St George, St Osytho and St Richard
5 Part of the jawbone of St Mark
6 Fourteen teeth of St Mark
7 Part of St Eustace's brain
8 A stone which had helped stone St Stephen

Five ways in which Queen Victoria remembered Prince Albert's death

1 Conservation

For the 40 years between Prince Albert's death and her own, Queen Victoria kept her husband's room exactly as it had always been. Hot water was brought in each morning, his chamber pot scoured with all the others in the household, fresh towels and bed linen laid out, and a clean nightshirt placed upon his bed.

2 Multiplication

She decreed that every future heir to the throne should be given the name Albert. Though King Edward VII, King Edward VIII and King George VI were all called Albert, each chose a different name for his reign. In the present Royal Family, Prince Andrew alone is called Albert (as a second name).

3 Communication

Queen Victoria attended seances organised by Robert James Lees, a friend of both Disraeli and Gladstone, in the hope of contacting the spirit of Prince Albert. Alas, her other half remained firmly on the other side.

4 Impersonation

For years after Prince Albert's death, Queen Victoria slept with his nightclothes in her arms.

5 Abstention

During her 40 years of widowhood, Queen Victoria never went to a theatre or concert; neither did she give nor attend a court ball.

Five official reasons for the death of King George IV

1 Dropsy
2 Nephritis
3 Rupture of a blood vessel in the stomach
4 Gout
5 Alcoholic cirrhosis

Seventeen last words of British monarchs

1 *'Shame, shame on a conquered King'*
  King Henry II, 1189
2 *'Youth, I forgive thee. Take off his chains, give him 100 shillings and let him go.'*
  King Richard I to his killer, 1199.
3 *'I will die King of England, I will not budge a foot! Treason! Treason!*
  King Richard II, 1485
4 *'I die a Queen, but I would rather die the wife of Culpepper. God have mercy on my soul. Good people, I beg you pray for me.'*
  Catherine Howard, before her execution, 1542
5 *'Monks! Monks! Monks!*
  King Henry VIII, 1547
6 *'Oh my Lord God, defend this realm from papistry and maintain their true religion.'*
  King Edward VI, 1553
7 *'All my possessions for one moment of time.'*
  Queen Elizabeth I, 1603
8 *'I go from a corruptible to an incorruptible crown, where no disturbance can be, no disturbance in the world.'*
  King Charles I, before his execution, 1649
9 *'Let not poor Nelly starve.'*
  King Charles II, 1685
10 *'I am not afraid to die.'*
  Queen Mary II, 1694
11 *'Can this last long?'*
  King William III, 1702
12 *'Pray louder that I may hear.'*
  Queen Caroline, wife of King George II, 1737.

13 *'Wally, what is this? It is death my boy. They have deceived me.'*
   King George IV, 1830
14 *'Good little woman'*
   Prince Albert, 1861
15 *'Oh that peace may come. Bertie!'*
   Queen Victoria, 1901
16 *'No, I shall not give in. I shall go on. I shall work to the end.'*
   King Edward VII, 1910
17 *'How is the Empire?'*
   King George V, 1936
   (Some suggest he said, 'Bugger Bognor.')

Burial Places of Kings, Queens and Consor since the Conquest

Name	Date of Death	Place of Burial
William I the Conquerer	9 Sept. 1087	Abbey of St Stephen, Caen
Matilda of Flanders	2 Nov. 1083	Church of the Holy Trinity, Caen
William II Rufus	2 Aug. 1100	Winchester Cathedral
Henry I	1 Dec. 1135	Reading Abbey
Matilda of Scotland	1 May 1118	Westminster Abbey
Adeliza of Louvain	23 March or April 1151	Afflighem, Flanders
Stephen	25 Oct. 1154	Faversham Abbey
Matilda of Boulogne	3 May 1152	Faversham Abbey
(Empress Matilda	10 Sept. 1169	Bec Abbey)
(Emperor Henry V	23 May 1125	Speyer)
(Geoffrey Plantagenet	7 Sept. 1151	Le Mans Cathedral)
Henry II	6 July 1189	Fontévraud
'Henry 'the Young King'	11 June 1183	Le Mans; later transferred to Rouen)
Margaret of France	1197 or 1198	Acre)
Eleanor of Aquitaine	31 March/1 April 1204	Fontévraud
Richard I	6 April 1199	Fontévraud
Berengaria of Navarre	about 1230	L'Epau Abbey, near Le Mans
John	19 Oct. 1216	Worcester Cathedral
(Isabella of Gloucester	about 18 Nov. 1217	Canterbury Cathedral)
Isabella of Angoulême	31 May 1246	Fontévraud
Henry III	16 Nov. 1272	Westminter Abbey
Eleanor of Provence	24 June 1291	Amesbury, Wiltshire
Edward I	8 July 1307	Westminster Abbey
Eleanor of Castile	28/29 Nov. 1290	Westminster Abbey
Margaret of France	14 Feb. 1317	Grey Friars Church, London
Edward II	21 Sept. 1327	Gloucester Cathedral

...me	Date of Death	Place of Burial
...elle of France	22 Aug. 1358	Grey Friars Church, London
...ward III	21 June 1377	Westminster Abbey
...hard II	6 Jan 1400	Westminster Abbey
...ne of Bohemia	before 3 June 1394	Westminster Abbey
...elle of France	13 Sept. 1409	Abbey of St Laumer, Blois; transferred to Church of the Celestines, Paris
...ary IV	20 March 1413	Canterbury Cathedral
...ary de Bohun, first wife of ...ry IV, died before his accession	4 June or July 1394	St Mary's Church, Leicester)
...n of Navarre	9 July 1437	Canterbury Cathedral
...ary V	31 Aug. 1422	Westminster Abbey
...herine of France	3 Jan. 1437	Westminster Abbey
...ary VI	21 May 1471	Chertsey Abbey; transferred to St George's chapel, Windsor
...rgaret of Anjou	25 Aug. 1482	Angers
...ward IV	9 April 1483	St George's Chapel, Windsor
...zabeth Woodville	8 June 1492	St George's Chapel, Windsor
...ward V	unknown	unknown
...hard III	22 Aug. 1485	Grey Friars Abbey, Leicester; bones later thrown into River Soar
...ne Neville	16 March 1485	Westminster Abbey
...nry VII	21 April 1509	Westminster Abbey
...zabeth of York	11 Feb. 1503	Westminster Abbey
...ary VIII	28 Jan. 1547	St George's Chapel, Windsor
...herine of Aragon	7 Jan. 1536	Peterborough Cathedral
...ne Boleyn	19 May 1536	Chapel of St Peter-ad-Vincula in the Tower of London
...e Seymour	24 Oct. 1537	St George's Chapel, Windsor
...ne of Cleves	17 July 1557	Westminster Abbey
...herine Howard	13 Feb. 1542	Chapel of St Peter-ad-Vincula in the Tower of London
...herine Parr	5 Sept. 1548	Chapel of Sudeley Castle, Glos
...ward VI	6 July 1553	Westminster Abbey
...e	12 Feb. 1554	Chapel of St Peter-ad-Vincula in the Tower of London
...rd Guildford Dudley	12 Feb. 1554	Chapel of St Peter-ad-Vincula in the Tower of London
...ry I	17 Nov. 1558	Westminster Abbey
...lip II, King of Spain	13 Sept. 1598	El Escorial
...zabeth I	24 March 1603	Westminster Abbey
...nes I	27 March 1625	Westminster Abbey
...ne of Denmark	4 March 1619	Westminster Abbey
...arles I	30 Jan. 1649	St George's Chapel, Windsor
...nrietta Maria of France	31 Aug. 1669	St Denis
...arles II	6 Feb. 1685	Westminster Abbey
...herine of Braganza	31 Dec. 1705	Santa Maria de Belém, Lisbon
...nes II	6 Sept. 1701	Church of the English Benedictines, Paris; transferred to St Germain-en-Laye

(Anne Hyde, 1st wife of James II, died before his accession	31 March 1671	Westminster Abbey)
Mary of Modena	7 May 1718	Chaillot
William III	8 March 1702	Westminster Abbey
Mary II	28 Dec. 1694	Westminster Abbey
Anne	1 Aug. 1714	Westminster Abbey
Prince George of Denmark	28 Oct. 1708	Westminster Abbey
George I	11 June 1727	Leineschloss Church, Hanover; transferred to Herrenhausen aft World War II
(Sophia Dorothea of Brunswick-Zelle)	2 Nov. 1726	Zelle
George II	25 Oct. 1760	Westminster Abbey
Caroline of Brandenburg-Ansbach	20 Nov. 1737	Westminster Abbey
George III	29 Jan. 1820	St George's Chapel, Windsor
Charlotte of Mecklenburg-Strelitz	17 Nov. 1818	St George's Chapel, Windsor
George IV	26 June 1830	St George's Chapel, Windsor
Caroline of Brunswick	7 Aug. 1821	Brunswick
William IV	20 June 1837	St George's Chapel, Windsor
Adelaide of Saxe-Meiningen	2 Dec. 1849	St George's Chapel, Windsor
Victoria	22 Jan. 1901	Royal Mausoleum, Frogmore
Prince Albert	14 Dec. 1861	Royal Mausoleum, Frogmore
Edward VII	6 May 1910	St George's Chapel, Windsor
Alexandra of Denmark	20 Nov. 1925	St George's Chapel, Windsor
George V	20 Jan. 1936	St George's Chapel, Windsor
Mary of Teck	24 March 1953	St George's Chapel, Windsor
Edward VIII	28 May 1972	Royal Burial Ground, Frogmo
George VI	6 Feb. 1952	St George's Chapel, Windsor (King George VI Memorial Chapel)

NB The alleged murder of Edward V in the Tower of London has never been proved and there has been no satisfactory identification of the bones discovered there and subsequently reinterred Westminster Abbey as his.

295 Days of the week on which monarchs have died

Sunday:
Edward III, Henry VI, James I, William III, Queen Anne, Geor I.

Monday:
King Stephen, Richard II, Henry IV, Henry V, Richard III, George V.

Tuesday:
Richard I, Edward II, Charles I, James II, William IV, Queen Victoria.
Wednesday:
John, Henry III, Edward IV, Edward V, George VI.
Thursday:
William I, William II, Henry II, Edward VI, Mary I, Elizabeth I
Friday:
Edward I, Henry VIII, Charles II, Mary II, Edward VII.
Saturday:
Henry VII, George II, George III, George IV

Seven Royal corpses and what became of them

296

1 The fourth cervical vertebra of King Charles I
Having been sliced 'clean through' by the executioner's axe, it remained with the rest of the King's body until it was stolen by the Royal Surgeon, Sir Henry Halford, in 1813. Sir Henry employed it as a salt cellar for the next thirty years, until Queen Victoria found out and ordered its prompt return.

2 The corpse of King Henry VIII
Soon after the corpse of King Henry VIII was placed in the chapel at Windsor two weeks after his death, the lead coffin burst open and, according to one witness, 'all the pavement of the church was with the fat and the corrupt and putrefied blood foully imbued.'

3 The jawbone of King Richard II
It was stolen from his tomb in Westminster Abbey (where the skull of the King could be touched through an opening in the coffin) by a schoolboy in 1776. The schoolboy's family kept the jawbone until 1906, when they decided to return it.

4 The heart of Anne Boleyn
It was buried separately and secretly in a casket in a church near Thetford in Suffolk. It was discovered in 1830, and re-buried.

5 The corpse of Catherine de Valois
The body of King Henry V's wife, buried in 1437, was dug up during rebuilding work at Westminster Abbey during the reign of King Henry VIII. The mummified corpse was left on show to the public for the next 200 years, until 1776. On his 36th birthday, Samuel Pepys paid the verger of the Abbey a shilling and 'I had

the upper part of her body in my hands, and I did kiss her mouth, reflecting that I did first kiss a Queen.'

6 The head of the Duke of Monmouth

After five chops had eventually separated the head from the body of the Duke of Monmouth, it was realised that as the illegitimate son of King Charles II, it was important that his portrait should be painted. The head was sewn back onto the body, the joins were painted over, the body redressed and the portrait painted. It now hangs in the National Portrait Gallery.

7 The corpse of Henry IV

When Henry IV's body was being taken by boat to Faversham for his burial at Canterbury Cathedral, a great storm arose. The superstitious sailors threw his body overboard, and substituted another in the King's coffin. When the coffin was opened in 1823, the story was proved: the coffin hid an inner coffin of mean design and quite another shape; the body was dressed in no regalia, but common clothing, and surmounted by a cross of twigs.

297 *The Royal line of Succession*

1 HRH The Prince of Wales
2 HRH The Prince William of Wales
3 HRH The Prince Andrew
4 HRH The Prince Edward
5 HRH The Princess Anne
6 Peter Phillips
7 Zara Phillips
8 HRH The Princess Margaret
9 Viscount Linley
10 Lady Sarah Armstrong-Jones
11 HRH The Duke of Gloucester
12 Earl of Ulster
13 Lady Davina Windsor
14 Lady Rose Windsor
15 The Duke of Kent
16 Earl of St Andrews
17 Lord Nicholas Windsor
18 Lady Helen Windsor
19 Lord Frederick Windsor
20 Lady Gabriella Windsor

21 Princess Alexandra
22 James Ogilvy
23 Marina Ogilvy
24 The Earl of Harewood
25 Viscount Lascelles
26 Alexander Lascelles
27 Hon James Lascelles
28 Rowan Lascelles
29 Sophie Lascelles
30 Hon Robert Lascelles
31 Hon Gerald Lascelles
32 Henry Lascelles
33 The Duke of Fife
34 The Earl of Macduff
35 Lady Alexandra Carnegie
36 HM King Olav V of Norway
37 HRH Crown Prince Harald of Norway
38 HRH Prince Haakon Magnus of Norway
39 HRH Princess Martha Louise of Norway
40 Princess Ragnhild, Mrs Lorentzen
41 Haakon Lorentzen
42 Ingeborg Lorentzen
43 Ragnhild Lorentzen
44 Princess Astrid, Mrs Ferner
45 Alexander Ferner
46 Carl Christian Ferner
47 Cathrine Ferner
48 Benedicte Ferner
49 Elisabeth Ferner
50 HRH Princess Margarita of Roumania
51 HRH Princess Helen of Roumania
52 HRH Princess Irina of Roumania
53 HRH Princess Sophie of Roumania
54 HRH Princess Maria of Roumania
55 HRH Prince Tomislav of Yugoslavia
56 HRH Prince Nikola of Yugoslavia

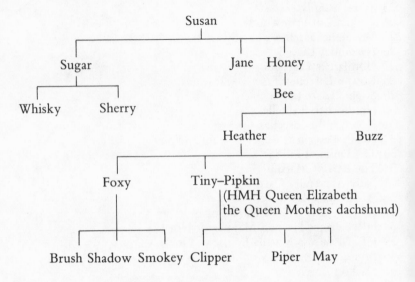

Susan
├── Sugar
│   ├── Whisky
│   └── Sherry
└── Jane Honey
    └── Bee
        ├── Heather
        │   ├── Foxy
        │   │   ├── Brush
        │   │   ├── Shadow
        │   │   └── Smokey
        │   └── Tiny–Pipkin
        │   (HMH Queen Elizabeth
        │   the Queen Mothers dachshund)
        │   ├── Clipper
        │   ├── Piper
        │   └── May
        └── Buzz

The Queen relaxes with three of her corgis

1 HRH Duke Albrecht of Bavaria (born 1905)

The Duke is the heir to the Royal House of Stuart by his descent from Henrietta, Duchess of Orleans, who was the sister of Kings Charles II and James II (who was forced to give up his throne and flee the country when his heir – the Catholic 'Old Pretender' – was born). Before the Coronation in 1953, supporters of his claim – which he does not press himself – tacked a Proclamation to the gates of Buckingham Palace to publicise his right to the Throne. Despite that, he and the Queen, who has stayed with him in Germany, are on good terms.

2 HRH Princess Elisabeth of Bourbon-Parma (born 1904)

Princess Elisabeth could claim to rival Duke Albrecht as heir to the Royal House of Stuart (and so rival his claim to the British throne). The dispute centres upon the claims of the descendants of the Duke's ancestress Princess Maria Beatrice of Savoy (1792–1840) who married her maternal uncle Duke Francesco IV of Modena (1779–1846). Such a marriage would be invalid under English law (strengthening Princess Elizabeth's claim), but it can be argued that English law recognises as valid marriages contracted outside its jurisdiction in countries where they would be regarded as legally valid (which confirms Duke Albrecht's claim).

3 The Duke of Buccleuch (born 1923)

The Duke of Buccleuch is the heir of the Duke of Monmouth, the first son born to Charles II. The King denied that he was legally married to Lucy Walter, Monmouth's mother, but this was disputed at the time, and has been ever since. If the Duke of Monmouth *was* legitimate, the present Duke of Buccleuch could sit on the Throne.

4 HRH Archduchess Robert of Austria-Este (born 1930)

This possible claimant to the Throne was born Princess Margherita of Savoy-Aosta, heir of the claim of Elizabeth, Queen of Bohemia, who was the eldest daughter of King James I.

5 Lady Kinloss (born 1944)

If Lady Kinloss, as representative of Lady Jane Grey (descending through her sister Catherine, wife of Edward Seymour, Earl of Hertford), were to press her legitimate right to the Throne (as her

ancestors could have done according to the will of Henry VIII),
she would be Queen Beatrice I of England.

6 The Countess of Loudoun (born 1919)
If the children of Edward IV and Elizabeth Woodville are regarded
as illegitimate, the heirs of Margaret, Countess of Salisbury and
the Plantagenet kings could claim the succession. The present
representative of this line is the Countess of Loudoun.

300 *Five oldest Sovereigns to ascend the throne*

1 King William IV *64 years and 10 months*
2 King Edward VII *59 years and 2 months*
3 King George IV *57 years and 5 months*
4 King George I *54 years and 2 months*
5 King James II *51 years and 3 months*

301 *Five Sovereigns who died youngest*

1 King Edward V *12 years and 8 months*
2 King Edward VI *15 years and 9 months*
3 Lady Jane Grey *16 years and 4 months*
4 King Richard II *33 years*
5 King Richard III *33 years and 1 month*

302 *Five Sovereigns who lived longest*

1 Queen Victoria *81 years and 8 months*
2 King George III *81 years and 7 months*
3 King Edward VIII (Duke of Windsor) *77 years 11 months*
4 King George II *5 days short of 77 years*
5 King William IV *71 years and 10 months*

Five youngest Sovereigns to ascend the throne

1 King Henry VI *8 months*
2 King Henry III *9 years and 18 days*
3 King Edward VI *9 years and 3 months*
4 King Richard II *10 years and 6 months*
5 King Edward V *12 years and 5 months*

Three years which saw three kings on the throne

1 1066 Edward the Confessor, King Harold, William the Conqueror
2 1483 Edward IV, Edward V and Richard III
3 1936 George V, Edward VIII, George VI

Six different views on the Duke and Duchess of Windsor

1 *'The Duke's love for her is one of the greatest loves of history.'* Sir Winston Churchill, 1948.
2 *'She would have made a good Queen.'* Adolf Hitler, after having tea with The Duke and Duchess in 1937.
3 *'The Duchess is quiet and easy to please.'* A female employee of Raymond's hairdressing salon in 1949.
4 *'Admit that man has charm.'* Harold Nicholson to H G Wells, who replied, *'Glamour'*.
5 *'We did it better in my day.'* Maxine Elliott, a sometime mistress of King Edward VII, in conversation with Churchill.
6 *He will be known for a long time – because of me.'* The Duchess of Windsor on the Duke of Windsor.

The Duke and Duchess of Windsor return to England for a brief visit in 1946

Hugh Montgomery-Massingberd's tantalising trivialities about eighteen favourite foreign Royal personages

'1 King Henry IV of France (1553–1610)

Henry of Navarre was born with a full head of teeth, causing havoc to the wet-nurse who attended him. This cheerful, bearded character was known as *Le Roi Galant* and changed his religion three times. He was stabbed to death in his carriage by a religious fantatic, having previously escaped assassination while relieving himself in a pig sty.

2 Mulay Ismail al-Samin, Sultan of Morocco
(c. 1646–1727)

This great ruler is credited with more wives, concubines and children than any other ruler in modern history. In 1703 he was said to have had 525 sons and 342 daughters. Forty sons are said to have been born to him in the course of four months in 1704. In 1721 some 700 sons were attributed to him; his last child, however, is reported to have been born 18 months after his death.

3 King Augustus I of Saxony (1670–1733)

This larger-than-life figure was known as "The Strong"; when King of Poland, he would pick up two of his State Trumpeters, one in each hand, and hold them at an arm's length for five minutes, while they played a fanfare. He kept a harem and left 354 bastards (including the soldier Maurice de Saxe, whose natural daughter was the grandmother of George Sand, the novelist). For all his lechery, gluttony and brawn, "The Ever-Cheerful Man of Sin" (as Carlyle called him) was a Baroque patron of the arts who beautified Dresden and presided over the Meissen porcelain factory. He found it difficult to keep track of his love-children and at least one of his daughters subsequently became his mistress. He died in 1733 after a drinking bout.

4 King Adolf Frederick of Sweden (1710–1771)

Described by a courtier as looking "gracious even from behind", he died suddenly at Stockholm following a supper of buns, sauerkraut, oysters, lobster and champagne.

5 King Ferdinand IV of the Two Sicilies (1751–1825)

"Although an ugly prince, he is not absolutely repulsive", his brother-in-law, Emperor Joseph II, wrote of this king. "He is clean, except for his hands; and at least he does not stink." This partial cleanliness seems to have been the only refinement of "*Nasone*" (as he was known on account of his prominent proboscis); in other respects he was gloriously coarse. At Court festivities he would indulge in boisterous horseplay, slapping the ladies' buttocks, kicking those of the gentlemen, shouting obscenities and vulgar jokes at the top of his high-pitched voice. He would make his courtiers stand around him and amuse him with their conversation while he sat on his *chaise-percée*. When asked how he liked his bride, he replied: "*Suda come un porco*" ("Sweats like a pig"). When standing on the palace balcony at Naples with his exalted and correct brother-in-law, who was paying him a visit, "he made a very unwarrantable noise" – excusing himself by saying that it was necessary for his health ("*E necessario per la salute, fratello mio*").

6 King Ernest Augustus of Hanover (1771–1851)

This one-eyed monarch, unfairly regarded as the wickedest of Queen Victoria's "wicked uncles", looked upon the more elaborate court ceremonial as humbug. To people who, when speaking to him, began with the traditional form, "Allow me to throw myself at Your Majesty's feet!" he would retort, "Rubbish! If you did, you would split your trousers!"

7 Emperor Ferdinand I of Austria (1793–1875)

After his reign was brought to an end in the upheavals of 1848, Ferdinand continued to hold his own little court in Prague and received the respectful salutes of the citizens as he took his constitutional stroll along the ramparts. He was also able to keep his title of Emperor; on one occasion he was to insist: "I *am* the Emperor and I *will* have dumplings!"

8 Vladika Petar II of Montenegro (1813–1851)

Six feet, eight inches tall, with the long hair and beard of an Orthodox ecclesiastic, Petar was a poet and author of *The Serpent of the Mountain*. He was also noted for being able to hit with a rifle shot a lemon thrown into the air by one of his attendants. "A singular accomplishment for a bishop," remarked an English visitor in 1844.

9 Mutesa I, Kabaka of Buganda (*c.* 1837–1884)

He is said to have told the Christian missionaries who stressed that he would have to give up polygamy if he wished to be baptised, "Give me Queen Victoria's daughter for my wife and I will promise to put away all of my wives."

10 Nasir ud-din, Shah of Persia (1831–1896)

The most able ruler of the Qajar dynasty who became well-known to the British public in Victorian times for his enormous moustaches. He publicly kissed Queen Victoria's photograph at Windsor railway station and when the formidable Baroness Burdett-Coutts, the philanthropist, was about to be presented to him, he proclaimed in an all-too-audible voice, "*Quelle horreur!*" When visiting an English prison, he was shown the gallows and asked whether he could see it in use; on being told that there was nobody who was about to be hanged, said, "Take one of my suite!"

11 Queen Elisabeth of Roumania (1843–1916)

"She was both splendid and absurd," wrote her successor Queen Marie, of this romantic poet who used the name "Carmen Sylva". She used to stand, at all hours of the day and night, on the terrace of her house overlooking the entrance to Constanza harbour calling out blessings to the departing ships through a megaphone. She would listen in hand-clapping rapture to her circle of writers, artists and musicians which included one old charlatan who imagined that he could sing equally well in tenor, baritone or bass.

12 King Frederick Augustus III of Saxony (1865–1932)

This plain-speaking monarch once asked the Kaiser whether he was planning to wear uniform or plain clothes in the evening during a visit to the Archduke Franz Ferdinand. The Kaiser expressed a preference for uniform. "Quite right!" exclaimed the King cheerfully. "You look hideous in plain clothes!" Even in exile after the First World War the blunt King retained the love of his people, a crowd of whom asked him to show himself at the window of a train carriage. Frederick Augustus looked down at his ex-subjects and said: "Well, I must say, you *are* a fine set of Republicans!"

13 Princess Magwende of Ankole

This unfortunate lady who killed herself in 1895 was forced to abort several pregnancies by her powerful mother Kiboga who decreed that it was not fitting that she should have children while her brother, the Mugabe Ntare V, remained childless. Eventually she concealed a pregnancy and gave birth to Kabututu (meaning "One who is obtained through sweat"), declaring "I will keep this last product of my sweat."

14 Khalifa II, Sultan of Zanzibar (1879–1960)

The Sultan had a passion for circuses and shortly before his death he travelled to Glasgow to see one. He also enjoyed the Coronation of Queen Elizabeth II, though disconcerted his English entourage by referring to his programmes for the ceremonies as his "pornogram".

15 Andrianamantania Paul Razafinkeriefo of Madagascar (1895–1977)

As "Andy Razaf" he collaborated with the great Fats Waller and wrote the lyrics for such numbers as *12th Street Rag* and *Ain't Misbehavin'*.

16 Queen Salote of Tonga (1900–1965)

This massive matriarch stole the show at the Queen's Coronation in 1953 when, refusing to have the covers of her carriage put up despite the driving rain, she beamed and waved at the appreciative crowds. Sitting in the coach with her was a Malaysian sultan of rather undernourished appearance. Watching this Procession, a friend of Noel Coward's asked "the Master" who the person was opposite the Oceanic Queen. Coward replied: *"Her lunch."*

17 King Farouk I of Egypt (1920–65)

This dissipated voluptuary was the subject of a lewd ditty sung by the British troops in the Second World War to the tune of the

Egyptian Royal Anthem. A celebrated glutton, he held the record for the biggest breakfast served at the Connaught Hotel in London until the arrival of the present contributor in 1972.

18 King Husain of Jordan (1935–   )
When he was at Sandhurst, the Sergeant-Major shouted at His Majesty on the parade ground: "King Husain, Sir! You're an idle monarch, Sir!" '

Hugh Montgomery-Massingberd edited Burke's *Royal Families of The World*.

307 *Nine Sovereigns born outside the British Isles*

1 William I the Conqueror: *born at Falaise, Normandy about autumn 1028.*
2 William II Rufus: born in Normandy between 1056 and 1060
3 Stephen: *born at Blois about 1096*
4 Henry II: *born at Le Mans 5 March 1133*
5 Richard II: *born at Bordeaux 6 January 1367*
6 Edward IV: *born at Rouen 28 April 1442*
7 William III: *born at The Hague 4 November 1650*
8 George I: *born at Osnabrück 28 May 1660*
9 George II; *born at Hanover 30 October 1683*

308 *Twelve birthdays of the Royal Family and the celebrities they share them with*

1 The Queen
21 April 1926 (Also 21 April: Norman Parkinson, John Mortimer, Anthony Quinn).
2 Prince Philip
10 June 1921 (Also 10 June: Saul Bellow, Lionel Jeffries, Maurice Sendak, John H Louis).
3 Prince Charles
14 November 1948 (Also 14 November: King Husain, Peter Phillips, Dame Elizabeth Frink, Aaron Copeland).

4 Princess Diana

1 July 1961 (Also 1 July: Debbie Harry, Trevor Eve, Olivia de Haviland, Jean Marsh, Leslie Caron).

5 Prince Andrew

19 February 1960 (Also 19 February: Dick Emery, Lee Marvin, Merle Oberon, Erin Pizzey).

6 The Queen Mother

4 August 1900 (Also 4 August: Sir Osbert Lancaster).

7 Prince Edward

10 March 1964 (Also 10 March: Lady Falkender, Sir Michael Havers, Dame Eva Turner).

8 Princess Anne

15 August 1950 (Also 15 August: Robert Bolt, Jack Lynch, Oscar Peterson, Jim Dale, Nicholas Roeg, Dame Wendy Hiller).

9 Princess Margaret

21 August 1930 (Also 21 August: Lord Goodman, Chris Brasher, Count Basie, Barry Norman, Dame Janet Baker).

10 Viscount Linley

3 November 1961 (Also 3 November: Lulu, Jeremy Brett, Ludovic Kennedy).

11 Lady Sarah Armstrong-Jones

1 May 1964 (Also 1 May: Rita Coolidge, Joanna Lumley, Joseph Heller, Steve Cauthen, Judy Collins).

12 Princess Alexandra

25 December 1961 (Also 25 December: Princess Alice Duchess of Gloucester, Little Richard, Noele Gordon, Lord Grade, Kenny Everett).

Ten Royal predictions by Kim Tracey 309

(Kim Tracey was the only clairvoyant to predict that Prince Charles would marry Lady Diana Spencer and the month of the wedding a year before it actually happened.) These were her predictions in January 1982:

1 The Royal baby will be a boy.
2 He will be followed by two girls.
3 The marriage of Prince Charles and Princess Diana will be a happy one.
4 Their boy will be artistic and will be known as the Artist King.

5 He will be a great diplomat.

6 He will marry around the age of twenty-two or twenty-three.

7 Prince Charles and Princess Diana's oldest daughter will marry someone unacceptable from the world of movies or sport.

8 Their second daughter will marry late. She will work in medicine or nursing.

9 Their granddaughter will be involved in a political scandal when she is seventeen or eighteen years old.

10 Prince Charles will become King in five years time, when the Queen steps down for health reasons.

310 *Nine significant predictions concerning Royalty*

1 Queen Victoria's glorious reign

George III's fourth son, the Duke of Kent, was told by a gypsy in Gibraltar that he would have 'many losses and crosses' but was to die in happiness – and that his 'only child would be a great Queen.' Recalling this prediction years later, he determined that his wife should make the arduous journey across the continent so that their child would be born in England. Although at the time of her birth the baby which they named Alexandrina Victoria seemed unlikely to succeed to the Throne, she was Britain's longest reigning monarch.

2 The Queen's marriage to Prince Philip

When the Queen was only 15, Chips Channon (Sir Henry Channon) wrote in his diary: 'An enjoyable Greek cocktail party. Prince Philip of Greece was there . . . he is to be our Prince Consort, and that is why he is serving in the Navy. 21 January 1941.'

3 Death on a Friday

King Edward VII's second valet, Hawkins, said that the King had often expressed the feelings that he would die on a Friday, which he did.

4 The Edwardian style

Upon the birth of Edward VII, the magazine *Punch*, itself only 5 months old, predicted: 'The time of the Prince will be glorified by good cooking and good cheer. His drumstick will be the drumsticks of turkeys, his cannon the popping of corks.' A strange comment on the birth of a child, but Edward VII became famous for his gastronomy.

5 Tragedy in the reign of Henry VI

Since an astrologer had warned King Henry V of the unluckiness of his wife's confinement at Windsor, the King was horrified to hear that his son had been born there, and prophesied disaster for the boy. When the child became King Henry VI, he suffered bouts of severe madness, which prolonged the War of the Roses, and was murdered in the Tower of London.

6 Death in Jerusalem

A fortuneteller once told Henry IV that he would die in Jerusalem. Years later the King was taken ill at Westminster Abbey praying in preparation for his departure on a Crusade. Reviving in the room to which he had been taken, he enquired if the room had a particular name. 'The Jerusalem Chamber', they said. The King then cried: 'Lauds be given to the Father of Heaven, for now I know that I shall die here in this chamber, according to the prophecy of me declared, that I shall depart this life in Jerusalem.' And so he did.

7 The Restoration

After he had been condemned to death, King Charles I told his attendant, Colonel Tomlinson, that the monarchy was at an end. Half an hour later the King announced that the Holy Spirit had given him assurance that his own son would reign successfully. Charles II was crowned eleven years later.

8 The Abdication of King Edward VIII

Before the ascendancy of Mrs Simpson was widely known, an astrologer who called himself 'Cheiro' wrote 'The Prince of Wales' chart shows influences that point to changes greatly affecting the Throne of England. He was born under peculiar astrological circumstances which make his character a difficult one to understand. There is an intense restlessness, a lack of continuity of thought, a difficulty of concentration, and an absorbing love for travel and a lack of a sense of danger. He is determined not to settle down until he feels a grande passion, but it is well within the range of possibility that he will fall victim to a devastating love affaire. If he does, I predict that the Prince of Wales will give up everything, even the chance of being crowned, rather than lose the object of his affection.'

9 The influence of Mrs Simpson

In the throes of divorce from her first husband, the future Duchess of Windsor visited a fortuneteller in New York, who said that she would have two more husbands and that she would become 'a famous woman'. Some years later, while she was divorcing Ernest Simpson, she consulted a famous astrologer, Evangeline Adams, to be told that there would be 2 more marriages, plus various crises; that she would have a normal life span, and that 'between the ages of 40 and 50 she would exercise considerable emotional power – this power would be related to a man.'

311 *Eight predictions which were confounded by events*

1 *'Charles to marry Astrid – Official!'* Headline in the *Daily Express*, 17 June 1974.
2 *'It will make things easier for your successor,'* said Lady Astor by way of congratulating King Edward VIII on his 'modern' manner of kingship.
3 *'The Beatles? They're on the wane.'* Prince Philip in Canada, in 1965.
4 *'I'm too old for marriage,'* said Angus Ogilvy in 1962. His marriage to Princess Alexandra took place the next year in Westminster Abbey. (On his first public appearance after the announcement of their engagement, he was seen carrying an American paperback book *The Secret Heart of Princess Alexandra*. It contained no mention of him.)
5 *'I think that everything so far is satisfactory – there is no cause for alarm.'* Sir James Clark, the Royal Physician, a few days before Prince Albert's death.
6 *'Let me introduce you to the last King of England.'* Edward VII went to his deathbed believing that his son would be the last king, so alarmed was he by the toppling thrones of Europe. It was with these words that he introduced the future George V to Lord Haldane.
7 *'He falls instantly in and out of love. His present attachment will follow the course of all the others.'* Winston Churchill on the subject of King Edward VIII and Mrs Simpson on New Year's Day 1936.
8 *'I understand no other designer has been approached by Buckingham Palace, which makes the choice of Zandra a mere formality.'* Jean Dobson, writing in the *Daily Mail* a few days before the announcement that the Emmanuels had been chosen to design Princess Diana's wedding dress.

Four omens which foretold the fate of King Edward VIII

1 A temporary statue

One of the attractions of the 1924 British Empire Exhibition at Wembley was a statue of Edward, Prince of Wales. It was modelled in butter.

2 A fallen jewel

As the coffin of King George V turned into Palace Yard during the funeral procession, the Royal Crown which was being carried on the coffin shed its bejewelled Maltese Cross. It rolled into a gutter. As a sergeant-major picked it up, the new King, Edward VIII, was heard to mutter, 'Christ! what's going to happen next?'

3 A telling stamp

Preferring his left profile to his right, King Edward VIII insisted on breaking a 300-year-old tradition when he informed the Post Office that he would only allow them to print his best profile. The crown on the stamps had already been printed, prompting *The Times* after the Abdication to remember 'the superstitious anxiety of those who shook apprehensive heads at the new stamps, because the head of King Edward VIII was turned away from the light, and forward into the gloom.'

4 Screeching crows

In May 1972, crows (the traditional birds of death) screeched and banged at the Duke of Windsor's bedroom window. Seventy-two hours later, he was dead.

Astrological signs of the Royal Family

1 *Capricorn (22 December to 20 January)*
Princess Alexandra; Princess Alice, Duchess of Gloucester; Princess Michael of Kent.

2 *Aquarius (21 January to 19 February)*
Prince Andrew.

3 *Pisces (20 February to 20 March)*
Prince Edward; Lord Snowdon; Lady Rose Windsor; The Duchess of Kent; James Ogilvy.

4 *Aries (21 March to 20 April)*
Lord Frederick Windsor.

5 *Taurus (21 April to 20 May)*
The Queen; Zara Phillips; Lady Sarah Armstrong-Jones; Lady Helen Windsor; Lady Gabriella Windsor
6 *Gemini (21 May to 21 June)*
Prince Philip; The Duchess of Gloucester.
7 *Cancer (22 June to 23 July)*
Princess Diana; Earl of St Andrews; Prince Michael of Kent
8 *Leo (24 July to 23 August)*
The Queen Mother; Princess Anne; Princess Margaret; Lord Nicholas Windsor; Marina Ogilvy.
9 *Virgo (24 August to 23 September)*
Mark Phillips; The Duke of Gloucester; Hon Angus Ogilvy.
10 *Libra (24 September to 23 October)*
The Duke of Kent
11 *Scorpio (24 October to 22 November)*
Prince Charles; Peter Phillips; Viscount Linley; Earl of Ulster
12 *Sagittarius (23 November to 21 December)*
There are none in the Royal Family

314 *Twenty Royal Masons*

The Grand Lodge of England was convened in 1717 and the following have been members of the Craft.
1 1737 Frederick Lewis, *Prince of Wales*
2 1766 Edward Augustus, *Duke of York*
3 1766 William Henry, *Duke of Gloucester*
4 1767 Henry Frederick, *Duke of Cumberland*
5 1786 King William IV
6 1787 King George IV
7 1787 Frederick, *Duke of York*
8 1790 Edward, *Duke of Kent*
9 1796 Ernest Augustus, *Duke of Cumberland*
10 1796 William Frederick, *Duke of Gloucester*
11 1798 Augustus Frederick, *Duke of Sussex*
12 1868 King Edward VII
13 1874 Arthur, *Duke of Connaught*
14 1885 Albert Victor, *Duke of Clarence*
15 1911 Prince Arthur of Connaught
16 1919 King Edward VIII (*Duke of Windsor*)
17 1919 King George VI
18 1928 George, *Duke of Kent*

19 1952 Prince Philip, *Duke of Edinburgh*
20 1963 Edward, *Duke of Kent (Elected as the present Grand Master, 1967).*

Nine omens of the fate which would befall members of the Royal Family

1 King Edward VII's broken ritual

One of King Edward VII's most firm traditions was to turn everyone out of Sandringham a few minutes before midnight every New Year's Eve. As midnight chimed, he would escort Queen Alexandra through the front doorway. On New Year's Eve in 1910, a young member of the Royal Family was late in coming out of the house and the ritual was ruined. 'We shall have very bad luck this year', the King predicted. By May he was dead.

2 The Queen Mother's childhood game

As a young girl, Lady Elizabeth Bowes-Lyon liked to dress herself up in the nursery of Glamis Castle. 'I am Princess Elizabeth', she would say.

3 Queen Elizabeth I's Coronation ring

For 45 years of her reign, Queen Elizabeth I refused ever to remove her Coronation ring. But by 1603 the ring had grown so deeply into her flesh that her doctors insisted that it be cut away. Within a week the Queen was dead.

4 Princess Diana's dormitory portrait

As a boarder at West Heath School for Girls, the young Lady Diana Spencer slept in a dormitory which was decorated with a portrait of the Prince of Wales at his Investiture. As fate would have it, Lady Diana was allotted the bed immediately beneath the portrait.

5 Charles I's marble bust

When Bernini's bust of him was completed, it was brought to Charles I who was sitting in the garden at Whitehall Palace. At the moment he asked for it to be uncovered, so that he could admire the sculptor's portrait of him, a hawk flew by with a bird in its beak and a drop of its blood fell onto the throat of Charles I's effigy. He was beheaded by Cromwell on 30 January 1649 as 'an implacable enemy of the commonwealth of England'.

6 Catherine of Aragon's motto

The motto and device of Catherine of Aragon was 'Not For My

Crown' and a pomegranate; at the time of her divorce from
Henry VIII, it was remarked that the crown of the pomegranate is
thrown away when the fruit is eaten.

7 Queen Mary's inquiry

It was thought remarkably kind and unselfish when, the hour after
her fiancé, the Duke of Clarence died, the future Queen Mary
sent to ask about the baby born that day to Lady Fermoy. It now
seems portentous: the baby was Princess Diana's grandmother.

8 The Queen Mother's gift

At a children's party aged 5, the Queen Mother took the cherries
off her own slice of cake, and put them on the plate of the child
sitting next to her. That child was her future husband, King
George VI.

9 The Duchess of Windsor's first husband

The childhood nickname of The Duchess of Windsor's first
husband, Win Spencer, was 'Duke'.

316 *Eight superstitious rules of Royalty*

1 Touch wood

If the Queen has a horse running at Ascot, she can be seen busily
fingering a star of light wood inlaid into the mahogany stairpost.
Queen Victoria was also a keen wood toucher.

2 Never wear black or green

During the war, the Queen Mother refused to wear black or
green.

3 Don't seat 13

King Edward VII would never sit down with thirteen at a table.
Once when it appeared that he had broken his rule, he pointed out
that one of the guests was pregnant. The Queen also holds to this
rule: if she cannot avoid thirteen at dinner, she divides the party
into two tables.

4 Stick pins

King George IV's difficult wife, Caroline of Brunswick, used to
make wax figures of her husband, give them horns, stick pins in
them and throw them on the fire. It had little effect – he died aged
68.

5 Beware the Koh-l-Noor

The central jewel on the Queen's crown, the Koh-I-Noor, is said
to bring bad luck to any man and good luck to any woman who
wears it.

6 Avoid May weddings

Queen Victoria wouldn't let any of her children marry in May, following the Scots in thinking it unlucky.

7 Surround yourself with blondes

The Duchess of Windsor thought that fair-haired people brought her luck. Consequently, she only employed fair-haired servants.

8 Chuck salt over the shoulder

Any salt spilt in Buckingham Palace is likely to find itself hurled over the Queen's left shoulder.

Ten Royal Ghosts 317

1 The Blacksmith at Nether Lypiatt

The sound of clanking metal is an occasional disturbance at Prince Michael of Kent's house. A blacksmith who was hanged for sheepstealing returns to fling open the gates that he fashioned when still alive.

2 Catherine Howard at Hampton Court

The fifth wife of Henry VIII can be heard shrieking in the haunted gallery of Hampton Court. Her figure rushes along the gallery and passes through the door at the end. It disappears into the chapel.

3 Lady Fanny Sinclair at the Castle of Mey

Lady Fanny Sinclair, daughter of the 13th Earl of Caithness haunts the bedroom in the tower of the Queen Mother's home in Scotland. She eloped with one of her father's servants, was brought back forcibly and locked in the tower. Within a few hours she had thrown herself out of a window, plummeting to her death.

4 Anne Boleyn at Hever Castle

It is said that the ghost of Anne Boleyn wanders in the oak panelled chamber of her old home singing sad songs in a low voice. When Lord Astor bought Hever Castle, he invited the Pyschical Research Society for Christmas week several years running, but they heard and saw nothing.

5 Anne Boleyn at Blickling Hall

On May 19 each year, the ghost of Anne Boleyn returns to her probable birthplace in a coach drawn by four headless horses and driven by a headless coachman. With its passenger's head sitting comfortably on her lap, the coach disappears as it drives headlong into the front door.

6 The Thing in the den

A 'thing' causing immense terror is said to lurk in the 'Den', an area by the River Meldrum, near Angus Ogilvy's family seat. It does not affect those in love. Angus Ogilvy and Princess Alexandra have never been affected by it.

7 King George III at Windsor Castle

Shut up in a bachelor flat in Windsor Castle, the increasingly mad King George III used to enjoy toddling to his window and saluting the guards as they passed. The ensign would always give the 'Eyes Right' command. A week after the King's death, the ensign saw him once more at the window. After a few seconds' hesitation, he once more shouted, 'Eyes Right'. Other ghosts at Windsor include: Herne the Hunter; a little grey man; Queen Elizabeth I; and the energetic Anne Boleyn.

8 King George V's sighting

As a naval officer, King George V was sailing in the South Atlantic, and, convinced he had sighted the phantom naval ship *The Flying Dutchman* only 200 yards away, he entered full details in the ship's log book.

9 Prince Andrew's sighting

Three teenage girls who were sharing a room at a Scottish houseparty in 1975 were surprised to be woken by Prince Andrew, who was a fellow houseguest. 'There's a ghost in my room', he said. The girls looked incredulous. 'There's a ghost in my room', he repeated, 'And so I'll have to stay in this room with you.' Managing to control their terror, the three girls ushered him back to his own room.

10 The Illness Bearer of Althorp

When Princess Diana's father, Earl Spencer, was seriously ill in 1978, he summoned his friend the Reverend Victor Malon to exorcise Althorp, believing that a ghost could be the cause of his pains. Earl Spencer's health improved after the exorcism, though his wife claimed some of the credit, having played a recording of his favourite opera, *Madame Butterfly*, over and over again.

Four peculiar locations for Royalty

1 The Vatican library
Many of King Henry VIII's passionate love letters to Anne Boleyn are to be found in the Vatican Library.

2 At the top of the hit parade
At the time of Prince Charles's Investiture, a Welsh Nationalist song, 'Carlo Windsor', topped the Welsh Hit Parade. 'Carlo ' is Welsh for 'dog'.

3 In a hippy musical
In 1969, Princess Anne caused a stir by dancing with the cast and audience on the stage at the end of the nude musical *Hair*. The Princess herself appeared fully clothed in a purple trouser suit.

4 On the Watergate Tapes
Prince Charles's one and a half hour talk with President Nixon supplied one of the most straightforward episodes on the Watergate Tapes.

Five unusual people presented to Royalty

1 Tom Thumb
On a visit to England in 1864, the 25-inch high General Tom Thumb was introduced to Queen Victoria. His appearance at court was recorded in the Court Circular: 'His impersonation of the Emperor Napoleon elicited great Mirth. . . . The General danced a nautical hornpipe and sang several of his favourite songs. The Queen presented him with gifts and a Coat of Arms.'

2 The Wild Boy
At the age of 13 'The Wild Boy' was discovered walking on his hands and feet 'with the agility of a squirrel' in the woods of Hanover. He was introduced to King George I, who greatly took to him. His portrait is painted on the ceiling of the main staircase at Kensington Palace.

3 Old Parr
Shortly before he died in 1635 at the age of 152, Thomas Parr, or 'Old Parr', was presented to King Charles I. The King was so touched by meeting the oldest man in the world that he allowed his body to be buried in Westminster Abbey.

4 Tee Yee Neen Ho Ga Prow and friends
Four Indian Chieftains, hoping for Royal support against the

French in Canada were presented to Queen Anne. Along with Tee Yee Neen Ho Ga Prow came Ga Ga Yean Qua Prah Ion, Elow Oh Koan and Oh Me Yeath Ion No Prow. To help win the Queen over, they presented her with belts of wampum, with which she seemed pleased.

5 The Shah of Persia

Before the Shah of Persia's first visit to Britain in 1873, Queen Victoria received this report: 'His Majesty generally dines alone, and when so, prefers to have his meals on the carpet. For that purpose a moveable carpet should be kept ready whereupon *his* servants will put the dishes, etc. brought to the door by the English servants. The Shah does not like to have to cut up his meats.' The British Ambassador in Berlin sent additional advice, warning that no one had dare tell the Shah that he should not put his arm around the Queen's chair at dinner, 'or put his fingers into dishes, or take food out of his mouth again to look at it after it has been chewed, or fling it under the table if it does not suit his taste.'

After she had finished reading all these reports, Queen Victoria asked the simple question, 'Why is he called Imperial, then?' and, so saying, removed the title from the Official Programme of the visit.

Though when the Shah arrived he failed to use the lavatories, organised a boxing match in the garden of Buckingham Palace, and ate all his meals on the floor, Queen Victoria took an unexpected shine to him, presenting him with a leaving present of a miniature of herself set in diamonds.

320 *Two American Presidents with ideas above their station*

1 President John Adams

The second President of the United States, John Adams, had plans to found an American dynasty by marrying one of his sons to a daughter of King George III. When George Washington heard of this, he went to Adams dressed in a white uniform to try to talk him out of it. When this failed, he returned, dressed in black. When even this failed, he dressed in his Revolution uniform and threatened to run Adams through with his sword. And so the American dynasty foundered.

2 President Richard Nixon

During his visit to America in 1971, Prince Charles found himself in the constant company of Miss Tricia Nixon. President Nixon's plans for his daughter's advancement soon became clear to Prince Charles when the President left the two of them together in a room, saying, 'My wife and I will keep out of the way so that you can really feel at home.'

Tricia Nixon and David Eisenhower talk to Princess Anne and Prince Charles

Fourteen Royal meetings with famous people

1 Princess Alexandra meets Bob Monkhouse

Shortly after her twenty-first birthday, Princess Alexandra, wandering around a television studio, bumped into comedian Bob Monkhouse, who did not recognise her.

'Hello darling', he said. 'You shouldn't be here, you know.'

'I must be getting back', replied Princess Alexandra. 'The people I've come with will be missing me.'

'All right, sweetheart', bubbled Monkhouse, 'If you want a

ticket for the show, ask for me at the door.'

'Okay, thank you', the Princess replied graciously.

2 The Queen meets Walter Annenburg

When President Nixon's Ambassador to Britain, Walter Annenburg, was presented at Court, the Queen asked him how he was settling into his new home.

'Very well, Ma'am', came the reply, 'Except for some discomfiture owing to elements of refurbishment.'

3 King George V meets Charles Lindbergh

On being introduced to the first man to fly solo across the Atlantic, King George V's first question was, 'What did you do about peeing?'

4 King George III meets Edward Gibbon

When Edward Gibbon presented King George III with the final volume of his *Decline and Fall of the Roman Empire*, the King said, 'Another big, thick, square book, eh? Always scribble, scribble, scribble, eh, Mr Gibbon?'

5 Princess Margaret meets J M Barrie

When she was a very small child, Princess Margaret had tea at Glamis with the playwright J M Barrie. Pointing to a cracker, Barrie asked whether it was hers. 'It is yours and mine', she replied. Barrie later put the line in his play, *The Boy David*, and gave the Princess a penny every time the play was performed.

6 The Duke of Kent meets Louis Armstrong

Soon after their first meeting, Louis Armstrong sent the Duke of Kent a twenty-first birthday telegram inscribed, 'To Black Jack – the sharpest little cat I know. Satch.'

7 The Queen Mother meets the Beatles

After a Royal Variety Show in 1964, the Queen Mother met the Beatles. 'And where are you playing next?' she asked. 'Slough', replied John Lennon. 'Oh,' said the Queen Mother, 'That's near us.'

8 Prince Philip meets Dr Allende

At a white-tie-and-tails state banquet in Chile in 1968, Dr Allende, soon to become President, was presented to Prince Philip. He was wearing a lounge suit. 'Why are you dressed like that?' asked Prince Philip.

'Because my party is poor, and they advised me not to hire evening dress.'

'If they told you to wear a bathing costume, I suppose you'd come dressed in one?'

'Oh, no, sir', replied Allende, 'Our Party is a serious one.'

9 Princess Alexandra meets Elton John

After a concert at the Rainbow Theatre in aid of the Queen's

Silver Jubilee appeal in 1977, Princess Alexandra asked Elton John whether he took cocaine to keep his strength up during performances. When news of this unorthodox Royal question became public, the Princess wrote the singer a letter apologising for causing him any embarrassment. In turn, Elton John apologised to her for repeating her remarks in public.

10 The Queen and Princess Margaret meet Neville Chamberlain

As children, the Queen and Princess Margaret were persistent nail-biters, no matter how much their governess tried to stop them. One day in the Palace they saw the Prime Minister, Neville Chamberlain, biting his nails. 'If he can do it, why can't we?', they asked.

11 The Queen meets Robert Graves

When Robert Graves went to Buckingham Palace to receive the Queen's Medal for Poetry, he said to the Queen, 'I don't know if you realise, ma'am, but you and I are descended from the prophet Mohammed.'

'Oh, really', replied the Queen.

'Yes.'

'How interesting.'

'I think', continued the poet,' that you should mention it in your Christmas message, because a lot of your subjects are Mohammedans'.

So far, the Queen has ignored this advice.

12 Princess Diana meets Elizabeth Taylor

After meeting Princess Diana at a charity preview of her play, *Little Foxes* in March 1982, Elizabeth Taylor said, 'The Princess was charming, gracious and beautiful. I was more than thrilled to meet her.'

13 Prince Charles meets Frank Sinatra

'Sinatra could be terribly nice one minute and, well, not so nice the next.' Prince Charles remarked after the two had met, 'I was not impressed with the creeps and Mafia types he kept around him.'

14 Princess Diana meets Chrissie Lloyd

'I'm so nervous about everything, I hardly know what to do', Princess Diana confessed on meeting Chrissie Lloyd at Wimbledon a few weeks before the Royal Wedding. Chrissie Lloyd assured Princess Diana that marriage was great and that she had nothing to worry about. She then asked why Prince Charles hadn't come with her to Wimbledon. 'It's because he can never sit still', came the reply, 'He is like a great big baby. But one day I hope to calm him down enough to enjoy it.'

And one famous person who failed to meet Royalty. . . .

Marlene Dietrich does not meet King Edward VIII

In 1936, Marlene Dietrich was so convinced that if she met King
Edward VIII she could convince him to abandon Mrs Simpson
that she persistently rang his homes and asked to speak to him.
When all her requests were refused, she presented herself at Fort
Belvedere. On being denied admission, she ended her campaign.

322 *Peregrine Worsthorne's list Ten Blessings of Constitutional Monarchy*

1 **Focus for national unity** It is useful to have a Head of State
whose authority remains unaffected by governmental failure.
because the monarch reigns without ruling, he or she can
remain popular even if the prime minister of the day falls from
grace. Thus there always remains one political institution
which inspires popular trust, however much the rest of the
political system may have become discredited.

2 **Long stop in the event of some threat to the constitution**
If some would-be prime ministral dictator of the left or the
right tried to use a temporary majority in Parliament, say, to
abolish elections, the monarch could always refuse to sign the
necessary enabling legislation, thereby giving public opinion
time to have second thoughts.

3 **Symbol of national continuity** However much everything
else changes, there is always the monarchy to remind the
British people of their historic roots. Thus, through the
monachy, people can identify with their past.

4 **Excuse for pageantry, ritual and ceremony** Royal
occasions provide uniquely satisfactory opportunities for the
nation to celebrate and rejoice.

5 **Model of family life as it ought to be lived** This is a
relatively new role but an increasingly important one. People
look to the Royal Family to set a moral example.

6 **Focus for the loyalty of the armed forces, who owe
allegiance to the Crown** This is an extra precaution against
any danger of the armed forces interfering in party politics.

7 **Wins foreign admiration for Britain** Royal visits overseas
arouse enormous interest. No other British institution enjoys
so much international acclaim.

8 **Attracts foreign tourism** It provides the best of all possible colourful spectacles – Changing the Guard, Trooping the Colour, etc. A major source of foreign exchange.

9 **Induces humility in politicians** Politicians have to bend their knees to someone more important than themselves. In the presence of their monarch, even the mightiest of subjects is made to feel small.

10 **Political wisdom and experience** Because monarchs tend to outlast prime ministers, they can often offer very useful political advice. This Queen, for example, has been on the throne ever since the last years of Winston Churchill. Thus her accumulated knowledge of statecraft is far deeper and wider than that of prime ministers who come and go.

Peregrine Worsthorne the distinguished essayist, is the Deputy Editor of the *Sunday Telegraph*.

Eight Royal Anniversaries to put in your diary 323

1 20 November 1997
The fiftieth wedding anniversary of the Queen and Prince Philip.
2 26 June 1983
The twenty-first birthday of the Earl of St Andrews
3 16 March 1985
The twenty-first birthday of Prince Edward
4 28 April 1985
The twenty-first birthday of Lady Helen Windsor
5 1 May 1985
The twenty-first birthday of Lady Sarah Armstrong-Jones.
6 22 February 1983
The fiftieth birthday of the Duchess of Kent.
7 25 December 1986
The fiftieth birthday of Princess Alexandra
8 7 September 2015
On this date the Queen will have achieved the longest reign of any monarch in British history. The Queen will be 89 years old, Princes Charles will be 67 years old, and Princess Diana will be 55 years old.

Index

280